MOST OF MY LIFE

MOST OF MY LIFE

G. S. Harvie-Watt

SPRINGWOOD BOOKS

© G. S. Harvie-Watt 1980

All rights reserved

Printed in Great Britain by
Butler & Tanner Ltd, Frome and London

0 9059 4798 3

Contents

1	Prologue	*1*
2	Youth and Upbringing	*5*
3	The Keighley Election	*12*
4	Keighley to Richmond	*20*
5	The Commons, the Bar and the Army	*29*
6	P.P.S. to the Premier	*41*
7	Winston on and off Parade	*50*
8	The House and Pearl Harbor	*61*
9	Intrigues in the House	*71*
10	Middle East Situation	*83*
11	Russia, the Desert and Libel	*95*
12	'The Fateful Year'	*107*
13	Scotland and Downing Street	*122*
14	Bombs and By-elections	*136*
15	Dominion Visitors	*151*
16	The Yalta Debate	*166*
17	Coalition Break-up	*185*

Contents

18	The 1945 Election	*197*
19	South Africa and Canada	*212*
20	Australia and New Zealand	*222*
21	Politics, Monotype and Gold	*232*
22	Consolidated Gold Fields	*245*
	Index	*257*

Illustrations

1	Churchill inspecting the House of Commons Home Guard	56
2	Christmas greetings card to the Author from the PM and Clementine Churchill	57
3	Churchill returning from the Atlantic Conference and greeted by Mrs Churchill and Author	72
4	The PM and Author going down to the House from the Annexe	73
5	The PM on his return from one of his many overseas journeys. Behind him, Herbert Morrison; behind Mrs Churchill, Lord Woolton	168
6	Welcome home. Leo Amery, Herbert Morrison, Author, Anthony Eden, Oliver Lyttelton, Clement Attlee, the PM, Mrs Churchill	169
7	V.E. Day. Churchill and Author on way to House of Commons	184
8	Title page inscription by Frederick Pile	185
9	Arriving at PM's entrance at the House of Commons after being greeted by the crowds. Author holding broken finger–it had been jumped on.	200
10	Letter from Clement Attlee	201
11	The Author as a piper	216
12	The Harvie Watt shaft at the Libanon mine	217
13	Signpost to the township of Glenharvie (Kloof Gold Mine)	217

Chapter 1

Prologue

In July 1941 I was commanding the 6th Anti-Aircraft Brigade with Headquarters at Radwinter near Saffron Walden. It was a warm summer's afternoon. I was watching some exercises of the regiments in my brigade in the heart of the county of Suffolk when out of the road dust near where I was standing with my Brigade Major a despatch rider rode up at speed and skidded to a halt beside me. This was obviously a message of some importance. Invasion or a sudden new move of the brigade.

I grabbed the message from the despatch rider. It was an urgent command from No. 10 Downing Street for me to report at once as the Prime Minister wanted to see me at 5.30 pm. I was amazed—why should he want to see me? However, I immediately got into my car with the blue flag of the 6th AA Brigade flying on the bonnet and dashed off to London.

In the car I began to wonder what this urgent summons could mean. I had read casually in the morning's newspaper that there was going to be some kind of Government re-shuffle, but I had paid little attention to this news. It had never entered my head, although I was still an M.P., that I might be included in a change of Government.

As I came nearer to London it did begin to cross my mind that I had been summoned to Downing Street for just that purpose, and already I had come to the conclusion that I should refuse as I would rather stay in the army.

I drove up to No. 10 Downing Street, a street I knew well since I used to go past No. 10 every day when I was a Government Whip; the Whip's Office was at No. 12. I was greeted by the doorman with whom I had often passed the time of day. I was handed over to a Messenger who accompanied me down the corridor to the open hall outside the Cabinet Room where most visitors waited for their appointment.

I sat there by myself for about ten minutes when out of the Cabinet Room came Brendan Bracken. Bracken was a tall man with bushy red hair and rather thick lenses in his glasses. He gave me a warm grin and said as he passed, 'You're next. Good luck.' Almost at once I was ushered into the Cabinet Room through the private office where the Private Secretaries had their desks.

The principal Private Secretary was John Martin. The others present that day were Leslie Rowan, John Peck and Jock Colville, all with brilliant careers ahead of them. I didn't know any of them, but they gazed in a friendly way as I walked towards the Cabinet Room door.

Winston Churchill was sitting at the Cabinet table, his back to the fireplace, looking out on the Horse Guards Parade and the garden. He waved me to sit down beside him.

It seemed ages before he spoke, then, looking at me with a rather cold, calculating stare, he said, 'You know what I want to see you about?' I replied, 'No'. He then explained about his Cabinet re-shuffle and consequent appointments, and said that Brendan Bracken, who was an old friend of his and had been his Parliamentary Private Secretary since the fall of the Chamberlain Government, was going to become Minister of Information, and that both Brendan and James Stuart, the Chief Whip, had suggested me as a suitable successor because I was well known in the House and was friendly with all the Chamberlain followers, which was important. He also said that he gathered that I was popular with many of the Socialists and Liberals. That was a useful background for me to have. I had also been P.P.S. to Euan Wallace when he was Parliamentary Secretary to the Board of Trade and later Financial Secretary to the Treasury. I had then been appointed an Assistant Government Whip and remained in that post until the war broke out when I was offered the post of a Junior Lord of the Treasury. I refused, however, as I had just received my mobilisation orders.

While excited by the P.M's invitation to be P.P.S., I felt it was only a staff job and I would be doing better service in the army. I said I had been in the Territorial Army for nearly twenty years and I thought that was where my duty lay. The

Prologue

Prime Minister seemed very taken aback by my rather lukewarm reaction to his proposal. It was certainly better and more important than being an Under Secretary to a Department, but I was hesitant. Then the Prime Minister said, 'What I am offering you is not a job down in the engine room. I am asking you to serve on the bridge.'

This sounded marvellous. I asked what my duties would be. I knew the ordinary duties of a P.P.S. to a Minister because of course I had been one myself. I didn't know what would be expected of me as P.P.S. to the Prime Minister in time of war. He immediately said, 'What I want is for you to keep the flies off the meat. It becomes bad if they are allowed to settle even for a moment. I am the meat and you must show me the warning light when troubles arise in the parliamentary and political scene.' So it was settled, and one red head followed another.

I asked leave to go to Scotland to get my civilian clothes. He grunted, 'Of course.' I left the Cabinet Room and again walked down the long corridor to the front door of No. 10 and towards where my car was waiting. I was really in a daze until a voice said to me, 'Hello Harvie. What's the matter with you? You seem in a trance.' At once I was back to normal and I saw it was Malcolm MacDonald, son of the Socialist Prime Minister, Ramsay MacDonald. I knew Malcolm very well. He was a National Labour M.P. and had held several Cabinet posts—Health, Colonies—and was shortly to become High Commissioner to Canada. I told him what had happened and he very generously said that I was just the man to fill Brendan Bracken's footsteps, that it was a better war job for me than to stay in the Army, that I knew the House so well and I would be a support to the P.M.

Needless to say I felt quite bucked up and strode off. Fortunately my driver was waiting for me. I had almost forgotten him. I jumped into the car and returned to my Brigade Headquarters to wind up my army affairs and hand over the brigade to my successor. I never met him, however, as when I told my General what had happened he said, 'You lucky man. Buzz off. You'll need all your time to get to Scotland and your new appointment.'

So I arranged to say good-bye to the brigade in the morning and had my battalion commanders to lunch with my brigade staff. The Brigade HQ gave me a rousing farewell. When we got to Audley End station the Brigade Major got out of the car, solemnly removed from it the brigade flag, a blue pennant with the numeral '6' in white, and handed it to me as a keepsake which I have to this day. I was most touched by this kind thought and I felt very sad. My army days were finished, at any rate for some time to come. It was then 9th July 1941.

I dined at King's Cross Hotel and caught the night train to Scotland. I was glad to see the family, for I had not expected leave for some time though I had not had any for nine months. It seemed strange to be no longer in uniform and I felt odd indeed in a civilian suit, which I had not worn since mobilisation. I was back in my native Scotland and in the area of the County of Linlithgow where I was born in 1903 in the small town of Bathgate—and here it all began.

CHAPTER 2

Youth and Upbringing

My early education was received at the local schools—first an infant school run by the Bathgate School Board and then at Bathgate Academy. This school was founded by a native of the town, John Newlands, who had made a fortune in Jamaica.

Some years before World War I my father had joined forces with a friend of his, James Wood of Wallhouse, a coal owner, and a Mr. Cunningham, an engineer, to establish the Atlas Steel Foundry Company in the adjoining town of Armadale, where they soon began to concentrate on the production of steel castings for ships built on the Clyde, and especially turbine casings for which the company became famous.

My time at Bathgate Academy came to an end in 1916 and I was soon alighting from the train at Waverley Station, Edinburgh, to begin my first day at George Watson's College. The school had been founded in 1723 by one of Edinburgh's successful businessmen.

It was not a boarding school, although there were boarding houses for some boys who had been sent back by their parents from overseas to be educated in their native land. Their fathers were usually Watsonians themselves. Watson's had some remarkable records. In the 1918 Parliament there were five Old Boys in the Government—Sir Ian MacPherson, afterwards Lord Strathcarron, the last Secretary of State for Ireland; Sir Eric Geddes; Sir Auckland Geddes; Sir Robert Horne, the Chancellor of the Exchequer; and T. B. Morison, the Lord Advocate.

My first priority when I reached Watson's was to join the school O.T.C. Being wartime the Corps met for parades at least three times a week because the older boys left to go straight into the forces.

At school I met two older boys in the Corps who were to

become great friends in the years ahead. One was David Maxwell-Fyfe, who ultimately became Lord Chancellor, and the other, who was my Platoon Sergeant, was Richard Snedden. Out of school in 1918, Snedden missed the war as he was commissioned in the Royal Scots just a few days before it ended. He had a distinguished academic career. I lost sight of him after he left school as our paths went different ways.

We met again in 1928. I had then started my final studies for the English Bar. However, I needed to earn a living and at about this time I applied for two jobs. One was with Conservative Party Central Office in London and the other with the Employers' Organisation. The latter asked me to see them in Edinburgh. When I went for my interview I found the Chairman of the Organisation was Forbes Watson, afterwards Sir John Forbes Watson, and the Assistant Secretary of the Organisation was Richard Snedden. It was the first time we had met since 1918.

I had the usual grilling, but I told them I had also applied for a job with the Conservative Party. After seeing Conservative Central Office officials, I decided to accept that job as I felt it would be more useful for a political career, which in fact it turned out to be. Richard Snedden and I resumed our friendship, and our interests became similar as the years went by. He was to help my legal career, particularly in my early struggles at the Bar.

However, I must retrace my steps to 1917, and especially to my days in the school O.T.C., for I was tremendously keen to be a soldier. In wartime the Corps was a very active organisation. We drilled regularly and had many field days with the other schools of Edinburgh—Loretto, Fettes, Heriots, Stewarts and Edinburgh Academy—sometimes marching eight miles out to our mock battle areas. Later I became a piper in the Corps and this achievement was to stand me in good stead throughout the rest of my life and throughout a great part of the world.

As the time passed I became more anxious than ever to get into the army. After the March retreat in 1918 and the heavy casualties which were suffered, I made up my mind that this was the time to enlist. So one morning on my way to school from the station, I put my cap in my pocket and walked into the recruiting office in Chambers Street. I was still only fifteen and not very large for my age. I stretched myself to my full height. It wasn't enough and the doctor turned me down. The Sergeant Major spoke quite kindly to me; I was encouraged and asked if I could enlist as a drummer or bugler. This was greeted with a blast from the Sergeant Major who said that at this stage of the war it was men they wanted, not schoolboys. I was furious and humiliated and slunk out, hoping no one I knew would see me.

My school career ended in July 1920. My father was anxious for me to go into the Atlas Steel Works and at any rate give it a try. This I did and I started working on the shop floor. Most of the men I knew because I had often played football with the younger ones and, of course, we were all locals.

At this time I was taking a keen interest in the Boy Scout movement. I increased the size of the troop from one patrol to many, with over sixty boys, and with a pipe band. As the County of Linlithgow champions we attended the Jamboree at Alexandra Palace, where the Prince of Wales inspected us. My troop won the County Championship three times in succession and we were twice in the first six troops for the Benmore Shield, awarded to the best troop in Scotland. This hobby helped me to get through the time I spent in the steelworks.

I had little enthusiasm for the various tasks that I had to do in the machine shop, pattern shop, drawing office, and as a bricklayer's labourer, and I was glad when after two years it was considered that I should go to the Royal Technical College, then an extramural college of Glasgow University and now Strathclyde University. The subjects I had to study were machine drawing, natural philosophy, mathematics and chemistry. I was bored, even more bored than when I was on the shop floor.

The pleasure and enjoyment at this stage of my career was in joining the O.T.C. in the Engineer Unit at Glasgow University in 1922. I thus started my long connection with the Royal Engineers in the Territorial Army. I was soon promoted to corporal and, after a course with the Royal Engineers at St. Mary's Barracks, Chatham, I was promoted sergeant and also took my Certificate A which at that time was the certificate for a commission.

I was commissioned into the 52nd Lowland Scottish Divisional Engineers—a very famous Scottish division—in 1924 and posted to 240 Field Company at Coatdyke. I was the only officer who had no medals. Practically all the officers and men had seen service in the War. After my first camp I was asked if I would like to join the regular army. But it was too late. I had made up my mind that my future lay in law and Parliament.

The army was to prove the greatest hobby in my life. I went on every army course possible, bridging, demolition, field works and riding—as a Sapper officer I was, of course, mounted. I also went on mechanical transport courses, driving and maintaining trucks and lorries. All of this I enjoyed.

During my time at the university I had become more disillusioned with the thought of working in a steel foundry and had quietly transferred to the Faculty of Arts without telling my parents. When I graduated in Arts, taking my degree at Glasgow, my father in particular was furious and said 'What do you think you are going to do now?' I replied, 'Become a barrister.' This was not at all popular. Careers are often changed during a student's progress through the university but few can have taken a sharper turn than mine. When I enrolled at the Royal Technical College and Glasgow University I was preparing to be an engineer and when I ended I was on my way to being called to the English Bar—although I had to put in a final year at Edinburgh University, where English Law was included in the curriculum.

When I was at Glasgow University I was at one stage on the Students' Representative Council. This is an important body at Scottish universities. During this period there was a Rectorial Election to elect a Lord Rector of the University. The successful candidate was Lord Birkenhead—another man who was going to play an important part in my life. During the few days he was in Glasgow I met him a number of times and got to know him quite well. We had many talks on politics. Birkenhead was the first person to suggest that I should stand for Parliament. My ambitions grew and I began to mull over this prospect.

Youth and Upbringing

My family upbringing was very much in a political atmosphere since my father was active in the Conservative Party and knew the local Conservative candidate, James Kidd, who, for a time, was Member and Junior Minister. He beat Manny Shinwell, who was afterwards Member for Linlithgowshire for many years. I also knew Shinwell quite well and in later years when I was in the House myself he gave me a very warm and friendly welcome.

It was now time to say good-bye to Scotland. I had finished my Arts and Law courses in Scotland and had enrolled at the Inner Temple to read for the English Bar.

When I left home I had no idea where I was going to stay when I reached London. At Waverley Station I bought the 'London Times' as one called *The Times* in Scotland, and in the train I perused the advertisements for digs. I found what I thought looked all right. The address was in Harcourt Terrace, near Earls Court, and the house was kept by a doctor's widow. It sounded respectable, and it was. I took a taxi from King's Cross, for I had no clue as to the whereabouts of Harcourt Terrace. For fifty shillings a week I got a first-floor bedroom and breakfast and dinner every day, with all meals at week-ends. I would have to draw on my modest savings unless I could earn some money somehow.

Like so many young men down from a university, I decided to write. I had already had some minor successes with newspaper articles in my student days and believed that there were editors in Fleet Street waiting for my contributions. How quickly disillusionment came. I churned out articles, but most of them were returned. Then my fortunes changed. Some of my articles began to appear in print. It was not enough and I had to give up my room for another and cheaper one in the same house—the higher one went in the building, the lower was the rent. In the end I landed up in a tiny attic with only a skylight which was not completely watertight, but the rent was only twenty-four shillings a week, including food.

I was offered, and accepted, the secretaryship of a small back-room organisation called the British Economic Federation at a salary of £250 per annum. Soon I was on the speakers' list of the Anti-Socialist Union, the Conservative Central Office, and later also lectured on legal subjects at the Polytechnic and L.C.C. evening classes. These offers came after I was called to the Bar by the Inner Temple in January 1930.

When still in Scotland I had joined the Inner Temple, one of the four Inns of Court. Passing the exams was not a difficult matter as I had covered some of the ground at Glasgow and Edinburgh Universities and had begun eating my dinners. Eating dinners is an historic practice at the Inns of Court. University graduates had to eat three dinners a term, and non-graduates six. It was a pleasant arrangement and I got to know a lot of people whose paths would cross with mine at the Bar, in Parliament, and socially as the years rolled by.

By this time I was more than interested in politics and in this field events were moving rapidly. There was a growing revulsion against the Baldwin Government of 1924–1929 and the by-elections showed no doubt about the turn of the tide. The dissolution of Parliament came in May 1929. Although I was very busy in my various small but money-earning jobs, I was able to take meetings in some of the London constituencies. The campaign was largely conducted in the open air. I used to make two, or occasionally three, speeches in an evening. Of course, the meetings were very rowdy, with a lot of shouting but, on the whole, good-natured. The campaign lasted three weeks. In that contest the lines were clear-cut.

Baldwin sought re-election on a 'Safety First' programme. Anti-Government feelings had been embittered by the Act of 1927 directed against the trade unions after the General Strike and there was a general unhappiness about unemployment. It was, therefore, no easy task for Conservative speakers to state their case in districts like Poplar, Bethnal Green and Stepney; most Conservative speakers wanted to speak in the safe, respectable constituencies. We knew that the cause of the depression was world-wide and that conditions were as bad, or worse, in other countries, but the electors throughout Britain were worried and showed us little mercy at the polls.

The second Socialist Government followed in 1929. After my call to the Bar in January 1930 I served my pupilage with F. W. Wallace, who had been three times Conservative candidate

Youth and Upbringing

for Dundee without any luck. While waiting for briefs I gave some time to journalism and speaking. The main questions agitating the country at that time were the profligacy of socialist finance, safeguards for British industry, and closer trading with the dominions and colonies.

I made money addressing political meetings at £1 per speech plus expenses. I never charged for speaking for the Conservative Party but I did charge the Anti-Socialist and the National Citizens Union. My fees for lecturing at the evening schools were about £1 an hour. It was very hard work, for I also did one or two parades a week, often at week-ends, with the 56th 1st London Division R.E. at Bethnal Green where their Headquarters was situated.

CHAPTER 3

The Keighley Election

By now I thought it was time to try to get a seat to contest at the next General Election. I had done so much speaking for the Conservatives that I again went to see the Deputy Chairman of the Party, Sir George Bowyer. He said that, of course, I would have to fight a hopeless seat for my first attempt. I quite agreed but laid down the stipulation that I must fight a Cabinet Minister.

He couldn't understand this, for, as he said, it would be a pretty desperate fight. I agreed but told him that if by any chance I fought a Cabinet Minister and there was a slide to the Conservatives, and by a miracle I won, I should have earned a good reputation. This is what ultimately happened. Bowyer said there was very few seats going. Coventry was one, and another was Keighley, Yorkshire, which was held for the Socialists by the Rt. Hon. H. B. Lees-Smith, President of the Board of Education. I said at once, 'Done, that's the one I'll go for.' Bowyer was sympathetic and said he would put my name forward to Keighley.

However, I had to get known. When I was called to the English Bar in 1930 I joined the North Eastern Circuit. I had no legal influence anywhere but I had thought that Yorkshire would be a good place to find a constituency. The southern counties were mostly safe Conservative seats and unless one had money and influence the chance of someone like me—a raw Scot with no money—would be pretty slim.

In the autumn of 1930 I was summoned to speak before the Selection Committee of Keighley. If I had not been on the North Eastern Circuit I'm bound to say I would never have heard of Keighley. I was at once impressed by the kindly reception I received. I was in quite good form, nevertheless I couldn't believe I could secure adoption at the first attempt.

The Keighley Election

When I returned to London I heard nothing and then I went home to Linlithgowshire for a brief holiday with my parents. Whilst there I got a letter from Keighley inviting me to an adoption meeting in September. The Committee had passed me and now they were prepared to recommend me to the Conservative Association.

This was a great excitement and so unexpected. I was twenty-seven, and had made it plain that I was not a rich young man and, therefore, the Keighley Conservatives would have to raise my election expenses. This was a great hurdle which they agreed to meet. At the meeting to adopt me as prospective Conservative candidate for the next election I was given an enthusiastic reception, and at once I knew this was going to be a happy relationship.

I enjoyed my years at Keighley. The Yorkshire people I loved; they spoke their mind bluntly but were never unfair. There were many small towns and villages in the constituency and, of course, I had to make speeches at them all. The division stretches from the outskirts of Shipley to the borders of Skipton in Yorkshire's golden valley, so named from the number of large fortunes made by pioneers in textiles and their dependent industries. Its people were thrifty, industrious, and maintained the high standard in education which, on account of the number of exhibitioners from its Technical Institute, once moved a university professor to ask 'Where is this Keighley?'.

At the time of my adoption in September 1930 it was evident that the country was about to turn in favour of the Conservatives. It was clearly seen in the victory in the neighbouring constituency, Shipley, at a by-election in November 1930. We captured the seat which had a Socialist majority of 5,000 in 1929. This time the Conservatives had a majority of more than 1,500. While one swallow never makes a summer, such a turnover in a neighbouring constituency was most encouraging. Keighley, however, was a much more difficult proposition. The Socialists had held the seat since 1922. The member was H. B. Lees-Smith, President of the Board of Education in the MacDonald Government, who at the 1929 General Election had a majority of 7,510 over a Liberal candidate, who had finished more than 1,000 votes over the Conservative.

I had to admit that the odds were heavily against me. I was not discouraged by the boast of the Socialists that no other man than theirs had a chance of success. Many of the Liberals, for example, who had put their candidate into second place had begun to have doubts about dividing the anti-Socialist vote but none of them quite knew how to end such a policy. I did my best to give them a lead and in speech after speech I said that there was still one section of the Liberal Party which could easily collaborate with the Conservatives, the section led by Sir John Simon, afterwards Lord Simon, the Lord Chancellor. There are not a great many points of difference between the point of view of the moderate Liberal and the Conservative, and particularly a progressive Conservative. I was certainly progressive—a man of my background was of necessity that kind of candidate. This I stated in my speech at the Annual General Meeting in March 1931.

In May 1931 Geoffrey Ellis, later Sir Geoffrey Ellis, the Chairman of the Yorkshire Conservative Association, gave a week-end conference for Conservative candidates in Yorkshire. Sir Geoffrey had been a Yorkshire member but was defeated in 1929. Now he was the candidate for Winchester. Among the candidates present were Richard Law, the son of Bonar Law, formerly Prime Minister, and Geoffrey Lloyd. Geoffrey Lloyd was to become a close friend of mine for whom I had the greatest regard. At that time he was Baldwin's Private Secretary. Later he held many Ministerial offices. The guest speaker for the weekend was Sir Philip Cunliffe-Lister, who had been President of the Board of Trade in the last Baldwin administration. The holding of this week-end conference was an excellent idea. We had brief lectures and questions and discussion periods on Conservative policy. We separated, not to meet again until the autumn of the same year when we all became Members of Parliament. There was only one principle upon which we did not agree and that was the age-old controversy on tariffs and free trade, but even in that particular aspect the lines which hitherto tended to diverge were then converging.

My visits to Keighley during the first half of that year had attracted notice, some in strange quarters. One day I was surprised to receive an invitation to lunch from Philip Snowden

The Keighley Election

and his wife. As I had never met them before I was naturally puzzled. What would the Socialist Chancellor want me for—a young Scot trying to make a way for himself in London? All I knew of him had been gained from his speeches which had generally been fierce and bitter attacks on his political opponents, but that did not help me in my search for an explanation of the invitation to 11 Downing Street.

I was thrilled as I turned out of Whitehall into that famous street which I had never visited before. I entered No. 11 where I was greeted by Mrs. Snowden, who herself conducted me to the Chancellor's room.

Beside one of the chairs stood the Chancellor leaning on two sticks for support, but nevertheless a man with a certain formidable dignity. All my preconceived ideas about him vanished at once when he spoke. Instead of the man with the grim mien and gesture and the acid tongue which had been seen and heard on platforms in every part of the country, I found a gentle and kindly person whose smile and sweetness would have disarmed the most critical opponent.

'I'm glad you've come,' he said, holding out his hand in welcome. 'I did want to see the young David chosen by the Keighley Tories to oppose the Socialist Goliath.' He added with a smile and twinkle in his eye, 'I'm a Yorkshireman and come from near Keighley and know it well, so I wanted to meet you. It is good of you to come.' I didn't know he was a Yorkshireman nor that he came from near Keighley. I now understood his friendly gesture and the invitation to lunch. I had read of his physical handicap caused by a bicycle accident when he was young, but I had no idea as to the extent of his disability until that moment. He did not resume his seat from which he had obviously risen on my arrival but suggested that we should pass to the dining room with its beautiful oak panelled walls and an unusual vaulted ceiling.

At lunch he talked about Yorkshire, returning several times to Keighley. The hamlet of Cowling where he was born was not in my constituency but a little outside its borders. However, the town of Keighley was the natural centre to which as a boy he had looked and he still had many friends there. He was interested in what I had to say about my experiences among the people and in what I thought of my prospects. Our talk ranged over a wide field and I was amazed to hear that this man, whose figure had loomed with almost vindictive menace and who in debate was apt to be acrimonious, had once been greatly interested in amateur theatricals. 'I have found the political stage equally interesting,' he said. 'I like watching the players on it.' He then suggested how some members of my party did not hold posts for which he thought they were eminently suitable. 'Baldwin does not give his able young men the chance they deserve.'

We left the table and Snowden made his way slowly out of the room. I had been long enough in their company to realise that, besides being an excellent hostess and a charming woman, Mrs. Snowden was a perfect match for her husband. Leaving the room in which so many Chancellors have attended to State matters we made our way to the street door. She shook my hand and her parting words were, 'You must come back and see us after you are in the House.' Was there a ring of prophecy?

1931 was a particularly busy year for me. I was determined to win Keighley for the Conservative Party so I paid frequent visits to the constituency and attended functions of all kinds. By this time I was in the chambers of John W. Morris K.C., a very brilliant lawyer and a delightful and friendly man who did not share my political views. Indeed two of my colleagues in chambers, Herbert Baxter and Emlyn Jones, were to fight elections as Liberals. John Morris became a Lord of Appeal and Arthian Davis and Gerald Thesiger, also in the chambers then, became Judges of the High Court. I was not long in these chambers because at that time I began getting briefs from the Shipping Federation through their solicitors, Botterrell and Roche. The Leader for the Shipping Federation was Lord Reading so I moved to his chambers.

This new source of briefs came through the good offices of Richard Snedden, who was now Secretary of the Shipping Federation. This proved a very valuable legal connection. At the same time I was lecturing in law at the evening classes of the London Polytechnic two evenings a week and this entailed a lot of preparation. I was also still writing but I was getting so busy that this side of my activities gradually came to a full stop.

The Keighley Election

When I came to London I had transferred from the 52nd Lowland Scottish to the 56th (London) Division at the end of 1928 and was promoted Captain the next year and on 1st January 1935 was given the Brevet of Major. The T.A. also took up a lot of time. My Drill Hall was at Bethnal Green. In Scotland the men were largely miners, but in the 56th they were Cockneys with all kinds of occupations, some on the railways, some cabinetmakers, joiners, builders and all kinds of odd-job men, but they were a cheerful lot and I enjoyed serving with them.

Whatever else I did I always found time for my first love—soldiering. I remained with the 56th Division R.E. until I left in 1938 to command the 31st Battalion R.E. in AA Command. I paraded every week with the T.A. and also attended the many social functions in the winter months. The culmination of the year's work was the annual camp. I was so keen that I usually commanded the advance guard to put the camp up and stayed with the rear guard to take the camp down again. Each year I tried to do a course with the regular army with the Sappers. These courses were either at Chatham or Aldershot, which I fitted into the vacations at the Bar. I did bridging courses, demolition courses, the R.E. Senior Officers course, and the General Senior Officers course for other arms as well as Sappers. Several times I was asked to transfer to the regular army, but much as I liked soldiering, I liked politics better.

Before the Socialist Party had its first tenure of office, in 1923, Winston Churchill said that Labour was not fit to govern. It was, I thought, an unfortunate phrase at the time because it was made to appear by astute Socialist electioneers as if he were insulting a class instead of merely criticising, as Churchill was, the leading personnel of a political party. Eight years after Churchill's statement more than half the country's adult population echoed that dictum and there was far more truth in it in the summer of 1931 than when it was uttered. Public expenditure had gone beyond the safety level. Public confidence in the national rulers had declined and there came the financial crisis which forced the Socialist Government to agree to vast economies.

The Cabinet authorised Ramsay MacDonald and Philip Snowden, who shortly became a peer, to apply the brake on spending and seek Conservative and Liberal support for their economic proposals. I have always had a feeling that, but for Snowden's grim determination to go through with the plan, MacDonald would have yielded to the dictatorial crack of the Trades Union Congress whip when it announced uncompromising opposition to the programme of cuts. Most of the Ministers accepted the view of Transport House.

Events then began to move quickly and culminated in the formation of the National Government in which MacDonald was joined by only a handful of his Socialist colleagues who were willing to co-operate with the other parties. He asked for a dissolution of Parliament, and the General Election was fixed for 27th October. Thirteen months after my arrival in Keighley I was in the throes of my first Parliamentary contest. During that period I had been in the constituency as often as I could leave London.

The hope in the constituency had been that there would be only two candidates, Conservative, or National Conservatives as we called ourselves at that election, and the Socialist. Keighley had a long Liberal history, but with the decline of that party and the rise of Socialism the political scene changed. The Conservatives had only once held the seat; that was in 1918 when a Coalition Unionist had been elected but beaten in 1922. From then on it had been a so-called safe Socialist seat.

Just before the election there was a Liberal flurry; the Liberals of Shipley said they would not contest Shipley if the Conservatives would stand down at Keighley. Countering that, the Conservatives had recently won a spectacular fight at a by-election a year ago in Shipley. However, the Liberals decided to fight me and their candidate, chosen at the last minute, was Mr. Crossland Briggs of Bradford.

The Keighley Conservatives were determined to make no deal, although a few did toy with the suggestion that I should stand down. There was no compromise and the election went on. I had never addressed such enthusiastic meetings. From the word go I had a feeling that I was going to win.

There were many rowdy meetings, both outside and indoors,

The Keighley Election

but I loved the heckling. I had been brought up in a tough school in Scotland and I knew something about such meetings and how to overcome the noise and make the audience listen, even if only in short gaps. I gained something of a reputation for my handling of meetings and this stood me in good stead. It was a hard-fought election but the Yorkshire people are great sports. When the count took place it was one of the most nerve-racking things I had ever experienced. But early on I realised I was going to win, and I did, with a majority of 5,887. Lees-Smith, the Socialist, got 13,192 and the Liberal 9,044.

Outside the hall where the count took place the crowds were massive, as they were too in the Town Hall square. When I went out on the balcony with the Returning Officer, the other candidates followed. There was a roar of cheers and boos. I got a tumultuous reception. This went on and on until we retired back into the hall. It was the most exciting moment of my life. No other election was the same.

Letters and telegrams flowed in, the first being from Stanley Baldwin. I was only twenty-eight and, with my background, it seemed young to me. A new world lay ahead.

CHAPTER 4

Keighley to Richmond

Before the House rose for the Christmas recess I made my maiden speech in November, not long after taking my seat. I got up twice but didn't catch the Speaker's eye the first time so I sat down again and I was very glad to do so. By the time I rose the second time I had cold feet but survived. I spoke on the Debate on the second reading of the Import Duties Bill.

I was interested in the Import Duties Bill because of my past experience in the steel industry and my new experience of the textile industry in Keighley. It is customary in the House of Commons for the speaker following a maiden speech to pay a tribute to the speech. When I sat down a generous tribute was paid by Mr. Neil McLean, Socialist Member for Govan, Glasgow. He congratulated me on the very able speech I had delivered. He said he did so with all the greater heartiness in that I was a fellow student at Glasgow University with his own son and he would be only too proud to see his son follow in my footsteps. Socialist Members intervened to say, 'But not in the same party!'

My speech received several good notices in the Press. 'Captain Watt is a good natural House of Commons speaker'—*The Times*. 'On the Conservative side there was an excellent Maiden Speech by Captain Watt (Keighley) which impressed the House very favourably'—*Yorkshire Post*. 'The House was considerably impressed by a Maiden Speech from Captain Harvie-Watt'—*Sheffield Daily Telegraph*. Notably the *Glasgow Evening Times* said, 'Of the many Maiden Speeches now being made in the House of Commons one of the most successful was delivered by Captain Harvie-Watt. Although he sits for a Yorkshire constituency in which he defeated the redoubtable Lees-Smith, Captain Watt is a past graduate of Glasgow University.

He was a popular figure in student life at Gilmorehill and was closely identified with the O.T.C.'

Lord Dunglass, later the Earl of Home and Prime Minister, also made his maiden speech that evening. I was glad this ordeal was over but, despite what the Press was good enough to say, I was never at ease speaking, or even asking a Question, in the House of Commons.

A greater event in my life was about to take place because I became engaged in April 1932. My fiancee was Bettie Taylor, the only daughter of Paymaster-Captain Archibald Taylor, O.B.E., R.N. She was an assistant to the Resident Director of the Chinese Maritime Customs.

We had known each other for about three years, gradually meeting more often until we both knew that this was it, and we arranged to get married at St. Columba's Church of Scotland on 4th June, a Saturday, by the late Rev. Archibald Fleming. It was a quiet wedding with close family and friends and we had a lunch party afterwards. Unfortunately we couldn't take much of a honeymoon, for I had a brief in court on Monday morning, so we went up the river to spend a week-end only. Our honeymoon proper would be in Scotland when Parliament and the Courts were in recess. Ours has been a very congenial and successful marriage and on 4th June 1977 we celebrated our sapphire wedding, forty-five years of happiness.

I must say that all the time I was in Keighley I worked hard with public meetings, answering questions, socials, dances, sporting events, kicking off at a Rugby League game, and even once preaching from a Methodist pulpit with my wife in the pulpit beside me. At the same time I was practising at the Bar and my practice was growing. I had also started asking Questions in the House because I realised this was the way to acclimatise myself to the House of Commons. I even asked a Question about sterilisation of the mentally unfit, although I knew nothing about the subject! Some organisation must have asked me to put the Question; I soon became wary, for M.Ps were constantly asked to put Questions in the House about subjects supported by various organisations, many of them cranky.

Apart from my frequent visits to Keighley, I spoke all over the country at by-elections and other meetings. By this stage my reputation as a good speaker for the industrial areas had been passed around and I was constantly being asked to speak in that type of constituency. I had to restrict my meetings to week-ends since I was still keen on asking Questions in the House and my practice was steadily expanding.

My next speech in the House was on the Army Estimates, when I moved a Motion urging the Government to do all in its power to encourage and stimulate T.A. recruiting and to maintain and increase the efficiency of that Army. This sentiment did not meet with approval from one of the Socialist back benchers, who interrupted me to ask, 'What is the T.A. for anyway?' I said, 'Defence.' He said, 'Defence against whom?' and another voice intervened, saying with a note of jocularity 'Against Scotland'.

Everyone knew I was a Scot because I used to wear the kilt occasionally if I was going to speak at some Scottish function and, of course, I couldn't, and didn't want to, disguise my accent. I remember at the Speaker's Levee I wore my kilt, so did Mr. Ramsay, M.P. for the Western Isles. The kilt had not been worn before at such Parliamentary functions and we both had to obtain the Speaker's permission to wear the 'dress'.

Not long after my speech on the Territorial Army in the House it was decided to form a T.A. Committee to look after the interests of the Territorials. All those Members who were also Territorials were invited to join. At the meeting Major J. J. Llewellyn, afterwards a Cabinet Minister and later Governor-General of the Central African Federation, was appointed Chairman and I was appointed Secretary. It was decided that members of the committee should ballot for an opportunity to open a Debate on the Army Estimates, calling attention to the pay and conditions of the T.A.

In all my political work my wife took a keen interest and was a great help. She made her maiden speech in the constituency in February 1934. She had often made votes of thanks and brief speeches. On this occasion, the Annual General Meeting of the Keighley Women's Association, she had to stand in for me because I was speaking at Lancaster that night. I was told afterwards she had made a first-class speech; I felt very proud,

Keighley to Richmond

but I knew alas this would let her in for other speeches, and it did.

My next speech in the House of Commons was in a Debate calling for some active steps to secure greater safety on the roads. I was alarmed at the rapid increase in accidents. Traffic was then increasing at an amazing rate, 80,000 more cars every year. It was calculated that since the war ended in 1918 until the end of 1933 about two million men, women and children were killed or injured on the roads of Great Britain, almost 75% of the total war casualties. This speech got a very good reception from all sides of the House.

Towards the end of October 1934 I was asked to stand for, and was elected to, the Council of the Royal Borough of Kensington, London, to represent the Redcliffe Ward, where I had lived since I arrived in London in 1929. I had long felt that there was something lacking in my political experience, and that was a knowledge of local government. This was now to be rectified, although it made my life busier than ever.

I had been candidate and Member for Keighley from October 1931 and it was now October 1934. In this period I had addressed 272 meetings of one kind or another in my constituency and 72 meetings outside it. These speeches did not include lunches, dinners, and lectures at the Bonar Law College, Ashridge, or other political schools. In the same period I had written over 6,500 letters. I was horrified when I collected these statistics. Furthermore, this took no account of any legal cases though my practice was rising all the time.

I was also carrying on vigorously my duties in the T.A. When I was awarded the Brevet of Major on 1st January 1935, I attended a King's Levee at St. James's Palace to be presented to His Majesty. It was a fascinating ceremony. I was presented by General Sir George Kirkpatrick, K.C.B., K.C.S.I. All those present were in full dress uniform. Mine was hired from Moss Bros. It would have been very expensive to buy and I doubt if I would have worn it again. The T.A. was greatly to the fore at this time, thanks to the T.A. Committee in the House. Roger Lumley, afterwards Lord Scarbrough, proposed, and I seconded, a Motion that in view of the important role assigned to the Territorial Army in the system of National Defence this

House considers that improvements in the pay, training, and conditions of service of the T.A. are needed to increase numbers and efficiency.

By this time more and more reports were appearing in the Press about my activities at the Bar. I had had plenty of devilling to do and many police court and county court cases, but in October 1935 I appeared in the King's Bench Division for the first time before the Lord Chief Justice, Mr. Justice Humphrey, and Mr. Justice Singleton on an appeal from one of the Metropolitan magistrates. I had appeared in this case in the magistrates court. The decision was in our favour.

By now, the 1935 General Election was getting under way. In 1931 I had polled the highest number of votes ever cast for a candidate in Keighley, but the Socialist and Liberal candidates combined had scored over 3,000 higher than my poll. It was hoped that this time it would be a straight fight between the Conservatives and Socialists. The Rt. Hon. H. B. Lees-Smith was again going to be my Socialist opponent. The first speculation of the election was what would happen to the Liberal vote. Early on, however, the Keighley Division Liberal Association decided not to put forward a candidate, the first time in Keighley that there had not been a Liberal candidate. I had arranged to speak at fifty meetings in every part of the constituency, but it turned out to be seventy speeches. In addition, of course, there was canvassing and the usual office work, not to mention preparation of notes for speeches.

I received messages of good wishes from the Prime Minister, Stanley Baldwin, Mr. Ramsay MacDonald and Sir John Simon. I realised I was up against it. You could get the feel of the meetings. It was harder than in 1931. I had some very rowdy meetings with masses of heckling—on the whole good-humoured, but at times it took all my efforts to keep the meeting under control. On these occasions Chairmen are not of great help because the bully boys won't let them intervene. It's the candidate they want to get at. Although it was hard work I always enjoyed an election. My eve-of-poll helper was Sir Philip Cunliffe-Lister, Minister for Air.

Polling day was dull and wet, which was not favourable to

me, for the small farmers in the Dales, mostly Conservatives, would not get to the polls. I had fought hard and so had my wife and the workers of Keighley. In an 80% poll the Socialist Party got a majority of 468, the lowest Socialist majority ever in Keighley. When I appeared on the balcony, second after Lees-Smith, I was booed and cheered and many sang 'He's a jolly good fellow,' but I was defeated.

It was little comfort to be held up in the Press as the best candidate the Conservatives had ever put up at Keighley. There was no recrimination from me. I had in fact nearly 1,000 more votes in 1935, 20,124 compared with 19,079 in 1931; but it was still a defeat. I had a telegram from Duff Cooper, 'Bad Luck. Congratulations on a fine fight,' and a letter from Cunliffe-Lister, 'I'm very sorry. You put up a good fight in a very difficult seat.' Baldwin also sent a telegram—'My sincere thanks for your fight. Sorry to lose your support in the House.'

By December I was back in the courts, and by January I was again speaking at political and social meetings, including proposing the toast of Robert Burns. And so the circle began once more but without a constituency. I was asked to fight Keighley again but I felt I could not do so because the next General Election would not be until 1940, or 1939 at the earliest, and I couldn't wait all that time nursing a constituency so far away from my work.

Fortunately I was busy at the Bar. It is difficult to keep, or build up, a practice when you are in the House and nursing a constituency. Briefs were frequent in December and January and I could now see that my prospects were improving with every case. Most of my cases were from the Shipping Federation and kindred clients. I much enjoyed this work.

On 22nd January 1937 it was announced in the Press that the Conservative Party candidate for Richmond, Surrey, following on the resignation of Sir William Ray, would be chosen from four names—Sir Albert Clavering, the Hon. Edward Jessel, Major Harvie-Watt and Mr. Frederick William Dean. Within twenty-four hours of Sir William's resignation Richmond Conservative Office received no fewer than seventy applications, including many ex-M.Ps. The four names selected were to be placed before the Executive Committee for them to make the final choice.

I didn't think much of my chances here. Richmond was one of the safest Conservative seats in the country. Clavering had been with Central Office at Palace Chambers for seven years as the honorary director of the party's film department. Edward Jessell, aged thirty-three, was a son of Lord Jessell and had practised as a barrister but was then in the City, and F. W. Dean, aged fifty-two, was an ex-Mayor of Marylebone. The Selection Committee of the Richmond Conservative Association after a two-and-a-half hour meeting made the announcement.

The names were put before the Executive Committee which packed the large room of the Conservative offices at Richmond on the evening of 28th January 1937. I was not very optimistic, for it was a plum for any Conservative candidate and I understood that whoever was selected would have to pay £500 a year to the local Conservative association, in addition to subscriptions to many local organisations and, of course, pay the election expenses. The *Daily Express* headlined next day in large letters, 'Red-headed Major is picked from 70 as Richmond Candidate.' In smaller print it went on to say, 'Last night four speeches were heard from the men whose names had been selected from the seventy applicants. Major Harvie-Watt won the speaking match unanimously.'

My candidature was won, but not without a struggle. As I've said, from the financial point of view I was a dead duck and so, not thinking I had any chance, I made a first-rate speech and got great applause. Then came questions, a few perfunctory ones on political subjects, after which I was asked what, if selected, would I be prepared to give to the association for election expenses and as an annual subscription. 'Ah,' I said. 'That is the important question. Not what we are going to do about defence in the face of the rise of Hitler, not what we are going to do about unemployment,' and so on I went. 'No, the most important question is, what is the candidate prepared to give to the Conservative association?' And I said, '*Nothing.*'

I then walked from the room, went upstairs, and sat with the other candidates. Clavering looked pleased with himself. I understood afterwards that his wife and daughter were in a large car outside, ready to sweep in when the name of the winner had been announced. After a very short time the Agent popped his head in rather sheepishly and pointed to me. I was amazed. I thought perhaps the jolly good audience below just wanted to say good-bye. When I walked in, however, I was greeted with almost deafening applause. I was asked a lot more questions. Actually I agreed they couldn't drop from £500 p.a. to nothing but I pointed out that it was their duty to raise the money and until they did I would help out with a diminishing sum.

My wife was absolutely staggered. She had never for a moment thought I would be successful because I could never afford the large sums of money which had been mentioned. But that night made us many friends who remained friends for the rest of our lives. Later three of my Young Conservatives, Ian Harvey, Bernard Braine, and Pat Hornsby-Smith, all members of the Richmond Association and later to become M.Ps and Ministers, took up the cudgels on my behalf and they helped to stop these extortionate sums being asked for in many of the safe Conservative seats.

My fight at Richmond began at the beginning of February 1937. I had been out of Parliament for just over a year. Richmond was a different kind of constituency altogether from Keighley. Keighley had been largely industrial and I loved the tough meetings I used to attend. Richmond was an outer area of London, and mostly residential.

This time I had a straight fight with the Socialists. George Rogers was the Socialist candidate and later got into Parliament for North Kensington.

In politics there are more kicks than half-pence, as the saying goes, and the *Sunday Express*, not a friend of mine in later days, said of me then, 'Ginger-haired Harvie-Watt with a burr in his voice, married five years, no children [couldn't afford them; my wife was also working], a fervid Territorial, a fine orator, educated at George Watson's College, Edinburgh, and the Universities of Glasgow and Edinburgh. Mr. Harvie-Watt is a poor man. He has no money save what he earns and he earns it at the English Bar. He is solid rather than exciting, capable and ambitious, a pocket edition of Mr. Baldwin. I predict a good future for him after his return to the House of Commons on Thursday.'

However 'the best-laid schemes of mice and men gang aft agley'. Although I was back in the House of Commons with a majority of 12,837 over the Socialist, I little thought that before I was to fight another General Election there would be a world-wide war, and my life would take a turn towards other interests.

Chapter 5

The Commons, the Bar and the Army

I had no sooner finished the election than I was back in the courts again. Indeed, I took several cases while the campaign was being fought, Richmond was so close to the county and police courts, where I usually operated.

In the midst of this very busy time at the Bar, Euan Wallace, Parliamentary Secretary to the Board of Trade, appointed me to be his Parliamentary Private Secretary, so now I had my foot on the lowest rung of the political ladder.

The general duty of a P.P.S. is to relieve his boss of many minor tasks in the House. For example, he has to keep in touch with Members, especially when Departmental Bills are going through the House, and to sense whether Members are in agreement or otherwise with what is being proposed. During the passage of these Bills, he acts as a go-between with the Department's civil servants who are in charge of the Bill, and has to provide information required by the Minister to answer criticisms put forward by the Opposition or by his own party. The P.P.S. also has many duties outside the House—for instance, taking constituency meetings or even speaking at functions when the Minister has a major speech to make in the House or elsewhere. He also helps with constituency correspondence, which can become quite a task. To become a P.P.S. is generally considered to be a first stepping-stone to ministerial rank.

This position did not interfere much with my Bar practice, except when there was any Bill going through the House where the Committee stage was taken in a Committee Room upstairs. Fortunately most of my cases were in the London area. The Senior Counsel to the Shipping Federation, Lord Reading, decided not long before the war to leave the Bar. He was Commanding Officer of the Inns of Court Regiment and a most enthusiastic territorial. When this happened David Maxwell-Fyfe began to lead me in many of my cases.

An interesting case came along when I had to go to Madeira. I took my wife with me as her father, a former Naval Officer, had an appointment in connection with the Navy's non-intervention activities during the Spanish Civil War, with an office in Funchal. I had to take evidence on commission for a shipping company and Alex Ross acted for the unions and looked after the legal interests of the crew.

We went out in the *Arundel Castle*. It was my first experience of a luxury liner and we treated the voyage as a holiday.

We sailed on 31st December and were supposed to return to England in the *Warwick Castle* on 7th January 1936. However, it didn't work out like that. Madeira was a leisurely place and no one was in a hurry. The population always seemed to be having a holiday. Finally, when evidence on commission was taken, I was rung up by the British Consul and was asked to go to see him at once, so both Alex Ross and I went together. We were staggered to hear that the shorthand typist had made a mess of the whole proceedings because she couldn't really take down the correct statements as her English was sadly lacking. So we had to wait until we could get a typist who really could understand English.

The result was that, instead of being in Madeira about a week, we were there for nearly three weeks. The case concerned a ship called the *Sea Rambler* which had sailed from the west coast of Africa. By the time it reached Madeira it had to put in to harbour because most of the crew were dead or dying. The case turned on the nature of the illness and the reason for death. The one side, that of the Shipping Federation for whom I was acting, said that the reason for this catastrophe was that the men had caught yellow fever, and the other side said it was due to bad water.

This case went from one court to another but, alas, from my point of view, it was a great disappointment because when it went to the House of Lords, where I had never before pleaded, I was mobilised. This would have been my chance but John Bassett took the case for 'Mr. Harvie-Watt on War Service'.

The Commons, the Bar and the Army

In 1938 I was exceptionally busy. I was really working from morning until night at the Bar and at the House of Commons as P.P.S. to Euan Wallace and had the T.A. at weekends, not to mention many speeches in the constituencies, including my own. Meanwhile the clouds were gathering, dark and menacing, on the European scene.

I had been just over a year as P.P.S. to Euan Wallace as Parliamentary Secretary to the Board of Trade. Now he was made Financial Secretary to the Treasury—a position that was considered a stepping-stone to the Cabinet. He asked me to continue as his P.P.S. and I was only too pleased to agree and delighted at this very minor improvement in my Parliamentary status.

It was not to be for long, for shortly afterwards I was entertaining a constituent to tea when one of the Whips' messengers came down to the Harcourt Room where we were and asked me to come up to the Whips' Office as the Chief Whip wanted to have a word with me. I wondered why but, as on all occasions like this, it suddenly flashed through my mind—could he want me for an appointment in the Whips' Office? This was then my greatest ambition.

I was ushered into the Chief Whip's room. He was Captain David Margesson, a tall, very well-dressed man, usually wearing a black morning coat with black and white checked trousers. He could put the fear of God into new Members, but otherwise was charming to meet. He was behind his desk and he asked me to sit down and explained that, in the change of Government, he wanted a new Assistant Government Whip (unpaid). I was thrilled. This was a real foot on the ladder and just the way up the ladder that I wanted. I would rather have been an unpaid Government Whip than a minor Under-Secretary in one of the Departments. The Government Whips' Office varies in numbers, but there is usually the Chief Whip and a Deputy Chief, who at that time was Captain the Hon. James Stuart, who was also the Scottish Whip. Then there were several Junior Lords of the Treasury, and finally several Assistant Government Whips, unpaid. There were also two Whips who held Court jobs. The Whips' Office was a very close community and most Junior Whips had to see that the fire was always stoked up in the winter time. It was like being back at school and in your first year.

In the Whips' Office one begins to feel nearer the centre of Government, and the Chief Whip's conferences each day were illuminating about personalities in the House and Government business. I started my duties on 18th May 1938. The routine was a varied one. In the morning I went to No. 12 Downing Street. Nothing much was done there except by the Chief Whip. Most of us dealt with our correspondence, although in my case I rarely attended because, being an unpaid Whip, it was permissible for me to carry on my practice at the Bar. So I spent most of my days in the Temple or in the courts. I usually only needed to get to the House after 4 pm. and I remained there until the House rose, at 11 pm. But in the year before the war, apart from all-night sittings, I seldom got home before midnight or even 2 am.

In the *Daily Telegraph* of 20th May 1938 it was reported, 'Major H. Watt, the newly appointed Assistant Whip, is evidently a glutton for work. Although he is a busy, practising barrister, he has undertaken this extra parliamentary work. His spare time he devotes to the Territorial Army, in which he is and has been for many years a serving officer. He will need all his ingenuity to fit in as many trips to his Richmond constituency as he has done up to now.'

In the *Richmond Herald* it was stated that I was the first M.P. for the Richmond Division to hold a Government office since Viscount Cave.

In May 1939 the Prime Minister sanctioned a scheme which included the appointment of a Conservative boss who would be the opposite number to Mr. Herbert Morrison, the Socialist Party Leader for London. I was appointed to the position of London Whip, probably the largest Whip area in the country. Part of my duties would be to act as liaison officer between the Conservative Central Office and the party in the House of Commons.

The Whip is supposed to keep in close touch with his area and to listen to all the problems, so that the Chief Whip gets a broad feeling of what is happening in the country and can report to the Prime Minister. Of course, if there are any serious rows he has to report to the Chief at once. He also has to take his place on the Front Government Bench, watch the business of the House, and see that it goes smoothly, and move some Motions on behalf of the Government. He must listen to criticism in Debate so that the Chief Whip can follow what has been taking place.

Another curious job a Whip has to do is to be 'On the Door' as it is called. This is the Members' Lobby which leads to the cloakrooms and doors out of the House. There is always a Whip on the door to tell Members if there are likely to be Divisions and if they have to return at any particular time. Most Members are co-operative and tell you their movements and when they will be back. Many times it is essential that they should return, and a Whip must prevent an M.P. taking French leave unless he has special permission or is paired with a Member of the Opposition.

The only two Members who ever gave me bother were Sir Alan Anderson, the Member for the City—a tall, snooty-looking man who had his head in the air and just looked at me as if it wasn't my business as to whether or not he was coming back for the Division. The other was Winston Churchill, who always walked in a purposeful way with his shoulders shrugged and his head down like a bulldog. When he passed me and I told him there would likely be a Division at a certain time, his face looked sterner and he adopted the bulldog look, but walked on. During the time I was in the Whips' Office I can't say I ever spoke to Winston.

By the summer of 1938 the international situation was looking grave. I was asked to transfer to the 31st Bn. R.E., an anti-aircraft battalion, with a view to taking command. I was very sorry to do this, but it was clear that the AA was vital should war come suddenly, and truly the threat grew more serious; shortly afterwards on 26th September 1938 I was ordered to join my battalion immediately. I got this order while motoring in the Highlands with my wife. Apparently the police had been contacted by my Adjutant, who knew roughly where we were going. We were stopped about forty miles to the north of Invergarry by an Automobile Association man. We were quite staggered. We did an about-turn and set off for London, driving all through the night. We stopped south of Carlisle for supper and heard Hitler ranting on the radio. I joined my unit in the afternoon. The war clouds were no doubt gathering fast but the immediate threat came to nothing and I was demobilised again. I was soon back in my usual routine in the courts and the constituency.

In January 1939 I was appointed to command the 31st (City of London Rifles) Anti-Aircraft Bn. Royal Engineers. I had been commissioned in 1924 and after fifteen years was commanding a battalion. I got a telegram from the Secretary of State for War, Mr. Hore-Belisha, congratulating me on my promotion.

1939 was just as busy a year for me as 1938 had been. I don't think I have ever worked so hard. My Bar practice was beginning to go really well; indeed, from a personal and legal point of view, the war came at the wrong time as my junior practice was shooting ahead fast.

On 17th August, immediately I returned from a partial mobilization, my wife and I, mingling business with pleasure, left Southampton in the *Capetown Castle* for South Africa. Apart from my short visit to Madeira a few years before, I had never had the opportunity to venture very far. But on this occasion I was going to South Africa and Rhodesia on business and to visit two gold mines in Rhodesia. They were the Globe & Phoenix and the Phoenix Prince gold mines, of which I had become a director. I was also on the Board of the Phoenix Mining & Finance Company, a central finance company interested in these Rhodesian mines. This trip, therefore, entailed a journey to Que Que, between Salisbury and Bulawayo, and would take in the Sebakwe district of Matabeleland.

The pleasure of the voyage had been spoiled by the news from home, and on the 24th August, while listening to the news, I received a cable ordering me to report to my unit as soon as possible. However, there was no way of getting back quickly; we had passed the homeward bound ship *Arundel Castle* much earlier in the day, so there was no question of transferring at sea and we would have to go to Cape Town.

On the 27th August (Sunday) the day started off badly by a

The Commons, the Bar and the Army

disturbing broadcast to all passengers and the ship's company by the Captain who informed us that the ship had been taken over by the Admiralty and had to be darkened at night in case of emergency. I had drinks with the Captain after the church service and he showed me some private cables to the effect that the Baltic and the Mediterranean were now closed to British shipping and all British ships in those seas had to make for open water.

It was quite eerie at night travelling in a darkened ship. All dead-lights and port-holes were closed and no lights were allowed on the decks at all. This was all rather depressing but nevertheless exciting. One evening I had to take the chair at a concert held in the lounge when Richard Tauber, the famous singer, sang many of his popular songs. He finished his selection with *Land of Hope and Glory* which he sang with great fervour, the whole audience rising to its feet. It was a memorable occasion.

We reached Cape Town in the early morning of 31st August. I had given the Whips' Office, my Adjutant, and my Clerk in the Temple my address as the Mount Nelson Hotel, but there were no messages so we proceeded north to Rhodesia by train. We stopped at Mafeking, famous for its siege in the Boer War. There we were told that Germany had bombed Warsaw and other Polish towns, and that Great Britain had given an ultimatum to Germany. Our problem now was how we were going to get home.

Colonel Ellis Robins, who had been on the ship with us and was now also on the train, said he thought the quickest way for us to return would be by flying-boat from Beira and that he would try to arrange the passage for us as soon as possible.

We arrived at Que Que in the early hours of 3rd September and we were in the Globe & Phoenix mine when we heard that war had been declared. Next day we were horrified to hear of the sinking of the *Athenia* with 1,400 passengers going to Canada.

We spent five days at the mine, inspecting all aspects of its activities. On 8th September we left Que Que to motor to Bindura to visit the Phoenix Prince gold mine. We had to go by Salisbury. There I went straight to the office of the British

South African Company of which Colonel Robbins was Resident Director. We were surprised, but glad, to hear that we were to fly back the next morning. I motored the sixty miles to Bindura and returned to Salisbury in time for dinner. It was indeed a brief visit to the mine.

We left Salisbury at 6 am. on 9th September for the two-and-a-half-hour flight to Beira, only 350 miles from Salisbury. It was a small plane, seating only six people. We came down once at Umtali. It was a very bumpy journey through mountainous country and we both felt sick when we left the plane for lunch and a four-hour wait until the Imperial Airways flying-boat arrived at Beira. From Beira to home it was like a trip on a magic carpet.

The day after we got back I joined my battalion, but not before I was offered the job of a Junior Lord of the Treasury. However, I refused. It was a reluctant refusal.

My life pattern was changing rapidly. Although now in the army, I did remain a Whip for a week or two and on 20th September I had to appear on the Government Front Bench as Lt. Colonel. I moved the adjournment of the House. The sight of uniforms was not common at that time and certainly not on the Front Bench. It must have been many years since a Member of the House had worn uniform on the Government Bench. Back benchers, of course, did wear uniform when on leave and this continued to be a practice for the rest of the war.

On mobilisation my battalion was spread out over Sussex and Surrey. We had searchlights in many out-of-the-way places. My Battalion H.Q. was first at Crawley, where I spent some months, then at the foot of the South Downs in a lovely house called Plumpton Place which was owned by Lord Manton.

In August 1940 I was cheered by the birth of my eldest son, James, in Edinburgh. Not the best time for my wife, for she had been listening to the thunderous broadcasts of Churchill about 'fighting on the beaches', the devastating threats from the air, and 'we shall never surrender'. As she said to me on the telephone, 'At least I shall be immobile.'

The Commons, the Bar and the Army

The raids began in earnest about the early autumn of 1940, and rumours of invasion began to spread. Many times I had to go up to the Downs with some troops to spy out the lie of the land which, by this time, we knew well. Many experiments were made in my battalion area and Lord Dowding often visited my Headquarters with General Sir Frederick Pile, G.O.C. AA Command. Pile was a tiny man with great sparkle and a first-class commander of troops. He remained head of AA Command throughout the war. He was always friendly to me and thought I had done a wonderful job with various experimental devices and with the battalion. He began to suggest I should get a brigade before long. Meanwhile, however, I had plenty to think about. Lord Dowding, the head of the Royal Air Force then, was a different kind of man—shy, quiet. In fact he was dead tired. He carried a tremendous burden in those days, so much depended on the Air Force in the autumn of 1940 and onwards. He visited my Battalion H.Q. on several occasions.

The planes often went over my area on the way to London. Here we were experimenting with a gadget called a U.P. rocket and G.L. Sets Radar. These rockets were most unpredictable things. You never knew if they would, or could, go at all or, if so, in which direction. They were supposed to be useful against low-flying bombers. They frightened us.

It was at this time that I got a signal from AA Command to say Sir Frederick Pile was bringing the Prime Minister to visit my experimental rocket site. They were going to visit first the famous Biggin Hill aerodrome where many of our fighter aeroplanes were stationed and which will always be associated with the Battle of Britain.

At an earlier stage I was caught by one of the first air attacks on Biggin Hill and it was not a very pleasant experience. There were many casualties but, fortunately for me, I escaped everything but fright. It was the first time I was bombed. After visiting Biggin Hill the Prime Minister came on to one of my sites north of Redhill where he wanted to see our experiments. It was the intention to demonstrate the rocket in particular firing against low-flying aircraft. It was a great trundling thing like a long tube, and had not yet been perfected.

I had come up from Plumpton to see my company shoot the rocket for the Prime Minister's delectation. Everything went wrong. First General Pile said to me the P.M. was frozen and in a bad temper and asked if I could give him a strong whisky. It was something we did not have on a site and I had to say that I would send a despatch rider to my nearest company H.Q. at Bletchingley, some miles away along winding roads, and it would take a little while before he could get back.

Pile said afterwards that I had told him there was about as much chance of getting a whisky and soda here as there was in the middle of the Sahara. The despatch rider must have taken awful risks in the blackout.

Meanwhile everything was going from bad to worse. The field was almost waterlogged and the rain poured down. Everything I tried to show the Prime Minister he had seen before. The U.P. rocket was fired several times. I never heard what happened to the missiles or what damage they caused to life or limb or property. I could only suppose that any destruction was blamed on the German bombs since there was a heavy but mercifully brief air raid that night.

Nonetheless, I had to keep the talk going and interest the P.M. I tried to keep him in all the driest places on the site, but there were not many. My Adjutant said in a jaundiced voice, 'It's a pity we haven't an umbrella, but they are not part of our issue.'

Fortunately the P.M. started talking politics to me. There had been a meeting of the Conservative Party to elect a Leader and there were some cliques in the party who said that Churchill should not become Leader and that he would be in a stronger position without too strong a party attachment. The advocates of this policy were clearly those who had been his opponents in time of peace and a few ambitious men who thought they might themselves get preferment to high office.

The Prime Minister asked me what I thought about these developments at Westminster. My reply was immediate, for I had often browsed over the political scene as it had developed since the war. I said it would be fatal if he did not lead the Conservative Party as the bulk of the party was anxious that he should be the Leader now we were at war. He was still suspicious of them and of their attitude to him before the war. I said it was only a small section of the party that took that line and that the mass of the party was with him. My strongest argument, however, and I felt this very much, was that it was essential for the P.M. to have his own party—a strong one with allies attracted from the main groups and especially the Opposition parties. But essentially he must have a majority and I was sure this majority could only come from the Conservative Party.

He was obviously interested in my proposals and questioned me quite a lot about the strength of Ministers and what influence they wielded. I replied that if you have a strong army of M.Ps under you, Ministers would be won over or crushed, if necessary. He seemed to appreciate my arguments and thanked me very much. Then he began to feel the cold again and agitated to get away. But I have often thought that conversation had something to do with my appointment as his P.P.S. not so many months later when there was a Government reorganisation.

In spite of my wet clothes I was now dry in more ways than one and the P.M. was getting edgy and anxious to get on as he was freezing. I was sweating, thinking of my poor despatch rider and praying that I had kept the ball in play long enough to get that drink for the P.M. before he froze to death. Pile kept fuming about the delay and getting angry with me. Then suddenly I heard the beat of an engine and the despatch rider drew up to a grinding halt. He got to us as we got to the General's car. The despatch rider had brought glasses and I filled them nearly full, and neat, and handed them to the P.M. and the General. The P.M. took a great half-tumbler full, then spluttered and gurgled and when he could speak he said, 'You have poisoned me.' Pile drank his glass more slowly and I took a good swig from the bottle, sprang to attention, and saluted as the car door banged and the car shot off. I thought I had done my cause no good.

After the war Pile wrote his memoirs, *Ack Ack*, and described the incident. He generously inscribed a copy for me—'To Brigadier Sir George Harvie-Watt, who served in Ack Ack before and during the War and was one of the first T.A. soldiers to make the rank of Brigadier. It was due to him and his likes that this story could be written. F. A. Pile'. Not the kind of inscription I thought I would ever see after the visit General Sir Frederick Pile and the Prime Minister had paid to my experimental company. After that episode I returned to my H.Q. at Plumpton and settled down again to my usual routine, with alarms and excursions from time to time to keep us on our toes. And so the weeks and months passed until my summons and appointment came in July 1941. By that time I was commanding a brigade in Suffolk.

CHAPTER 6

P.P.S. to the Premier

Clearly it is not possible for a Premier, who is also Defence Minister in fact as well as in name, who presides over Cabinet meetings and committees, attends Parliamentary sittings, answers Questions, acts for no small part of his time as Foreign Secretary, replies to notes and messages of all kinds, to do all this without a very strong team behind and with him. Hence the appointment of a Parliamentary Private Secretary or P.P.S., as he is called. There are several Personal Private Secretaries, each doing different jobs, but there is only one Parliamentary Private Secretary.

The P.M. is made aware of the minimum content of only the most essential communications. Before the P.M. decides on his own attitude, he may wish to be acquainted with the views of the influential members of his party and those outside his immediate circle. But if Members know where to find the P.P.S. they can be certain that their ideas will be set out in a report to the P.M. immediately, giving as much background explanation about any situation as may seem necessary. There is always a lot of work behind the scenes and the P.P.S. can take a great burden off the P.M's shoulders.

I went down to the House with Winston on the morning of 22nd July. It was a strange feeling to walk into the House with the P.M. and on such terms. I hadn't really ever known any P.M. well. I had, of course, met them.

I never got to know Baldwin, although I had an admiration for him; he was a much better Prime Minister than he was given credit. He only spoke to me once, and that was in a small lavatory near the Smoke Room of the House one evening. I was in a stall when I heard the footsteps of someone coming in. A voice said, 'Young man, please adjust your dress before leaving.' I turned round and I saw it was Baldwin. I suppose it was a joke, but he never spoke to me again. He did not deserve the hounding he got from the Beaverbrook Press on his statement on armaments and on his attitude in the abdication crisis. In later years Churchill said to me, 'Don't under-rate Baldwin. He is a shrewd and patriotic man.'

Chamberlain was the shyest man I have ever met. I never found him friendly on any occasion. He seemed to shrink from all social contacts. I don't think he ever knew his own supporters in the House. When Chamberlain became Prime Minister he selected as his Parliamentary Private Secretary Alec Douglas-Home, afterwards Prime Minister. Chamberlain was not at all convivial. He was definitely not a Smoke Room man and never looked at you when you passed him in the lobbies. Alec Douglas-Home knew this and did his best to induce Chamberlain to meet back benchers—not more than three or four at a time. He would arrange for Chamberlain to be in the Smoke Room on different nights. Then Alec would bring the P.M. and introduce him to those Members sitting waiting for him. He shook hands and sat down while Alec clucked around him like a mother hen. M.Ps are not known to be unsocial, but try as I might I never knew it to be so hard to converse with any man. The only time he really sparkled was when some Member knew something about fishing. A gleam would come to Chamberlain's eye and he would wax eloquent on the subject, of which I knew nothing. So I can fairly say that I never really had any conversation with Chamberlain, the Leader of my party.

However, Churchill was the exact opposite—that is, when he liked. As a rule he was a social animal and loved the Smoke Room of the House. I never saw MacDonald there, rarely Baldwin, and Chamberlain only when driven in by his P.P.S. Churchill, however, could be morose for quite long stretches and look at you as if you weren't there, or give the impression of just trampling over you. On the whole we got on well. Indeed I have read that I have served longer than any other P.P.S. to a Prime Minister.

When I got to No. 10 for my first day as P.P.S. I met my predecessor in that job, Brendan Bracken, in many ways one of the most remarkable men I have ever met. There was

P.P.S. to the Premier

always a mystery about his origin and how quickly he acquired fame. However, on the day I arrived at No. 10 I didn't really know him. He was very friendly and showed me the ropes of the P.P.S. duties. My office at No. 10 was in a room just off the Cabinet Room. It was a very pleasant room indeed. There was also a great building at the corner of Horse Guards and Birdcage Walk. This was called the Annexe where the Churchills had a flat; there were bedrooms down in the bowels of the earth in case of air raids. They were like cells in a prison with painted brick walls, a bed, a chair, a wash stand and a cupboard. The P.M. had the room next to mine. I have been told that this part of the Annexe has been left as a relic of the times, just as it was then. I have never revisited it.

It was observed that in my accommodation both at No. 10 and in the Annexe there was not one object in my room that belonged to me—not even a photo of my wife or children, or of the P.M. The impersonality and the informality of the room —its obvious ownership by tradition—seemed a little disconcerting to my many visitors. As one Member said, a startling contrast to the vigour and spiritual restlessness of the occupant. I was Harvie alike to jealous M.Ps, sympathetic friends, acid aquaintances, admiring dowagers, hostesses of taste and quality, but Harvie-Watt was ready to move out of that room at a moment's notice. I was four years in that room. One flattering comment made by a columnist at that time was that I had no stick, no umbrella, no bulging despatch case, no gloves and no airs.

My task was made more difficult by having to follow Brendan Bracken, who had had a long and close association with the Churchill family and whose services had won him promotion to the difficult post of Minister of Information. No one in the House of Commons had fallen more under the spell of Mr. Churchill than the Member for North Paddington and he was on terms of easy friendship with the chief he had served. I had still to win the Prime Minister's confidence, which I knew could only be gained on merit and service.

There was a belief among some of my friends that he was an extremely difficult man to work with, rather uncertain in his mood, hard to please and given to outbursts of temper, when he had a useful vocabulary with which to express his feelings. That filled me with dismay as I was anxious to make a success of the job. Weeks passed before I knew whether or not my work was giving satisfaction. The first words of encouragement came from Brendan Bracken, who told me the Prime Minister was pleased with what I was doing for him. Even after I had been in Downing Street for a month or two Churchill's silence on the subject worried me. At one point I began to wonder whether I had made a mistake in leaving the army. However, that mood did not last long.

My appointment came at an important stage in the war. Britain's pact with Russia had recently been signed and welcomed everywhere in the democratic world. At the time of my arrival at No. 10 it was easy to detect that something unusual was in the air. A few months later the Prime Minister put to sea to meet President Roosevelt 'somewhere in the Atlantic'. How the U-boats would have liked to know where that meeting took place! It was a top secret. Mr. Churchill and his party, including Lord Beaverbrook, Lord Cherwell, Sir Alexander Cadogan and the Chiefs of Staff, joined a train at a station outside London because they could climb into it without attracting too much notice, and travelled to the Clyde where the *Prince of Wales*, Britain's newest battleship, was waiting to carry them across the ocean.

Only a few knew whither they were bound. Naval and military officers who accompanied them were merely told to take sufficient clothing for a fortnight. Even the officers of the *Prince of Wales*, apart from the Captain, were unaware of the journey on which they were about to embark. They knew they were taking distinguished passengers, and so intrigued were they that they organised a sweepstake on their destination. Many guesses were made, and two of the officers found the correct answer. One of them said they were taking the Prime Minister to meet President Roosevelt and the other that they were taking Harry Hopkins, the President's special envoy who was already aboard, across the Atlantic. They shared the bumper kitty.

The first announcement of the meeting was made by Mr. Attlee, then Lord Privy Seal, in a five-minute broadcast which

P.P.S. to the Premier

was repeated in the world's principal languages. He disclosed the terms of the now famous Atlantic Charter—an eight-point plan for establishing a new order, not only in Europe but all over the world, based on a recognition of the principle of self-determination for all nations.

This speech ought to have had an electrifying effect on the nation and if Winston had been making it it certainly would, but Attlee was not an orator and he made the announcement seem rather dull and almost unimportant. I listened to it but could not help thinking it was something of an anti-climax instead of one of the most historic achievements of our time.

In the Annexe there was a Mess where we could have breakfast and dinner. This was a great asset. Brendan Bracken had started it, though after he became Minister of Information he rarely visited it or dined in. This was a pity from the Mess point of view as he was a most amusing controversialist.

The regular attenders were Jack Churchill, the Prime Minister's brother who was the complete opposite to him but a very nice companionable man. He was not a political figure but had been in the City a great part of his life. Another was John Martin, the Principal Private Secretary, who was a Scot and a son of the manse. He was extremely good at his job and when I got to know him well I realised that he was going to have a distinguished career. The others were Leslie Rowan, who was more of an extrovert, and I was not surprised when in later life, after making a name in the Civil Service, he went into the City where he became Chairman of Vickers. Alas he died young. John Peck, one of the younger members of the team, was to move to many important positions and finished up as Ambassador to Ireland. Of all the Private Secretaries at No. 10 I thought Anthony Bevir one of the deepest personalities. He had a great deal to do with recommendations on the appointment of bishops. He knew more about Church of England dignitaries than any one I have ever known. He was also a kindly man. The youngest of the team was Jock Colville, who was an amusing character and seemed to be a personal friend of the Churchill family. He gave me a warm welcome. He was determined to get into the Services, which he did and soon left to join the Air Force. He did his training, or a lot of it, in Rhodesia. Towards the latter part of the war he returned to No. 10 and after various posts he went to the City. By that time I was also in the City and I was about to invite him into Consolidated Gold Fields but found he had already been snapped up by Kenneth Keith and his group of financial companies.

Some former Parliamentary Private Secretaries to Prime Ministers were in the House with me. In addition to Alec Douglas-Home and Brendan Bracken, there was Geoffrey Lloyd, P.P.S. to Baldwin, who became Minister of Fuel in the war-time coalition and later, after the war, held other offices. There was also Tommy Dugdale, who had been a P.P.S. to Baldwin—a Yorkshire Member who had just returned from the Middle East and later became Chairman of the party. He was a shrewd politician.

One of the minor delights I had at No. 10 was a key for the garden gate leading to the Horse Guards Parade. This gave me a quick way to London's clubland and especially to the Carlton Club. This was one of the leading clubs in London which I only joined after I became P.P.S. It was essential that I should go there and hear the political gossip of the time. In fact, I had never been so popular before, and until my association with Churchill ended I don't suppose I was ever so popular again.

Shortly after I arrived at 10 Downing Street I had to motor down to Chequers, taking Dorothy Thompson (Mrs. Sinclair Lewis) with me. She was a well known American writer. I wasn't very sure what the drill was about clothes, but thank goodness I asked John Martin who told me it was dinner jacket. I hadn't thought I would need evening clothes in London and I had left mine in Scotland at the outbreak of War. I had to hire from R. W. Forsyth. I did collect my own on my next leave but I rarely ever wore them again during the war.

The Prime Minister frequently wore a dinner jacket, but as the war dragged on he took to wearing a boiler suit more and more, which always surprised people who saw him in it, especially Tom Johnston, Secretary of State for Scotland—a Socialist. He was a first-class man but he couldn't understand the P.M's wearing what was to him an ordinary working man's boiler suit.

P.P.S. to the Premier

When we arrived at Chequers Mrs. Churchill met us on the lawn. She was most charming and an admirable hostess. The P.M. was wearing the boiler suit with no collar or tie. However, he changed for dinner into a dinner jacket. Another of the guests was Harry Hopkins—a rather frail-looking man, personal aide to Roosevelt. He broadcast to the nation that evening on very pro-British lines. It was good to know we had such American backing. I had met Kennedy, the father of the future President of the U.S., several times. He was the American Ambassador to Britain. He was not very pro-British and he didn't think there was much chance or hope of Britain winning the war, or even withstanding the German air raids. Another of the guests was Averell Harriman and his daughter. He was a tall, academic man and very good-looking. He was also very friendly to the British cause.

The chief guest was, of course Dorothy Thompson, aged about fifty, good-looking, intelligent and a bright conversationalist. Lord Cherwell (Professor Lindeman that was), Mary Churchill, the P.M's youngest daughter who was most attractive, charming and bright, Jack Churchill, John Martin, the Principal Private Secretary, Commander Thompson, and Sir Maurice and Lady Bonham-Carter—a famous Liberal name with Asquith associations—made up the house party. It was a most cheerful evening. Winston as usual dominated the dinner table with his powerful personality and wit.

I drove the Bonham-Carters and Dorothy Thompson back to London. The conversation all evening was mainly about United States assistance to the United Kingdom. All the Americans I met at this time were very pro-British. It was encouraging to hear their views and I didn't feel quite so cut off from the New World. This made one more optimistic about the results of the war. We needed encouragement at that time. The situation in the West looked pretty grim.

Later that week Dorothy Thompson addressed a meeting at the House of Commons. She was a brilliant speaker and her speech was first class. She got a great ovation, partly because of her style and because she was so pro-British. It is always nice to hear good things about your own country when all around is gloom.

The next day, before the Cabinet meeting, I met Lord Beaverbrook for the first time. He was quite affable though not particularly so, and he remained like that to me for the duration of the war though our paths frequently crossed. No doubt he sensed I did not like him. He was a great friend of Brendan Bracken's and held some high offices in the Government but with little or no popularity in the Conservative Party. Indeed, in the House of Commons as a whole they didn't take to him, and for reasons I never knew they didn't seem to trust him. He had, however, an agile and competent mind and undoubtedly at times gave strength to the war-time coalition.

This had been a busy few days because, after the visit to Chequers, we had a full dress Debate in the House which Winston opened. I met the P.M., Mrs. Churchill and Mary Churchill at the House in the P.M's room behind the Speaker's Chair. I then took the ladies up to the Speaker's own Gallery which had an excellent view of the Commons Chamber and then went back to Winston and we entered the Chamber, he to his place on the Front Bench and I to the Second Bench behind him.

He was apprehensive about his speech which had taken him a long time to prepare. His speeches and their formation and lay-out interested me very much, for they were written, made up, and spoken word for word. The notes looked like hymn sheets, not just like a page from a book but with short paragraphs that could be spoken in one breath. This was most effective. You never got the impression he was reading a speech. It all looked and sounded as if he was speaking extemporarily. He could put a speech across better than any man I have ever heard. In conversation he could be brilliant—no notes here—all cut and thrust with tremendous humour flung in for good measure.

One of my many tasks was to be friendly with Members of all parties and so I had a good deal of entertaining ouside—drinks, lunches and dinners. Many names of Members, then important in the House, are unknown to the present generation yet they were giants at the time. Even war-time Cabinet Ministers are now forgotten. I doubt if any present Ministers could recite even ten of their names, although they have been brought up with a political background.

P.P.S. to the Premier

I spent endless hours in the Chamber of the House of Commons listening to the pearls of political wisdom that emerged from people well known in their day but now forgotten. It was a relief to get to the Smoke Room and listen to light gossip and chatter, as when Choppa Titchfield, the Marquis of Titchfield and afterwards the Duke of Portland, talked of medals and how he got his first medal for gallant conduct at the age of seven at the coronation of Edward VII. He was a cheerful personality and quite a wit. It was refreshing to meet in the political world someone with no ambition whatsoever.

It was about this time that some well-known figures of outstanding merit, mainly from the business world, were brought into the Cabinet—Lord Leathers and Lord Woolton went straight to the House of Lords. Lord Leathers was quite frank that he was not really a politician and would not like to fight a by-election. He felt he would be out of his depth. He was probably right but he was a first-class administrator. Lord Woolton made a wonderful Minister of Food, but I thought he ought to have come into the House of Commons in the ordinary way. Sir Andrew Duncan and Sir P. J. Grigg both decided to come into Parliament through the House of Commons. Grigg was a top Civil Servant and was made Secretary of State for War. Sir Andrew Duncan also preferred to face the hustings and heckling and come through the hurly-burly of a by-election. He became President of the Board of Trade. These four men made a great contribution to the war effort.

It was natural that, as Parliamentary Private Secretary to the Prime Minister, I should meet all the Ministers. After all, I was in Parliament and that was my job. Curiously, however, I acquired in different ways non-Parliamentary links with countries like Poland, Yugoslavia and Austria, all of whom had emigré governments in the United Kingdom. I also met many top United States representatives. These contacts proved most helpful.

At this time I began to meet General Sikorski, the Polish General, and also members of his government, military and political. Through General Sikorski I got to know many of his soldiers, for a substantial Polish army was being built up in the United Kingdom.

CHAPTER 7

Winston on and off Parade

To return to the political arena, some of my Conservative friends were becoming anxious that the party and its policies might be neglected and felt that we ought to have meetings from time to time to keep the Conservative ship afloat and to consider what Conservative lines we should take when the war came to an end. Somehow we never thought that there was the slightest chance of the Allies being beaten and felt that we should be ready for the usual political fray when the battle was won.

I had a long chat with the Prime Minister in the Cabinet Room, after he returned from the Atlantic meeting with Roosevelt. He was most affable, and optimistic about relations with America. At times he had a charming and delightful personality and at others he growled like a bear. We talked about the meeting he was having that evening to speak to the Ministers who were not in the Cabinet which he said I had to attend. It was an excellent idea, for many Ministers felt a little bit in the cold.

Those who attended on this first occasion were Lord Simon, the Lord Chancellor, Lord Sankey, Secretary to the Cabinet, Lord Leathers, Sir Andrew Duncan, Leo Amery, Geoffrey Lloyd and Moore Brabazon (all Conservatives), and Hugh Dalton, David Grenfell (Socialists), W. S. Morrison, Ernest Brown and myself. The P.M. gave a résumé of the war so far, with particular emphasis on his recent trip in the *Prince of Wales* to see Roosevelt. He was in a particularly cheerful mood. There had been great progress towards harmony with the United States. I also had a talk with Lord Halifax but he was not so cheerful at the way things were going in the United States. He was rather an aloof man and did not seem to get to grips with the ordinary M.P.

Another Cabinet Minister who was not so easy to get on with

Winston on and off Parade

was Anthony Eden. Nonetheless I liked him and admired his capacity as a Minister. He didn't like me much and was always ready to criticise my comments to the Prime Minister. My last talk with him was going through the Voting Lobby during the Suez Canal crisis in 1956. His eyes were sunken and I've never seen a man so exhausted, but he was really friendly with me for the first and only time. Perhaps it was because I said that his policy was correct, and if we were not successful then the whole of Africa would soon be fighting and squabbling, and our status would be reduced to nothing and destroyed.

At this stage there were by-elections pending at Wrexham, Scarborough and Lancaster. The Chief Whip, James Stuart, and Sir Robert Topping of Conservative Central Office had to discuss with me the tactics to be taken at these elections. It was often my job to draft letters from the Prime Minister to send to the Government candidates. The P.M. was anxious that there should be no bad results lest it gave the idea of disunity to the Germans.

With regard to these pending by-elections, Douglas Hacking, Chairman of the party machine, came to see me about helping him to get letters from Attlee, the Leader of the Socialist Party. Apparently the constituencies held by Socialists wouldn't accept any messages from the P.M. What rubbish! Such a rule should be in abeyance during a period of coalition government. There was no reason why the Socialist Leader shouldn't send a message to a Conservative or Liberal candidate. It was an absurd situation.

In the circumstances of a wartime coalition there were bound to be, and there were, many intrigues, with Members jostling for position. Members had so little Parliamentary work to do in the usual sense. There were always some people seeking to sack a Minister and suggesting themselves for the job. I got to know the schemers very well and will have more to say on this subject later on.

My wife had tea with Mrs. Churchill and really met her for the first time. I was also there. We had tea at the Churchills' flat at the Annexe. She was a wonderful person and my wife, like most people, was very impressed with her charm. They got on well and I was amused at the domestic touch when Mrs.

Churchill told us that Winston didn't like darns in his socks and so she bought six pairs at a time. He was also a daily dipper and liked to wear a clean pair of socks every day. She told me that I was of great assistance to Winston and took a lot of burdens off his shoulders on the political side of his work.

Apart from the Cabinet Room and the downstairs secretarial rooms, I had not seen much of No. 10 Downing Street. I had been too busy, but I felt I must now have a Cook's Tour of this famous house. It was a huge rambling place, added to by the Asquiths and reconstructed by the Chamberlains. It must have been a difficult house to run. The kitchen was vast. On the first floor were the reception rooms for the more social engagements. The bedrooms were on the floors above.

Winston usually, if at all possible, had a rest at some time in the afternoon, then rose and had a bath. Depending on his engagements, he would put on his boiler suit. Many times I had to report to him when he was in the nude rubbing himself with a towel while I gave him the news about the Debate in the House. To begin with I was very shy. I was not used to reporting to people in this way and especially to a naked Prime Minister. He was quite unconcerned and I got used to such interviews.

A minor political bother was raised at this time to the P.M. and myself by Eugene Ramsden, afterwards Lord Ramsden. He was one of the central figures in the party machine. I'm afraid he was a better businessman than a politician. At any rate he never had any personal axe to grind, which was a relief. I had no idea there were so many political axes to grind until I got into the Whips' Office and it was even worse at No. 10. No wonder the Prime Minister wanted someone to keep the flies off him.

We met in the Cabinet Room. The point that he raised was in respect of the repeal of the Trade Disputes Act which action was demanded by the T.U.C. Apparently there were strong demands for this from some of the unions. The P.M. was naturally not anxious to have any troubles with the unions but wanted no commitments in time of war if possible. He was all out to have friendly talks but no commitments now. We had, at all costs, to avoid any clashes in wartime.

Winston on and off Parade

He was prepared to take a strong line as Leader of the Party, but as Leader of the Government he preferred amicable settlements, especially as not all trade unionists were Socialists and it was reasonable to be friendly with them. Speaking of the Russians he said he didn't care what their political views were so long as they killed Germans.

He also expressed the view at this long-ranging discussion, or rather monologue, that there should be a continuance of the coalition of the parties for some years after the war to get over the necessary period of reorganisation and reconstruction. It was all most interesting but I couldn't believe the political parties would wish to carry on a coalition after hostilities had ceased.

During my first few months at No. 10 I was fascinated by the P.M's habits. He was a heavy smoker of cigars—I would say about sixteen a day. He smoked the first third, chewed and re-lit frequently the second third and then disposed of the remainder, which was usually pretty messy. I was most interested in his smoking habits becuase I was a minor cigar smoker myself, though even at my worst I smoked no more than six or seven a day and they were much smaller cigars. He also took snuff, though not much. His brother Jack was a considerable snuff-taker. I regret to say I acquired this habit, much to the disgust of my wife who thought both smoking and snuff-taking were filthy habits.

In the autumn of 1941 the Cuban Minister presented to the P.M. a magnificent cabinet of the very best Havana cigars of different brands, some 50 boxes of Punch, Laranaga, Romeo y Julieta, Bolivar and other varieties. I was green with envy! This cabinet was brought into my room. Winston came with it as cheerful as a schoolboy. 'What a pity,' he said, 'these boxes have to be tested in case they are filled with poison or explosives or have been interfered with in any way.' I said I would be very happy to do the testing for him. He looked startled and said, 'But you might be poisoned. We can't have that. At any rate this is a matter for Scotland Yard.' The cabinet remained in my room for some days but I was glad when it was removed. I've never before seen such a tempting display.

At this same time an Anglo-American delegation going to

Russia had a lunch party at which the P.M. presided and I was in humble attendance. There were many parties of this kind. Attlee and Walter Citrine, Chairman of the T.U.C., were similarly entertained. Citrine I thought extremely able, a friendly grey-haired man who, in the course of his life-time, went steadily to the right and certainly even at that time was not apparently very Socialistic at all. Attlee was a modest little man. Winston once said of him 'He has a great deal to be modest about.' Rather a harsh judgement. I liked him very much but he was not of the type that leaders are made. After the war, when the Socialists were swept into power, he made a reasonable Prime Minister though any man following Winston was bound to be overshadowed.

During the last week-end in September 1941 I went down to Sussex at the invitation of my old regiment. The C.O., Col. Eric Jones, sent a car up to London to drive me down to Lingfield, the Battalion H.Q. It was wonderful to see my old unit again. Everywhere I went I got a most warm welcome and I had tremendous feelings of nostalgia. On the Saturday there was a Mess Party representative of the unit as a whole, when I was presented with two incribed tenor drums and photographs of the battalion to mark my retiral from its command, although I had commanded a brigade in the interval. It seemed odd to be in civilian clothes while all the others were in uniform.

I got back to No. 10 on the Monday morning. The P.M. wanted to see me as he wished to discuss the 'Appeal to the Parties'. The matter was still nagging him. Fortunately, after some more talks with other Leaders, agreement was reached the next day with the Chief Whip. The Liberals had agreed but didn't want the appeal used at the by-election at Lancaster. I told the P.M. He was adamant. 'They either support or they don't. I don't want to discuss the matter any longer.' Neither did I. I had had enough of this marching backwards and forwards. I mention all this to demonstrate how difficult it was to get the coalition going in all its aspects, although the parties were in total agreement on the main and broader issues of the war.

One major subject discussed by the Conservative Committee was the amount of communist propaganda. The Tories felt that there might be an electoral truce but there could not be a political truce and that the left were exploiting the Russian struggle for their own ends.

One of the busy bees was a Scottish Q.C., Erskine-Hill. He was a most ambitious man, Chairman of the Conservative Back Bench Committee. It was the most powerful Committee in the House. He gave many little working dinner parties throughout the war and did admirable work for the Conservative Party. I was, as P.P.S., invited to many gatherings in order to meet the back benchers and to hear their comments on the running of the war and the running of the party. These meetings had their uses; since it was my duty to keep my ears to the ground, I learned a lot about reactions to Government policies and actions. Despite all this great effort, Erskine-Hill did not get Government office, although when it was all over he was given a baronetcy.

I have said that early on in my days at No. 10 I got in contact with many of the Polish exiles. My friend, Harold Mitchell, who was Chief Welfare Officer at AA Command and a liaison officer to General Sikorski, asked my help on several occasions to take an interest in Polish affairs. I was too busy to do much, but if I had the odd leave and happened to be in Scotland I would pay brief visits to his home, Tulliallan, to meet General Sikorski and General Kukiel, C.-in-C. of Polish Forces, and also Count Lipski.

On several occasions I met a most amusing Colonel of the Cameron Highlanders, Col. Alastair McLean. After the war he was to run the Edinburgh Tattoo for many years with tremendous success. At dinner once at Tulliallan there was a discussion about pipe music. The Poles loved the stirring tunes. Kukiel asked me if I played because Alastair McLean had just said he did. I said I could also play the pipes. McLean thought I was pulling his leg and challenged me to a piping duel after dinner in the Long Gallery. He took his pipes about with him wherever he went. The guests, mostly Polish generals, and my host, Colonel Harold Mitchell, all trooped out to watch me face the challenge. McLean was in the kilt and I was in a plain suit. I was challenged to play the March Past of the Cameron Highlanders, *The Pibroch o' Donal Dubh*. Fortunately although I had not played the pipes for years, this was a tune I knew well so I immediately struck up and marched and counter-marched along the Gallery. Alastair then played, so the pipes changed hands while gradually the spectators drifted off to bed. We played into 'the wee sma' 'oors'.

Next morning early I returned to London, a bit the worse for wear, and had rather a tedious evening of interviews with James Stuart, the Chief Whip, and the Prime Minister. My heart was still in Scotland and not with the by-election at Lancaster which was the centre of our discussion. This had been a very long drawn-out affair which I thought had been settled. Winston was laying down the law, and quite rightly. He wanted to avoid this kind of controversy in future by-elections. Archie Sinclair would have to sign the appeal if Ernest Brown, the Liberal National, did. Winston did not see why Brown should sign since his brand of Liberalism and his group had supported the Conservative Government since 1931. Sir Archibald Sinclair claimed there was only one Liberal Party and organisation and that was his. It was all rather a petty squabble but it took up a lot of time. The unfortunate thing was that the P.M. did not like Brown but he did like Sinclair, who was a debonair aristocrat with great charm. Brown had none.

One day at the House I was discussing some business with the Prime Minister. We heard a loud voice speaking in an ante-room outside. It was very loud, and went on and on. Winston became very annoyed and told me to go and see what was happening. I went out and found Mr. Ernest Brown, who was at the time the Secretary of State for Scotland, speaking into the telephone. His secretary was with him and I asked, 'What is he shouting about?' The secretary replied that Ernest Brown was speaking to someone in his constituency in Scotland and that it was a very bad connection.

When I returned Winston looked at me with a scowl and said, 'Well?', and I told him it was Mr. Ernest Brown speaking to his constituency near Edinburgh. The Prime Minister looked astonished and said, 'Well, go and tell him to use the bloody telephone.'

It was a relief to get away from this backstairs squabble and to go to meet Brendan Bracken, who was always a stimulating

1   Churchill inspecting the House of Commons Home Guard

2. Christmas greetings card to the Author from the PM and Clementine Churchill

character. He wanted me to meet Jan Masaryk, the Czech Ambassador. He was tall, very bald and square, but spoke good English and always dressed immaculately. He was going to America for six weeks to attend an I.L.O. Conference. The temper of the Czechs was very bad at this time. They had had a difficult period during the Occupation—horrible shootings and tortures. They were a very brave people but their prospect was not bright. Jan Masaryk impressed me tremendously. I met him on many occasions during the war. He told me his peace aims were simple. 'I want to go home and I want to be able at any time I like to ride in a tramcar down the Wenceslaus Square in Prague and say I don't think much of our present Government.' I saw him a very short time before he went back to his own country where he was assassinated, although there was some pretence that he fell out of a window and committed suicide. I have never believed that story.

For the rest of the war I was constantly in touch with the Poles, Yugoslavs, French, Dutch and, to a much lesser extent, the Czechs.

A few days after I had met King Peter at the memorial service to King Alexander of Yugoslavia, he called at No. 10 Downing Street to see the P.M. and I had to entertain him for some time while he waited for Winston. He was shy and nervous but, of course, he was young. He had driven down from Cambridge in the uniform of his Air Force. He spoke English well and told me of the wonderful fight his people were putting up against tremendous odds. The Yugoslav Army was growing and there had been many local successes against the Germans and Italians. He was anxious that we should invade Yugoslavia. This was what he wanted to see the P.M. about, but I didn't think there would be any comfort for him as a landing on the Dalmation coast would certainly not be on.

The next day I met General Simovitch of Yugoslavia and his Cabinet. They were not downhearted and were most determined and ready to fight under whatever circumstances. I was much impressed by their attitude, but alas it was not Simovitch but Tito who was to lead the Yugoslavs after the war.

That same evening I accompanied the Prime Minister, complete with detectives, to the Savoy for dinner with Lord

Hyndley, who was giving a party to say bon voyage to Mr. Attlee who was also going to the I.L.O. Conference. Among those present besides the P.M. and myself were Kingsley Wood, Arthur Greenwood, Jenkins, who was P.P.S. to Attlee, James Stuart the Chief Whip, Tom Johnston, David Grenfell, Ernest Bevin, A. V. Alexander, and Hugh Dalton—a good cross-section of the Cabinet.

Bevin was terribly fat, indeed gross. He spat his food about when eating and, as I was sitting next to him, several times I had to pick bits off my hand and sleeve. It was not a pleasant habit. For all that, he was a great man and tremendously able. He was very vain and pleased with himself. He boasted a good deal of his successful speeches and his successes with the T.U.C. He and the Prime Minister got on well, although there was a great contrast between the two men—one born an aristocrat and the other in very humble circumstances.

The Prime Minister was in admirable form and very friendly towards me. Many topics were touched upon at that top-level dinner party—the progress of the war and help to Russia, which was a growing priority. It was sad to see Kingsley Wood, as he really was past it on the active front. He had done a first-class job for the Conservative Party and for the country. He died not long afterwards. I drove back with the P.M. but he was now gloomy and not at all talkative. He was slumped in the car and when we got out at Downing Street he merely grunted and raised his hand.

My rounds at this time seemed endless and the amount of intrigue was really fantastic. Tom Dugdale and Malcolm McCorquodale, both well up in the party hierarchy, arranged to see me because they wanted a talk. They related many stories to me about the efforts amongst Conservatives in the House, stirred up by Beaverbrook, to oust Bevin. There was also an anti-Beaverbrook lobby and this was growing fast. Beaverbrook was a natural schemer and he was not popular, especially in the Conservative Party.

I had now been with the Prime Minister for over a year. I was naturally a very shy person, although no one thought so, and I had the reputation of being an extrovert. I had to put on that kind of front to hide my inner feelings. I had felt that my relations with Churchill were very slow in thawing. He liked to have people about him whom he knew well and I was an incomer. It was difficult for me.

One evening at this time late in 1941 we were going to a small private dinner at the Savoy. He told me to meet him in the Cabinet Room at 7.30, I duly went along. The P.M. was sitting at his usual place at the Cabinet table. It seemed ages before he looked up, gave a grunt, then rose and I helped him on with his coat. He seemed to accept my help reluctantly. We then walked out of the room, down the long corridor to the front door which was opened by the porter, then we went outside and were saluted by the policeman. We got into the car, and still not a word was spoken. I could not think of anything to say. Finally I felt I had to say something so I ventured, 'It is very dark tonight, Prime Minister.' He growled and then said, 'Well, what do you expect? It is dark every night in the winter time.' I was flattened. We drove on in silence in the black-out until we stopped at the Embankment entrance to the Savoy where we got into a small lift to take us up to the private rooms. In the lift he put his hand on my shoulder and, without saying a word, he literally beamed at me, and arm in arm we walked along to dinner. I felt the ice was broken.

I spent some time with Winston most days, either at No. 10 or at the House, for he liked to hear what was going on and to keep his finger on the pulse of political feeling and to know all the gossip about Members and what they were saying about current affairs. He also liked to talk at me about matters which were troubling him or interested him, just to get them off his chest or try them out on the watch dog, namely me.

At this stage he was somewhat critical of Air Marshal Tedder, whom he thought was rather weak, and General Auchinleck, who was rather slow. If only they would get a move on it would help to relieve German pressure on Russia and settle the critics of the Western and Eastern fronts and other amateur strategists. When the offensive took place it might be too late and we might have to fight on two fronts. It seemed as if we were pandering to popular opinion. During this conversation, or rather monologue, he was in one of his many tantrums–usually of brief duration.

I seemed to be the recipient of all complaints, for no sooner had I left the P.M. than Viscount Bridgeman, who was one of the top Home Guard Commanders, came to ask me to forward to the P.M. a complaint about the new role laid down for the Home Guard. This was a mobile role, but the Home Guard was raised for the defence of their locality only. However, I noted what he had to say and said I would pass it on, which I did—not to the P.M. but to General Ismay, the P.M's Military Adviser. I managed to soothe the noble Viscount.

Another of my functions was to deal with the political correspondents. Most of them were high-class journalists on the political front and they were very good at cross-examination, getting as much information as they could out of you. You had to be very careful to spill not even a bean, but occasionally to drop some hint which could help the Press and do no harm to the general situation.

At this time I had my first meeting with Mr. Winant, the new American Ambassador—a great improvement on Kennedy. I had nearly an hour's talk with him in my room at No. 10. He was an exceedingly shy and reserved man, tall and dark. I immediately fell for his charm. I met him many times and our relationship was always of the friendliest during the time he was in London.

On this occasion he said he thought England would be invaded. But he hoped that by that time, probably June 1942, the Americans would be in Britain fighting with us for the defence of our homeland. He was very pro-British and didn't hide his feelings. He believed that we were going too slowly at this stage, which was not helpful from the American point of view. I always found my talks with Winant stimulating and encouraging.

CHAPTER 8

The House and Pearl Harbor

The Prime Minister always took a keen interest in any military developments and, of course, he was himself a considerable strategist as I knew from personal experience. Now, in late 1941, we motored down to Chequers one morning, arriving at 10.30. He was exceedingly friendly in the car and I talked about the night he visited my experimental site. He remembered all about the evening, especially the whisky and what I had to say on the then political situation and on his leadership of the Conservative Party. I felt that he hadn't been all that interested at the time.

We went out to the ranges at Princes Risborough where Lord Beaverbrook and Lord Cherwell, more commonly known as the Prof, and also Sir Alan Brooke, Commander-in-Chief, joined us. We witnessed a demonstration of Banfords Spigot Mortars. They were very good. The shooting at the vital parts of tanks at 200 yards was amazingly accurate. Winston was in his element and he fired off two pans of ammunition. While all this was going on Lord Beaverbrook walked and talked with me, leaning on my arm. This was the first time he had shown any friendliness to me. He was a great character and a veritable dynamo, although not popular with the politicians. We returned to London in two cars, the P.M. and Beaverbrook in the first car and Lord Cherwell and myself in the second. The Prof complained bitterly about the stupidity of the War Office. He advocated raids on the coast to keep the Bosche on his toes and as a mild help to the Russians.

I felt very important as I drove in this cavalcade back to Downing Street, driving through red lights and going round the wrong side of the traffic islands. The gongs were ringing and I felt I was in a police chase—very impressive. From this exciting military day I returned to the political scene again.

At Downing Street I found that the Chief Whip wanted to see me. The political pot was always boiling. He wanted to discuss the Chairmanship and Vice-Chairmanship of the Conservative Party. Apparently Anthony Eden wanted Jim Thomas, who was a great friend of his and his P.P.S., to become the Chairman of the party. This would not have been a good appointment. Thomas was a close friend of Eden's so from Eden's point of view it was understandable, but Thomas was not popular. He was definitely one of the old type who came into Parliament with influence and money. I never heard that he had done anything but politics and he couldn't have lived very well off that. The Chairmanship problem would remain with us, for there was tremendous intrigue to get this job.

The Prime Minister then wanted to discuss other matters with me. One was the suggestion that there should be bombproof shelters at the House of Commons. He was not against the principle but was insistent that there should not be firstclass shelters and third-class shelters. If there had to be shelters they had to be open to all and no division between the sheep and the goats.

I took the opportunity to tell him about my talk with the Chief Whip on the question of the Chairmanship of the party and told him the Chief Whip preferred Tommy Dugdale to Jim Thomas and that I agreed with him as Dugdale would be more acceptable to the party. He concurred with this proposal. He then said he would like to appoint some Labour peers, the suggestions being Wedgwood Benn (whose son later gave up the title to go into the House of Commons, and became a Socialist Minister), Nathan, and Commander Fletcher. He agreed to refer them to the Cabinet. In due course they all appeared in the Upper House.

At the beginning of a new session of Parliament the King's Speech is always read by the Prime Minister to the Members of his Government the evening before. This is usually done in the Cabinet Room, but on this occasion it was read in the P.M's room at the House of Commons. The Chief Whip stood with his back to the Members of the Government present to watch the door and prevent any interruption while the P.M. read the speech.

It was never of any great length as the King would read it in the House of Lords at the Opening of Parliament, when the faithful Commons were summoned by Black Rod—an official of the House of Lords—to go to the House of Lords. This they did in procession, two by two, the Government pairing off with the Opposition. The Prime Minister led with the Leader of the Opposition. It was quite an impressive sight even in wartime. The King was in naval uniform.

On 11th November 1941 Waldron Smithers, a bumbling sort of chap with his heart in the right place, asked some critical questions in the House about Lord Cherwell and hinted that he was an alien. The P.M. was livid, rightly so, and said in an aside to me 'Love me, love my dog, and if you don't love my dog you damn well can't love me.' Afterwards Winston left the Chamber of the House with me and went to the Smoke Room. I've never seen him in such a temper before. Later Waldron Smithers came up with his tail between his legs and started grovelling to Winston who told him to get the hell out of here and not to speak to him again. Poor Smithers got the shock of his life.

Later that morning Brendan Bracken, who was closest of all Members to Winston, told me that Winston was very pleased with me and that I was going down well. He was thinking of giving me another job—one that I would like very much and which would enable me to continue as P.P.S. at the same time. I wasn't sure this was a good thing, for to be P.P.S. was a full-time job in itself, especially when Parliament was in session.

A lot of Members were coming under Winston's displeasure at this time and his wrath fell next on H. G. Williams for a speech he had made in his constituency at Croydon. He was critical of Winston's handling of the war. I spent an hour calming Winston down and discussing drafts for by-election messages. The Chief Whip joined us at this stage and the P.M. said he wanted to withdraw the Whip from Williams. However, we calmed him down again.

At this stage he couldn't stand any criticism of his handling of the war or of his friends in or out of the Government.

Next day Winston had forgotten all these fairly petty matters and was waxing lyrical about the attack in the Middle East.

He was eloquent about the young men in their tanks dashing across the desert in the crisp air, with the vast stretches of sand. He was always thrilled by this kind of thing and the soldier in him was never far from the surface.

By the late afternoon his mood had again changed because of a carping speech made by Wilfred Roberts, the P.P.S. to Sir Archibald Sinclair, a great friend of Winston and Leader of the more critical part of the split Liberal Party. It was not the 'done thing' for a P.P.S. to a Minister to criticise the Government, and the Prime Minister in particular. Winston was very sensitive about the House and the conduct of Members.

I was kept busy soothing Members and soothing the P.M. To make matters worse the news from the Middle East was not so encouraging. The attack seemed to be going more slowly. Winston related all this to me for half an hour in his room at the House and then saw Wilfed Roberts, and gave him a good ticking off. Roberts was most truculent and was not at all pleased.

After all this the P.M. switched his mind to more pleasant things. He had to go into the Chamber of the House where he made a congratulatory speech in celebration of Mr. Speaker's golden wedding. It was a most felicitous affair. Pethwick Lawrence spoke for the Socialist Party, Percy Harris for the Liberals and Jimmy Maxton, the Leader of the Independent Labour Party (I.L.P.), made a first-class speech. He was brilliant and a very nice man in spite of his ultra-leftish views. He also, like me, was a graduate of Glasgow University. He had great personal admiration for Winston which was reciprocated. Afterwards in the Committee Room Mr. Lloyd George, the famous World War I Prime Minister and now Father of the House, presented a cup to Mr. Speaker and Mrs. Fitzroy. The place was packed for this major and unique occasion. Lloyd George, as was expected, made a brilliant speech.

It was a long day of continuous events. In the evening we had our first dinner of Conservative Members to meet the P.M. This was something I arranged to bridge the gap which I felt might exist between the Leader of the Conservative Party and his supporters in the House. We met in a private dining and ante-room at the Savoy. The Members present were Rab

Butler, Jay Llewellin, Alan Chapman, Charles Waterhouse, James Stuart, Leslie Pym, Harry Willink, Erskine-Hill, Henry Brooke, Malcolm McCorquodale and Harold Mitchell, most of whom were to become Ministers of the Crown.

The P.M. was completely relaxed and made a very amusing speech. It was a most successful evening and did a lot of good. Members felt that they were closer to their Leader and there was little between them and the big issues. I intended to repeat these dinners for other Members from time to time as they would help to keep the wheels well oiled.

In the car, both going to the Savoy and returning to No. 10, Winston told me what was happening in the Middle East. He was really rehearsing what he was going to say in the House the next day. He usually called me Brigadier and only occasionally by my first name, but he was now tired of that and called me Harvie. All my friends call me Harvie, and those people who think they know me well, but don't, call me George. I always called Winston Prime Minster.

On 20th November Winston made a statement in the House on the Middle East situation. This was the first time that the House had been informed of what was taking place in that war area. News was still scarce since the troops were not using their wireless so as not to give their positions away. The House was agog. This information from the Prime Minister would no doubt help to calm the agitation which had been growing for a Second Front—an agitation which was mainly coming from the extreme Left and odd mischief-maker.

Winston's favourite restaurant was the Savoy and I think during the war I must have been in every private room in that estimable establishment. Winston much enjoyed dinner there with perhaps only a few cronies. Indeed I was with him there several times alone. He felt he could relax and range widely over his problems.

One of my favourite restaurants was the Carlton Grill and it was there that Tommy Dugdale asked me to dine towards the end of November. He told me he was to be the next Chairman of the party and he understood that Winston would like me to be Deputy Chairman but to continue as his P.P.S. This sounded all right. The alternative was to be for me to be Deputy

Chief Whip as well as P.P.S. to the Prime Minister. The latter would be a more agreeable job for me as I had already been an Assistant Whip. However, I thought and decided that being P.P.S. was completely full time, with all the party political problems that constantly arose. I still thought so when I was later asked to become Chairman.

At this time I thought it would be a good thing if I wrote weekly Parliamentary reports to the Prime Minister as he liked to ponder over reports and then ask questions, if any, afterwards. These reports I continued to write till the end of the war. Many times Winston told me how helpful he found them. It was rather like writing an essay at school every week. Some were short, some were long, but they provided a useful background to Parliament in the war. I have kept these reports—many with Winston's comments.

In one of my many talks with the P.M. about the Middle East when things were going well, he started to yarn and told me how during the blitz he was on his way to spend the weekend with Ronnie Tree, who lived in the country at his house, Ditchley.

On this particular night the R.A.F. told No. 10 that there was going to be a very heavy raid. Actually this was the raid on Coventry—one of the worst raids in the war. When Winston heard there was going to be a big raid he thought it was going to be on London so he ordered his car back to the capital. He wasn't going to miss anything.

However, when he got back nothing much was happening so he went up on the roof with his brother Jack and Brendan Bracken. It was a cold night. The others had coats but Winston hadn't. They complained of the cold but Winston said he didn't feel it. He was sitting on the parapet and at that moment a man came on to the roof and walked across to the P.M. who asked, 'Well, what do you want?' The man replied that the fire in his room was smoking. Winston was astonished and said, 'Well, what's that got to do with me?' The man then sheepishly replied that the P.M. was sitting on the chimney—no wonder he was the only one who didn't feel the cold!

The news from the Middle East was not good. The Germans were putting up a stiff resistance. It was a vital battle. The whole course of the war depended upon it and the position of the Government depended upon it too. Whenever there was a set-back in the field there was always trouble in the House. This time it came from Admiral Sir Roger Keyes, a distinguished sailor of World War I. He made a violent attack on the Staffs of the fighting services. Winston, although furious, said he was not going to the House. He was in an ugly temper. He didn't give a damn what the House thought—there was a bloody war on. He told me to tell Arthur Greenwood what he should say to the House as he wasn't going down. However, the storm blew over and Winston had time to simmer down also.

In the dying weeks of 1941 the news from the battle fronts was distinctly better. In Libya the tussle continued with a slight advantage in our favour, and in Russia the successful counter-attack at Rostov-on-Don threw up a gleam of hope. This was a great relief, but what a long way there was to go.

In a Debate in the House Winston opened on the subject of manpower. It was a factual speech so there was little scope for his eloquence, poetry and drama. The Socialists kept on about the conscription of wealth and property—a subject which naturally did not suit Winston. He just sat and glowered. He rarely sat through the Debates and I had to report to him later as to what happened. This was a dreary day.

Winston was not at all pleased with the Debate. He hated criticism from the House and especially from the Conservatives. He thought in some odd way that the Conservatives had let him down. He was inclined to be more friendly to the Socialists and Liberals. He still harked back to the pre-war days. It was essential, however, that he should have a solid backing and, although there was always some sniping at him, the great mass of the Tory majority was extremely loyal. They wanted to back him but his occasional crack at the party did not help him.

Sir Arnold Gridley, a rather conceited and smug Tory but a nice chap, came under the lash at this time for a speech he had made in the House. Winston said that Gridley had no right to criticise in view of some of his speeches before the war. He wanted to write to his constituency protesting. I told him 'This is most unreasonable and won't do.' The Prime Minister was sometimes very suspicious of the Conservative Party, yet he would be in an impossible position if he had no real party backing. He would be torn to shreds by the Socialists and some of the Liberals. Some Conservatives considered that Winston's philosophy was that the Conservatives should always be quiescent while the Socialists and the supporters of Sir Archibald Sinclair could do the criticising and get away with it. This would never suit the mass of the Conservative Party who would be bound to get restive.

However, this problem solved itself and unanimity was restored by the startling news of Japan's declaration of war on the United States and Britain in December 1941. America was apparently caught napping at Pearl Harbor; a great deal of damage had been done to shore establishments and ships. Parliament was immediately summoned. I went down to the House with the Prime Minister. He was wildly cheered by large crowds. The House was packed, in spite of the short notice. Winston got a great reception. The House was obviously delighted and relieved that Britain had now another ally. This was bound to alter the whole course of the war. The House only sat for the P.M's statement and comments from the various party leaders—all brief. The talking took place in the Smoke Room. Winston returned to No. 10 to study the new problem that had emerged.

The cheering did not last long, for the news which came through was very black indeed. The battleships *Prince of Wales* and *Repulse* had been sunk by the Japanese. The P.M. was much upset and returned to the House. It was an entirely different mood on this occasion. The whole balance of naval power in the Pacific and Far East was now changed. The P.M. was anxious to go to the United States.

He made a statement on the new war situation. The House was not cheering or jubilant. It was gloomy and even apprehensive. The P.M. was very peevish with Members who resented his suggestion that he should make his statement on the wireless. He was irate with an inoffensive Socialist Member called Bellenger. He was furious with somebody nearly every day. It was most trying as it was usually left to me to pour oil on the seething waters.

I met another foreign dignitary, this time Prince Bernhard of the Netherlands. He had called to see the P.M. because the 1st Dutch Battalion had petitioned their Queen to send them out to the Dutch East Indies. They felt they wanted to get in some real fighting against an enemy of Holland. The Prince was dressed in naval uniform with wings. He was pleasant and easy to talk to. He spoke English with a slight American accent.

This was a hectic afternoon, for Winston was to depart for the United States. He was going from Euston to Glasgow to embark in the *Duke of York* in the Clyde. I was sorry I couldn't go with him but, of course, my job was a political one and I could be of no help in a high military conference.

Before the House rose for the Christmas Recess on 19th December 1941 there was a secret session. The Commons and the country seemed very dissatisfied at the way the war was going, especially in the Far East with the loss of battleships and aerodromes. The Government would have to look out because the country could not stand many more reverses of a similar kind.

I had plenty to tell the absent Winston in my report. 'On Friday of this week the House went into Secret Session. The day, on the whole, went badly for the Government. Both Mr. Attlee and A. V. Alexander were batting on sticky wickets and the speeches did not please the House at all. The House was in a restless mood and criticised very strongly the action which led to the loss of the two battleships and the aerodromes in Malaya and Burma. The day was reminiscent of the Debate which followed the evacuation of Norway. Feeling, although not so strong as on that occasion, undoubtedly ran high. Lord Winterton opened the Debate in a severely critical speech which had a lot of support from all quarters of the House. An interesting and significant feature of the Debate was that none of the usual critics took part, although they were all present and indicated their sympathies by interruptions and cheers. The chief points brought out during the Debate were—
1. Why were the battleships employed without an attendant aircraft carrier?
2. Why had they been sent from Singapore when smaller ships might well have done the work, owing to the lack of air support?

3. Why had the aerodrome at Kota Bharu been inadequately defended so that it was lost so easily?

'Both Lord Winterton and Admiral Sir Roger Keyes criticised you personally as they considered that it was you who directed the policy and, therefore, you must take the blame, if any is deserved. Winterton considered that there appeared to be a tendency to blame Generals, Admirals and Civil Servants instead of the Ministers who were responsible.

'Keyes considered that it was madness to send the *Prince of Wales* and *Repulse* to Singapore, and that what had taken place in Malaya was nothing short of muddle and foolishness. Admiral Phillips on the spot was not so much to blame as the First Lord of the Admiralty. He also said that one aircraft carrier would not have been enough and it was essential to have had shore-based aircraft under the complete control of the Navy. The loss of the aerodrome at Kota Bharu had obviously disturbed Members who could not understand why it could not have been held after our experience in Crete.

'Some Members considered that the American Fleet should be sent to Singapore as it would be disastrous to the common effort should this fortress be lost or its utility in any way impaired. There was much disgust felt, not only in the House but in the country, not only at the way affairs had been handled in Malaya but also with the general conduct of the War. It was no good building aerodromes if we were not going to take adequate means to defend them.

'There was, according to some Members, a growing feeling of opinion, irrespective of Parties, which was tired of listening to stories of how we were retiring to prepared positions. Who was responsible for the muddles? This was the cry of many. On the whole, there was a very lively and critical feeling against the Government. Fortunately the House had gone off for the Recess and will, therefore, have time to cool off. I do think, however, that it might be a good thing if, on your return, the House could be summoned again for a further Debate on the War situation, preferably in Open Session.

'I hope you are fit and well and that you have every success in your mission to the United States. Harvie.'

CHAPTER 9

Intrigues in the House

1942 started with many political manoeuvres for changes in Government positions and also individual positions. I was always surprised how open some people were about desire for Government appointments and their own prospects and how well they could fill almost any job. I had had many talks with Brendan Bracken on this subject. He had no illusions. Neither had I. In a position like P.P.S. to the Prime Minister one became very cynical about human nature.

Brendan was a curious man, exceptionally well read in many subjects—American fortunes, architects of Government buildings, headmasters of public schools and bishops. He had great ability. He always wanted his finger in the political pie. He and Max Beaverbrook were very close whenever there were any prospects of Government changes. Sometimes he was very friendly to me and sometimes aloof. When there were any political squabbles about, then he was in the thick of it. He liked to be a king-maker. There were many king-makers about in the House, in all parties. On the Liberal side Lord Nathan liked to have his finger in the pie. I attended many of his dinners to meet some of his friends, such as Gil Lloyd George, Sir Geoffrey Shakespeare, Lord Woolton and Sir William Beveridge, who all became Ministers.

It was inevitable that there should be some shuffling for position. As I was in close contact with the Prime Minister and the man behind the scenes, the news usually came to my ears. In consequence, I was quite a popular figure, in great demand for drink parties, dinners, luncheons and têtes-à-têtes when I had to listen to all kinds of proposals as to what the Government should do, mostly in home situations and in appointments of people who would do much better than the present incumbents—usually themselves. Scarcely a day passed when I was not asked out to meet somebody who was an aspirant for office.

The beginning of 1942 was a kind of scramble for ambitious men. I could understand someone recommending a name for me to put before the Prime Minister, but in many cases it was their own name they wished to put forward. One evening Shakes Morrison, as he was called, probably because of his initials W.S., asked me to dine at the East India and Sports Club to discuss changes in the Government. During the conversation he casually suggested that he himself might be a possible Tory Leader. He may, of course, have been joking or pulling my leg but I didn't think so. He had a very good presence and great charm but I doubted if he had the iron to be a great Leader.

Curiously enough just after I had been called to the Bar and had got into the House of Commons, Shakes and I were in the Smoke Room of the House when I asked him how a young barrister got on to the Attorney's List. I felt I could ask him that as we had been at the same school and university. He asked if I knew anybody who knew the then Attorney-General, Sir Thomas Inskip, who could introduce me. I said, 'No'.

I thought it was very odd as he was P.P.S. to the Attorney-General, and even odder still when a few minutes later the Attorney-General walked into the Smoke Room and sat down beside us. I didn't know him and Shakes didn't introduce me. He merely carried on a conversation with the Attorney ignoring me, so I rose and left the Smoke Room. I thought this was a pretty poor show. Later, after the war, Shakes Morrison became Speaker of the House of Commons and then Governor-General of Australia and was a great success in both appointments.

On 17th January I lunched at the Senior with Desmond Morton and we picked up the Chief Whip at White's and went to Paddington Station to meet the Prime Minister on his return from America. Considering the supposed secrecy, there was quite a large turnout of the public. There were many Cabinet Ministers, of course, and Press men and Principal Secretaries, with hordes of cameramen, police and station officials. Naturally Mrs. Churchill and the family, including Randolph, were

3 Churchill returning from the Atlantic Conference and greeted by Mrs Churchill and Author

4 The PM and Author going down to the House from the Annexe

there. Mrs. Churchill, of course, greeted him first with a hug and a kiss. There were simply roars of applause and greetings of welcome. There was a terrible scrum—police, Ministers, officials—all mixed up in the welcoming mob. I managed to shake hands with Winston and then got separated in the crowd. We then drove back to No. 10 where the P.M. went to bed for an hour and held his cabinet at 6 pm., dressed in his comfortable boiler suit.

Next morning I had a long talk with him. He was sitting up in bed in a gaudy-coloured dressing gown surrounded by papers and smoking his usual cigar. Apart from a cold he seemed to be in good form. He said there would be no Government changes and strongly objected to any criticisms. He said the country and America were behind him. He said he would sweep dissident Members away; after all, it was the 1935 Parliament that had brought us to this mess. I knew he was merely flying a kite but it was a dangerous view. I doubt if the country wanted Parliament to be interfered with. It would be a disaster—any hint of dictatorship would cause grave dissent. The nation would be split.

Later that day Mrs. Churchill, James Stuart, John Martin, Sir Louis Greig, Mary Churchill and I went to Sir Archibald Sinclair's room at the Air Ministry where we saw a very good film show, unexpurgated, of the P.M's visit and speeches in America and Canada. This was a pleasant interlude. Mrs. Churchill walked back with me to No. 10. She was worried about the attitude of the House and asked me if I thought it was right for Winston to put off the Debate on the Far East situation for a week. Had he been well advised to do so? I think she sensed the opposition more than he did.

There was an idea floating around just then that Beaverbrook and the P.M. were toying with the idea of having a General Election. This sounded ridiculous. I didn't see what good it could do. It would finish up as a 'coupon election' and would savour too much of the Nazi pre-war elections to the Reichstag. Beaverbrook always liked to keep the pot boiling, or at any rate stirring.

On 20th January 1942 the House resumed after the Christmas Recess. The P.M. answered quite a number of Questions.

He got what I thought was a very subdued cheer when he entered the Chamber. I thought he would have had a tumultuous reception after his American trip. He informed the House that he would leave it to a free vote as to whether or not his speech should be broadcast.

In the evening James Stuart and I had to see the P.M. in his bedroom. He wanted to talk to us about the recording of his speech. He was in a furious temper at the expressed opposition to his intended broadcast to the nation. He called it a hostile Parliament and a guilty Parliament and said that a General Election might be necessary. Lord Beaverbrook said the same thing when I saw him later in the day.

The trouble was that in war the House had not enough to do, hence the bickering and the jostling for position. None the less Shinwell, Lord Winterton and Percy Harris, a Socialist, a Conservative and a Liberal, wanted to see me. We met in the Commons. They were all critical and wanted to see a reorganisation of the Government but Winston did not want to give in to this. I thought, and told him, that he was making a mistake and that a minor reorganisation embracing all parties would keep everybody quiet for another spell.

Things were still not going too well on the war fronts—Libya and the Far East. Winston had, and felt, a tremendous responsibility and burden. It was easy to see how he got short-tempered about political matters which seemed less important. The political clouds had not yet cleared, for he was again in a furious temper over the reports of the reactions of the Conservative Back Bench Committee. The Chairman, Erskine-Hill, was summoned. He was rather a stout man and readily sweated with the least expenditure of energy and had continuously to wipe his brow with a coloured handkerchief.

Winston sent for me afterwards. He was fuming with rage and walked up and down the Cabinet Room. He said that, after the magnificent reception in the United States and Canada, it was disgraceful to come back to the scurvy treatment of a snarling House of Commons. He said he alone had stood between the Tory Party and extinction. He seemed to hate the Tory Party for any criticism. They had no right to criticise. He was an amazing man. He shouted and stormed at me. He

Intrigues in the House

was determined to have a vote of confidence and, if necessary, a wartime election.

He then thanked me for my advice and help and gave me a colossal cigar. He said this was a present. 'It may blow up but don't blame me.' He then told me an anecdote of his visit to Roosevelt. He was in his American quarters when he heard a knock on his door. He shouted, 'Come in,' and there was the President, who was somewhat taken aback. He was in his wheel-chair. Winston was naked. At once he said to the President, 'Well, you see, Mr. President, I have nothing to hide from you.'

I read the P.M's speech which he was to deliver in the House. It was very strong meat. Tempers were not helped when he read the comments in the Press, and particularly those of Hannen Swaffer in the *Daily Herald* who pointed out that the newsreel of the P.M's return from America had been received in cinemas without a clap or a cheer. This was extraordinary and was certainly not the impression I had received from my enquiries. Any stick was good enough to beat the P.M. and Hannen Swaffer was not a particularly likeable man, as I found out for myself later on in the war.

Winston's speech on 27th January was a great success. I'd never seen the Chamber so crowded with Members and public—every seat was taken, with many Members standing behind the Speaker's Chair and at the Bar of the House. There was certainly great interest taken in the Debate.

Winston spoke for an hour and a half. It was a well-reasoned speech and, although there was not much cheering, the Members were delighted. I thought it would bring the criticism of the Government to an end for the time being. After the speech Winston and I sat in the Smoke Room so that he could greet Members and he asked me to introduce Members he didn't know. We had a drink together. He said he didn't mind people voting against the Government provided there were not too many of them. He was very sensitive to the opinion of the House, no matter what he said to the contrary. He was like a small wayward boy.

There was one group of Members he always talked to and that was the Clydesiders—all very left-wing but characters each one of them, especially Jimmy Maxton who started life as a Conservative at Glasgow University but was a pacifist in World War I. He insisted, however, on going to France as a stretcher-bearer. On his death a few years later Winston sent a wreath to his widow with a most friendly inscription. Another one was John McGovern, who suggested that I should give a dinner for them to meet the Prime Minister. They ought to get some recognition for occasionally helping the Premier. The P.M. said how about being made a Privy Councillor but McGovern said he would rather be a Lord and as he had started life as a plumber, how about Lord Plumber? This kind of badinage amused Winston. He had a very soft spot for the Clydesiders, and especially Maxton.

The Debate came to an amazing end after all the criticism, the noise and the bickering. The vote was 464 votes to 1. The P.M. was skilful in winding up the Debate. He took the broad view and did not hit his critics too hard. He got an amazing ovation after the result was declared. He was obviously relieved.

When Winston, Clemmie and I were walking along the Lobby to his room we met Waldron Smithers. It was only a few weeks since he tore strips off him. Winston called after him and shook him by the hand and said, 'Let bygones be bygones.' This, I thought, was a very fine gesture. The tears poured down Waldron Smithers' cheeks and he said, 'God bless you.' It was a very touching incident.

As we went on Clemmie said, 'Who was that,' and Winston replied, 'Only a bloody fool.' Poor Waldron. He meant well but always put his foot in it with the P.M. The P.M. said that he had had a long busy day and he was tired. He said he had made a peer and a Privy Councillor and wasn't certain that he hadn't deposed the King.

At the beginning of February the Lord Chancellor, Lord Simon, called at No. 10 to take me out to dinner at Claridges. On the way he gave me his view on the Reform of the Lords. He would like to see—1. the restriction of hereditary peers to only those with valuable public service behind them in the Commons or in local government, and elected rather like the Scottish system by election at the beginning of each Parliament; and 2. the creation of Life Peers; and 3. the retention of the powers of the Parliament Act 1911 but with safeguards to prevent the abolition of the second Chamber.

Simon was a smooth man and was not very popular when he was in the House of Commons. I'm bound to say, however, I always liked him and got on well with him. He it was who, towards the end of the war, suggested that I should take Silk and become a K.C.

However, I am digressing from the dinner at Claridges. The other guests were Hugh Dalton, afterwards a Socialist Chancellor of the Exchequer but at that time Minister of Economic Affairs, and several foreign emigré Ministers and servicemen. Simon spent a long time telling a story I knew well but apparently the others didn't, for they laughed their heads off. Simon was a golfer but not a very good one, and he told the story about the great Lord Birkenhead who was also a keen, but not very good, golfer. He and some of his cronies went to Le Touquet for a week-end golfing holiday. It was also a very social occasion. After a late and alcoholic evening he went out to play golf with, among others, Sir Robert Horne, a past Chancellor of the Exchequer. Birkenhead addressed the ball and missed. He tried again and missed. He turned to Horne and said, 'It's bad enough when you can't see the ball but when you can't even see the course it makes the game just bloody ridiculous.'

One of the really first-class brains behind the Prime Minister was that of the Prof, or Lord Cherwell. The P.M. relied upon him a great deal for advice on many military developments that were taking place. I admired him very much.

I remember once when Chamberlain was being criticised the Prof said to me that Winston had made a big mistake, indeed a tragic one, in not having made Neville Chamberlain Leader of the House of Commons and head of political affairs, for that was Chamberlain's metier. This would have allowed Winston to run the war full time, and which was what he really liked doing. He got impatient with the House and all the intrigues that went on and the jockeying for position. There was something in this argument but it would not have succeeded in our Parliamentary system. It was essential that the Prime Minister should work with, and lead, the House of Commons wherein lay the real power of the nation.

The trouble was there were too many prima donnas. Brendan Bracken was one and, early in February, he wrote to the Prime Minister wanting to resign from the Ministry of Information because he didn't feel he was properly treated. Winston had always treated him well and really Brendan owed everything to the P.M. The P.M. had enough to bother him without these petty squabbles. They were endless.

The next grumble I got was from Hugh Dalton, the Socialist, who had asked me to lunch as he had something he would like to say to me. He was an odd man, with curious eyes—opaque and dead at times—and a booming voice. He could be very amusing and witty, very much an opponent of Sir Stafford Cripps arising, I think, from jealousy. He said it would be fatal to put Cripps in high office and displace Attlee or Greenwood.

At this time I think Winston was feeling the burden of the moment. The whole war picture had really got bigger than any one man was capable of handling. Hore-Belisha, who had been Secretary of State for War at the outbreak of hostilities and had been dropped from the Government by Churchill, told me that he thought Winston had lost his hold on the House and that he was really on the wane. At the same time Hore-Belisha was anxious to get another job. He was able, flamboyant and a good speaker. Like many leading Members at that stage of the war, who were out of office, he felt he could run Parliament and the war better than Churchill. This was blatantly ridiculous.

While Parliament was going through one of its many throes of unrest, the news from the various fronts was not good. The situation in the Far East in 1942 was steadily deteriorating and the shipping position was pretty grim. Beaverbrook was steadily becoming more unpopular in the House. His appointment as Minister of Production was not at all well received. He did the Prime Minister a lot of harm as the Commons did not trust him. Winston was always loyal to his friends but the pressure against Beaverbrook was mounting. The criticism in the House had come out into the open and was not bubbling under the surface as it had been for some time.

The Prime Minister had to make two statements, one on the situation at Singapore and another on the passage of the German warships through the Straits of Dover. Both situations had alarmed the House. It was now clear that, as feeling was running so high, the Government must be reorganised, otherwise Churchill would be forced to resign by the march of events. That would be a catastrophe. However, Winston was now alerted. I had given him all the gossip and growlings from the House. The next day Government changes began. Cripps addressed a large all-party meeting at the House in the large Committee Room. He was a coming man in this Parliament and in the Government.

Beaverbrook had been dropped from the Administration. This was a great blow to Churchill. I think it was the best thing that could have happened at that juncture. The P.M. felt his hand had been forced and was not at all happy. He and Beaverbrook had been friends for many years but I don't think he was a good influence on the P.M., despite his drive and ability.

From time to time I was asked my views on promotions, both by the Prime Minister and the Chief Whip, and especially regarding Under-Secretaries, although I was often asked by the P.M. what I thought of so-and-so for a Cabinet job or for a change in Cabinet. On one of these occasions he asked me about J. J. Llewellin, who was then President of the Board of Trade; Winston wanted to make him Minister of Aircraft Production. This had become a key job and he was very successful in that vital post.

It was a fascinating experience for me to be so close to all this Cabinet-making. It seemed a kind of haphazard affair—calls put out to Ministers and then cancelled, often within ten minutes or quarter of an hour. It was like a jig-saw puzzle fitting everyone in. James Stuart and I had our heads together all during this period. I had to prepare a complete new list of Under-Secretaries, showing sackings and suggestions for inclusion in the Ministry. It was quite an experience. I had never been so popular until the names of the new Government were announced, then I found I had made new friends and I had lost some others. I didn't lose them for ever, because there were always new minor changes taking place and hope for them was eternal.

The reorganisation of the Government was completed and

then began a two-day Debate in the House on the war situation, especially in the East. Winston opened the Debate but he was not in good form and left as soon as he could, asking his son Randolph and me to go with him to his room behind the Speaker's Chair. The P.M. was most depressed. He thought he was wrong to succumb to the clamour for Government changes. I told him that I thought he had (at any rate) a better Government. He was also upset by the way the war was developing.

He was thoroughly bowed down by the fall of Singapore and the surrender of the British troops with scarcely a fight. We were standing there in gloom when one of his Private Secretaries, Leslie Rowan, came into the room to say that the Archbishop of Canterbury had been on the 'phone to suggest a Day of Prayer. Winston stood stock-still. He looked absolutely astonished and said with a scowl, 'A Day of Prayer. Yes, by all means. If we can't fight let's bloody well pray.'

The Debate continued the next day and there was a deep gloom hanging over the House. Stafford Cripps wound up for the Government in a first-class speech. The House was greatly relieved. Some Members had been looking round tentatively for a possible successor to Churchill as a wartime Prime Minister. Here, at last, was someone who could possibly take his place. Cripps himself had nothing to do with it. However, he had a brilliant brain and was not shop-soiled by being in the House too much during the war. He was in a position not unlike that of Cromwell during the Civil War nearly three centuries before. Cripps could lead the nation to victory.

The Prime Minister at that time was certainly feeling great strain. Winston sent for me and we had a long talk, but that meant he did most of the talking. He was in the depth of depression about the war. I hadn't seen him so 'down' before. He felt he had made a mistake in changing his Government and should have fought Parliament. He said, 'I need a holiday.' This certainly shook me. I'd never heard of him wanting a holiday before. In fact, he rather scoffed at holidays. This was certainly a bad sign. He thought it would be a good thing for him to go to the Middle East. I thought to myself, some holiday. What I did say was that that might prove disastrous, for while the cat's away the mice might play—indeed would almost certainly play. He couldn't possibly stay away so long from the centre of affairs. It might be a good thing, however, if he had a short visit to the Middle East. Such a visit would cheer up the troops as well as himself.

He put his hand on my shoulder and said, 'I hope I haven't made you too depressed.' He had to speak intimately to somebody. It was rather pathetic but disturbing to see the nation's leader so cast down in spirits. He concluded by saying he valued my advice, although he didn't always agree with me. His chat seemed to cheer him up.

He was most complimentary and then laughed when he said that I was probably one of those Conservative Members who went through the Lobby before the war with all his opponents. I reminded him that not only did I go through the Lobby against him but, as a Government Whip, I helped to put many others through the Lobby against him as well. It had been my job at the time. Winston gave a wry smile but was now rapidly recovering his usual good spirits.

There was always the brighter side. We were on our way to one of our quiet dinners in the Savoy—naturally in a private room—on a bitterly cold evening. When we were turning out of Downing Street he suddenly grasped my arm and said, pointing, 'There is a good-looking girl for you. At least she would be if she wasn't so blue with cold.' This kind of aside he frequently made when he felt skittish and in a light mood.

India was the topic of the moment with its threat to secede from the Empire. Cripps was going out there to try to get some agreement with her on the next developments which virtually amounted to independence. This was a problem we had not expected to arise, but of course now that Britain was so heavily involved and things were not going well for us it was the obvious time for her to snarl at our heels and try to get deals from us. India naturally thought we were so heavily involved that we might be forced to give way, yet vast armies from India were fighting with the British in many parts of the world.

At that time I was also having many talks with the Dutch Prime Minister, Gerbrandy, who naturally was most perturbed at the events in the East Indies where most of the Dutch

Colonies were situated. The fall of Singapore seemed to him to be not only a Dutch disaster but a world disaster, as indeed it was. He nursed the idea that Holland should become part of the British set-up, which could have been the beginning of the Common Market. He thought the Dutch felt more attuned to our way of life than to that of the Continent. Alas, his ambitions in that area never came to fruition.

CHAPTER 10

Middle East Situation

On my suggestion the Prime Minister had the Under-Secretaries to his room at the House. I felt that they were left out in the cold a bit and that such a meeting would make them feel that they were closer to the Leader and part of the Government team.

The P.M. stated that India must be strengthened in every way by troops and equipment. It must be defended. He paid high tribute to the Dutch. Australia, in the event of real invasion, would rank before the Middle East or any other theatre of war and we must also do everything we could to take the strain off the Russians. On the Battle of the Atlantic and the American losses, the P.M. said we were helping them with our anti-submarine experience. The Americans were willing to learn but not anxious to be taught. Winston said, talking of bombing, it was like the old lady who said, 'Well, it does take your mind off the bloody war.'

I attended a most interesting meeting of the Poles. It was convened by General Sikorski to meet General Anders who had just marched his army over mountains, rivers, snows and desert to the Middle East—a remarkable feat. The Poles had great guts and were first-class soldiers. I was tremendously impressed by Anders. He looked a 'real soldier'. I then had dinner with some of the Poles at the Savoy. There I met General Kopanski, Leader of the Carpathian Brigade. He told us the saga of the unique experiences of these fighting men in their endeavour to join the Allies in the Middle East. It was an amazing achievement. I also met Dr. Rettinger, recently Polish Chargé d'Affaires in Moscow. We had an interesting talk about the proposed Anglo-Russian Treaty respecting the Baltic States.

My next issue was to do with the Yugoslavs. Their Prime

Minister, Simovitch, asked me to go and see him. He was very perturbed at the treatment his soldiers were receiving from our soldiers in the Middle East. Apparently a General Stone, who was associated with them, was alleged to treat the Yugoslavs as if they were serfs. I calmed him down. This was not an issue for me so I passed him on to the appropriate military authority. It was scarcely a job for the Prime Minister or his Parliamentary Private Secretary. I met all these Allies so often that I sometimes got landed with things that had nothing to do with me. It is an example, however, of the wide range of subjects and people I had to deal with.

There were a number of by-elections during the war, many of them uncontested but others fought with some bitterness. In May 1942 there was a by-election at Putney, usually a safe Conservative seat and a residential suburb of London. Sir Archibald Sinclair, the Leader of one of the two groups of Liberals in the House, discussed it with the P.M. He thought that it would be better to send the candidates messages from each of the Leaders, then the candidate could put them up in the village hall. Winston looked astonished and then made us all laugh by saying 'Come come Archie, there are not many villages left in Putney.'

Archie tried to shuffle out of that one by emphasising the difference between Liberals and Liberal Nationals. They were like the North and South Poles. Winston felt the two brands were the same but the Liberals didn't see it that way and Archie Sinclair said that if Ernest Brown signed a message he would not sign, while Brown said that if Sinclair signed he would not do so, for he would take it as a great insult. I felt that the Sinclair Liberals were being very unfair and that they were just playing at politics. However, the matter was resolved satisfactorily after discussion with the P.M. and Chief Whip, the Chairman of the Party and myself.

In the evening Winston had another small dinner party for a few Conservative Members when he waxed strong on Northern Ireland. Ulster, he said, had been our salvation. The Conservative Party must always stand by Ulster. It was our duty, an absolute duty, not to desert Ulster since, but for Ulster, we might have had to undertake the conquest of Southern Ireland

Middle East Situation

in order to preserve the sea lanes to America. He ranged over a wide area of subjects.

Lord Beaverbrook was returning home from a trip abroad. The P.M. hoped he would really go back to Russia again as he could be a nuisance here, stirring up trouble and even running candidates against the Government. The man was a menace and his Second Front speech in America was a great embarrassment.

When speaking to Americans before they came into the war, they would ask what we would have done if Germany had conquered us and the P.M. would reply, without hesitating, 'With our dying hands hand on the torch of freedom to the New World.' The Prime Minister subsided in the car on the way back to No. 10; he was now dead tired.

During the war my wife was rarely in London, as our three children were born in 1940, 1942 and 1944, so she had her hands full. When she did come south it was usually for something to do with constituency work or to help me to entertain on some occasions when wives were included in any function. (There were few occasions during the war involving wives. It was a masculine life, even in the political field.) From time to time when my wife did come to London it was a relief to have her to talk to and to enjoy her company.

It was not until 1942 that she really met the Prime Minister. We were invited to lunch at No. 10. Mr. and Mrs. Duncan Sandys (Diana Churchill), Mrs. Churchill and Kathleen Harriman were there. We had sherry in the garden before lunch and then sat out again afterwards. The P.M. talked about the old tabbies of the House of Lords, the position in Madagascar and the Putney by-election.

That day my wife certainly got her fill of political entertaining, for in the evening we dined with Leslie Hore-Belisha, who had a very nice house in Stafford Place, Westminster. When we arrived he was exotically dressed in a green velvet dinner jacket and trousers. Lady Willingdon was the other guest. Hore-Belisha presented the ladies with sprays of orchids and me with a red carnation. He, of course, was very Jewish and he modelled himself on Disraeli. Indeed he had a bust of

Disraeli on a plinth in a prominent place in the room and no doubt saw the mantle of Dizzy on his own shoulders.

I had to leave early because I had to go back to No. 10 Downing Street and then accompany the Prime Minister in his car to King's Cross where we joined a special train with sleepers, dining car and a saloon car for a journey to the north. The other members of the party included Mr. Attlee, a nice man but not very stimulating. It was incredible to think he was the Deputy Prime Minister.

Dr. Evatt of Australia, Minister of External Affairs, was also there. I was not at all impressed by him. He was conceited and a bully-boy type and very anti-British, although I think the week-end did him a lot of good, for Winston was in tremendous form. He was most anxious that help should be given to the Australians against the Japanese. He particularly wanted ships and fighter planes.

The party also included General Ismay, afterwards Lord Ismay, John Martin, Principal Private Secretary, and Commander 'Tommy' Thompson who had much to do with the P.M's travel arrangements and went on all his journeys. We sat talking until about 2 am. Winston was in great form as he often relaxed late at night, or rather early in the morning. He said his heart was in the United States. The U.S. may preach isolationism but unless we were careful Hitler would enforce it. He had a feeling that Hitler was done. Our fighters and bombers would lead us to victory. He hadn't hated the Germans in World War I but he did this time.

He and I sat for quite a time together. He was wearing his slippers, black with W.S.C. embroidered in gold. He liked hot water bottles with pink covers both when he went to bed in the afternoon and again at night. At this stage he rang for his valet and kept on ringing because the valet didn't appear. So I asked if I could get him what he wanted. He said he wanted his sleeping pills. I was surprised because I never realised he needed sleeping pills and thought all he had to do was to put his head on the pillow and he was off. He couldn't do that at night, only in the afternoon, but he never could get to sleep in a train without sleeping pills. I had the same problem so I told him I likewise could not sleep easily in sleepers. He replied, 'My dear boy, you must have my prescription.' I got it from him in due course and used the sleeping pills for many years on my night journeys to Scotland and my many visits to all parts of the world.

Next morning we visited the Linton and Leeming aerodromes in Yorkshire. They were both Halifax bomber stations. We saw a plane landing blind as it would do in fog or darkness, also the latest 1,000 and 2,000 lb. bombs—all very impressive. The P.M. expressed the view that there should be less container material and more explosives.

We lunched in the train and then visited a bomb-filling station at Aycliffe not far from Darlington. It was a colossal factory with nearly 17,000 employees. We toured the buildings and then motored round the works to the resounding cheers of the employees. The P.M. sat up in the back of the open car and received the plaudits from the crowds of employees. He got a wonderful reception. On his leaving the factory a young girl of about seventeen presented him with a cigar. In return he kissed her to the loud cheers of the workers.

We spent the night in a siding at Staple Ripley. It was a lovely evening and we went for a walk along the river Nidd after dinner. The next day we went on to Leeds and toured the streets, visited two factories, a Civic Centre and the great Town Hall. It was a lovely day and there were massive crowds everywhere. It was estimated that in and around the Town Hall square there was a crowd of 25,000 people. I'd never seen anything like it. The P.M. made a brief speech. Dr. Evatt also made a brief speech but it was an anti-climax. We then rejoined the train for lunch.

In the afternoon we got out at a place called Lalom Heath near Newmarket where Winston inspected the 9th Armoured Division. We saw a tank battle and a drive-past of the tanks. It was most impressive. Later the P.M. surprised us all when, while facing some scout cars and their drivers, he quietly watered the horses, or in civilian language, had a pee. He didn't bother to find a sheltered spot or turn his back. We were all somewhat embarrassed and didn't know where to look. There he was, unperturbed, with a cigar in his mouth and his black hat on the back of his head. Why should he bother? The troops didn't bat an eyelid or turn a hair. Why should they?

The P.M. left the train at Wendover to go on to Chequers by car for what was left of the week-end while General Ismay, Dr. Evatt and I returned to London. Dr. Evatt was beginning by this time to thaw and become more friendly. I think he was overawed by the P.M. In the train he said to us that popular songs in Australia at that time were *Tipperary* and *Long, Long Trail*, which reminded the Australians of the glory of the First World War.

I gave a dinner at the Paddington Hotel when Gil Lloyd George was made Minister of Fuel and Power in June 1942. This was a mixed dinner of mainly Socialists and Liberals but also a few Conservatives. I had present on this occasion Sir Harry Fildes, Ernest Brown and other Liberals; Oliver Baldwin, Moelyn Hughes and other Socialists; A. J. Sylvester, the Private Secretary to the former Prime Minister David Lloyd George, and John Carvel, a well-known Lobby correspondent. We didn't break up until after midnight.

Also in connection with Gil Lloyd George's appointment Winston asked Gil and his wife, Edna, down to Chequers. I drove down to Chequers with them. Edna was a charming person and I got to know them both very well. They often stayed with my wife and me in Scotland after the war.

We arrived at Chequers just before dinner. Clemmie was not well so she didn't appear that evening. The only other people for dinner were John Martin, Tommy Thompson, Pamela Churchill and Pug Ismay—rather a No. 10 party with all of us on the inner staff, except Pamela. I had not met Pamela often but she was most attractive with fine reddish hair.

The P.M. was in superb form. We had an excellent dinner of soup, salmon and strawberries with sherry, champagne, port and brandy. After dinner there was a cinema show. We saw *The Younger Pitt* with Robert Donat and Robert Morley in the leading parts. It was an excellent film with speeches that might have been made in the present crisis. The staff of Chequers and the military guard on duty also attended. The P.M. put on his dressing-gown.

Afterwards he read telegrams from the Middle East, one of which said, 'To stand and fight it out or retire to the Egyptian frontier. Battle going badly.' The P.M. sent his telegram back—

'Stand and fight it out. Bless you all.' Retreat might be a rout. The battle now depended on will power.

The P.M. was very worried. He tramped up and down the room, having put on the gramophone, playing records of military band marches then sentimental tunes. Finally he felt optimistic about the result of the battle and he played Harry Lauder's song *Keep Right on to the End of the Road*. This was one of his favourites. We didn't get to bed until 3.30 am. The ladies, of course, had drifted away long before then. I slept that night in an ornately decorated four-poster bed; on the walls of the bedroom were paintings of Cromwell, Stafford, Robert Walpole–the first Prime Minister—and William Pitt.

In the morning the Lloyd Georges, Mrs. Churchill and I went for an hour and a half walk. Mrs. Churchill was a very keen croquet player and after the walk we played croquet for most of the day. Duncan and Diana Sandys came to lunch. The Lloyd Georges hadn't been to Chequers since 1922 when Gil's father was Prime Minister.

In the afternoon the P.M. went up to London for the United Nations parade. I'd never seen so many medals as Winston had. He handed them to me to feel the weight. They must have weighed a good many pounds. He was quite roguish about them.

After dinner we saw Charlie Chaplin in *The Gold Rush*. The Lloyd Georges and I left Chequers at midnight. We got back to London at 2 am. I don't know how Winston stood these long hours except that he did go to bed in the afternoon. I then had some letters to draft for his signature. I hated doing these. He was so much more able at that kind of thing. However, I got used to it. I found myself imitating Churchill, both in style of writing and in talking. With the passage of years I have alas gone back to pure Harvie-Watt in every way. I have no longer got the master's voice or touch.

Bendan Bracken had a long talk with me after I got back from Chequers. He was not very happy in his job. He wanted to get a change. He had said this before and I had no doubt he would say it again, but I really thought he enjoyed it. I know I liked my job and I wouldn't swop it for any other.

* * *

Winston had again gone off on his travels. He left London for Stranraer at mid-day. He was due to leave Stranraer at 11 pm. by flying-boat for Baltimore. General Ismay and his doctor, Charles Wilson, went with him.

That evening we had dinner at the Savoy—Stafford Cripps, Rab Butler, Geoffrey Lloyd, Gerald Palmer, Harold Mitchell and Donald Somervell, the Attorney-General. We discussed the question of coalition after the war to deal with the peace and domestic problems. Cripps was in favour of this course, provided we started now and worked out a policy with common goodwill. Apparently Anthony Eden, Oliver Lyttelton, Attlee and Ernie Bevin had talked with him on the subject. There was also the possibility of a centre party and this was what he had already talked over with Eden and his group. It might not have been a bad idea but I feared that party politics were a bit too strong at that time to agree to a coalition.

However, these matters paled into insignificance compared with the shocking news from the Middle East. The fall of Tobruk stunned the nation. This would have grave effects on our prestige, our shipping and our morale, not only in the United Kingdom but in the Middle East, North Africa and Malta. We seemed unable to snatch a victory anywhere. All this bad news would be reflected in the House and the morale of the country generally. Thank God for Churchill, with his abounding confidence, gallantry, determination and, above all, his outstanding leadership. That for me was the most desperate day since Dunkirk.

That night I had Geoffrey Lloyd and Charles Peat to dine with me in the Mess but the only uplift of spirit I had was in a story Geoffrey told about J. H. Thomas, a well-known pre-war Socialist Minister—a very nice man who had risen from the ranks. He was sitting beside a Chinese at a public dinner. The Chinese was very quiet. Jimmy, in broken English, at each course said, 'Soopee, Fishee', etc. At the end of the dinner the Chinese got up and replied to the toast in magnificent English. When he sat down he turned to Thomas and said, 'How you likee my speechee?' Jimmy Thomas was a great story-teller in his day.

While Winston was away I had lunch with Mrs. Churchill

and Mr. Attlee at No. 10. Mrs. Churchill was a most charming and vivacious woman, exceedingly striking in appearance. Attlee's more acid critics said his speeches were on a par with those of an Urban Councillor representing a very small Urban Area; nevertheless he was a very nice and kindly man and had been a gallant soldier at Gallipoli. Walter Elliot, a former Tory Minister, said to me, rather cruelly I thought, that there should be a new calendar called the Attlee Calendar, containing a platitude for each day of the year, beginning on 1st January with 'Every avenue will be explored'.

Clemmie asked me to stay and chat after lunch and put her in the picture about the feelings in the House. She talked about some of the women in the House. Irene Ward always had her arms filled with letters and papers which were constantly spilling on to the floor. The same process happened again and again—very clumsy but endearing. However, the woman who intrigued her most was the Socialist Edith Summerskill. She thought she was very bright and would go a long way which, of course, she did when the Socialist Party came into power after the war. Clemmie rarely talked about the women Members.

When Winston returned from his visit to America I went to Euston Station to meet him. The crowds this time were small and not very loud in their acclamation. Only the War Cabinet and a few other Ministers were at the station. Clemmie and the family were, of course, also present. Winston looked well but he was in a very bad mood about the feelings in the House. At the moment he tended to be truculent. The House and the country were truly upset and anxious about the Middle East and it would not do to upset the House with arrogance. I told him this and he was not at all pleased. He had a Cabinet meeting at once and then went to Chequers.

The Chief Whip, James Stuart, and the Chairman of the Party, Tom Dugdale, and I met to discuss the week's proceedings in the House. If the news continued to be bad then feeling and criticism in the House was likely to be strong and there would be demands for a Debate.

During this time the P.M. was at Chequers and was busy with the first draft of his speech. I read this. It was quite good but I thought he ought not to go for Shinwell yet. The ending was rather peevish, about resigning if not allowed to remain P.M. and Minister of Defence. I made suggestions to water these points down a bit. He said he would think about it.

The next day Winston was back from Chequers and he made a short statement to the House to the effect that General Auchinleck had taken over command of the 8th Army from General Ritchie. Although the news continued to be bad from the Middle East, Members were tending more and more to rally round the Prime Minister and the Government. Some Members thought there should not be a Debate but the P.M. was insistent and, in view of the criticism, he was quite right to insist on a Debate so as to bring all the criticism out into the open. Any other course would tend to enhance the prestige of Sir John Wardlaw-Milne, a Conservative back bencher who had quite a following and appeared to be growing in stature. He was a tall, impressive-looking man with a monocle and was a good speaker and effective critic of the Government.

The 1st July 1942 was the beginning of the great Debate. The P.M. sent for me to go to his bedroom to tell him of the progress made and what was being said. He had just come from his bath and was standing naked in his bedroom. I was a bit taken aback but he started to dry himself as if he were alone and then began to dress, walking up and down the room, asking me questions about the Debate. It was all rather disconcerting and at first I had difficulty in concentrating on my verbal report. I saw every detail of dress, up to his false teeth and oiling and brushing his hair. He had been having his usual afternoon sleep when he pulled the curtains and put a black band over his eyes.

I was able to tell the P.M. that Wardlaw-Milne had made a terrible gaffe in the House. He started off most impressively and had the complete ear of the House. Then he made the absurd suggestion that the Duke of Gloucester should be made Commander-in-Chief of the armies. The House collapsed in ribaldry and his danger as a critic had gone. The extraordinary thing was that, once the outburst of laughter and jeers had died down, he did succeed in getting the ear of the House again. This was quite a remarkable feat. I had never known such a complete comeback. However, the real threat had passed. He was never again a menace to the Government.

The House sat on until 3 o'clock in the morning when one of the Members, McGovern of the I.L.P., called a count. There were only thirty-three people in the Chamber. The House adjourned. A. P. Herbert, the well-known writer and humorist, who was a bit tiddly, did not want the House to adjourn and was furious. He made to set on McGovern. They had to be separated by the police. I had never seen a scene like it before. However, it was soon over and the House was glad to adjourn.

Later that same day, when the House resumed its sitting at the usual time, the Chamber was packed—as crowded as I had ever seen it. Winston rose to the greatest heights of oratory in winding-up the Debate, although the best speech was made by the Socialist Aneurin Bevan. He was very bitter but eloquent. He too was a great orator. In the Socialist Government after the war he became Minister of Health but, alas, he died prematurely, for I think he would certainly have become Prime Minister.

Although there was a huge Government majority, it was the writing on the wall unless the war took a turn for the better. There was now a considerable body of opinion, even among those who voted with the Government, against the Prime Minister and the direction of the war.

On the day after the vote, Mrs. Churchill sent for me to tell her all that took place and especially about Wardlaw-Milne. When I got there she was not in a fit state to see me and I had to speak to her through her bedroom door. She said she had not got her make-up on yet and was not looking very beautiful. However, after I had been talking to her for a bit she said that this was absurd and came out with her face shining with cream and wearing a white dressing wrap. She still looked very beautiful and was her usual charming self. She and Winston were both very natural people but I was more used to speaking and reporting to people in their offices. I found that easier than outside the bedroom door or in the bedroom with Winston in the nude.

On the following Saturday, I was walking in St. James's Park when I ran into the Chief of the Imperial General Staff, General

Sir Alan Brooke, afterwards Lord Alanbrooke. I had known him since before the war as at one time I was a Lieutenant-Colonel under his command. He was not then a popular general with the Territorial Army. However, he rose to the highest rank in the war.

On that particular day we had a long talk in the park where we were both taking our exercise. We talked particularly about the prospect of a visit by Winston to Cairo. The C.I.G.S. was all against it from the military point of view, while Auchinleck was fighting the battle and there was a Resident Minister in the Australian, Casey. He thought it would do more harm than good, apart from the danger of his plane being shot down in that very disturbed area. I knew none of these matters would deter the P.M. if he was determined to go.

The trouble with all these trips was that I could never be included because I was the Parliamentary Secretary, and I had to keep my ear to the ground even more when the P.M. was on his travels than when he was at home. Keeping my ear to the ground also meant using my mouth and my digestive organs from morning until early the next morning.

It was on 8th July 1942 that I first met Generals Eisenhower and Clark at lunch. I was much impressed by them. They had great assurance and were here to help get the war finished. I was to meet Eisenhower many times before the war ended and I was always inspired by his personality.

Chapter 11

Russia, the Desert and Libel

About this time Winston had been having his portrait painted. He was rather 'let in' for this by his wife, I think, who had been pestered by the artist Frank Salisbury. Winston refused to sit for him. However, after some argument, Salisbury was given permission to get into the Secretaries' Bench in the House. This was where the top Civil Service people could sit and help with any notes demanded by their masters. The artist could then watch Winston from about fifteen yards distance and do his sketches to take back to his studio. Salisbury was introduced to me to seek my help and make the necessary arrangements.

When the painting was finished Salisbury showed it to me. I didn't think it was very good. He hadn't got Winston's eyes or hair-colouring right. However, I knew very little about painting. It was arranged that it should be brought to No. 10 so that Churchill and others should see it. It was to be placed on an easel in my room suitably prepared with a special light. The portrait was possibly for Harrow, Winston's old school.

In due course I told him that the painting was ready for him to see. Unfortunately he had been in a bad temper all evening. When he came into my room he stood gazing at the portrait and then grunted. I asked, 'What do you think of it?', and he replied, 'Bloody awful', glared at me and walked out of the room without a word.

Next day Mrs. Chirchill was most upset, for she had been kind to Salisbury and hoped the viewing would go well. Salisbury also spoke to me the next day on the phone but I could not say that the P.M. thought it was bloody awful and I had to water down Winston's comment. However, Salisbury was a nice man and I think Mrs. Churchill did something about it, for I never saw it or heard mention of it again. For some time afterwards if I had something in my room I wanted the

P.M. to see he would say, 'Not another bloody portrait, I hope.'

The next night I had a political dinner for the Prime Minister with another cross-section of Members to meet him. The P.M. was very pleased with his speech in the House. He had received an excellent reception. He talked a good deal about the usual criticism in the House and thought that our side should be more tough and should strike back at people like Aneurin Bevan. He was more optimistic about the war, especially in Libya. Shipping losses were our greatest problem and danger, but he thought he could see the way through once the USA got more experience of convoy and anti-submarine work.

There would soon be a million Americans in this country. We must get friendly with them. A Second Front was necessary, but we were not going to have any more bloody failures as on the beaches of France. No more Dunkirks. Winston also talked about the bombing policy. Air Chief Marshal Harris had a simple philosophy. He was A.O.C. Bomber Command. He said, 'Never mind the army, navy or fighters—only bombers, bombers and more bombers.' Poor Harris; despite his brilliant record in the war he thought afterwards he had been let down and went to live in South Africa.

I was now meeting more and more of the United States service people and Winston asked me to come in and meet General Marshal and also Admiral King of the US Navy. The Americans I met were all good, tough types of commander. From this session with Americans I had to go straight to a session with General Sikorski and his top Ministers, the Ambassador to this country and Dr Rettinger, the eminence grise and a kind of Harry Hopkins of the Polish Government in exile. This had become a very international day, for in the evening I dined with Oliver Lyttelton, Averell Harriman and our Fourth Sea Lord, Admiral Sir John Cunningham.

At this time I was seeing a lot of Captain Butcher and Captain Lee, both A.D.Cs to General Eisenhower. One of the topics that interested me and surprised me was that the Americans were rather worried about their negro soldiers and the British girls. There was a good deal of fraternisation. I didn't see what could be done about this. Many American soldiers, black and white, married English girls who went out to live in America after the war, and I presume they lived happily ever after. It was certainly a good thing for us to have this influx of English girls to the USA, for they brought more British blood into the friendly American circles.

On 29th July 1942 there was quite an exciting day in the House on the Old Age Pension Debate which caused a split in the Socialist Party; I had to keep in touch with the P.M. It was often very odd reporting and speaking to the P.M. on the 'phone. He didn't somehow begin or end. He didn't say 'Good morning' or 'Good-bye' or use comparable sounds to that effect. Occasionally there was a grunt but usually a dead silence— a blank which was quite disconcerting. I never knew whether I was left speaking to myself or not. Although I was frequently on the 'phone to him from the House or he to me, I never got used to this type of 'phoning. I couldn't go on saying, 'Are you still there?' You felt damned stupid. I often used to wonder if he did this for fun.

The Debate on pensions proved to be the most stormy and heated discussion which had taken place for some time. There was considerable feeling of a personal nature between Shinwell and a few of his friends and Bevin and other Socialist Members of the Government. Ernest Bevin, in winding up for the Government, made an excellent speech and again his reputation was enhanced.

There was also an important all-party meeting. Sir Percy Harris, the Liberal elder statesman, was in the chair and some 250 Members of both Houses of Parliament of all Parties attended. The Russian Ambassador addressed the meeting. He stressed the grave situation in Russia, especially in the valley of the Don. He said that in the last war only one-third of the German army was engaged on the Eastern Front and that two-thirds were pinned down on the West, whereas today more than 80% of Germany's effort was directed against Russia. In addition, there were all the other armies that had been forced into her service in one way or another. The main points which he made, however, were—

1. That there was no informed war strategy on the side of the Allies. Every Ally had different conceptions of what

was required and a different strategy. It was impossible, therefore, to obtain properly synchronised action. Only by a unified strategy could the resources of the Allies be mobilised and concentrated at the decisive moment at the decisive place.

2. He urged an immediate Second Front in Europe. This suggestion had first been made by the Soviet Government as far back as July 1941 and had since been repeated again and again. He considered that a Second Front this year was an absolute necessity as the military power of the U.S.S.R. was at it peak. Next Spring the Russian forces would be weaker and, therefore, no advantage would be gained by postponing an invasion of Europe until then.

Dealing with casualties, the Ambassador said the losses of the Russian army in killed, wounded, missing, and prisoners were five million and those of Germany were ten million. It was a mistake to talk about the inexhaustible manpower of the U.S.S.R. because more than fifty million of the population were now under German control. With regard to supplies of raw materials, there had been large losses. Half their iron and steel production had gone whilst, owing to the loss of the Ukraine, the food situation in 1943 was likely to be most difficult.

This speech made a profound impression on Members of all parties present.

There was tremendous excitement because the P.M. wanted to go overseas to the Middle East. John Anderson, Stafford Cripps, and Charles Wilson (Winston's doctor) tried to dissuade him, without success. Personally I thought they were too weak in handling the situation. The P.M. was furious at being thwarted and kicked his legs in the air, completely losing his temper, and he shouted, 'Damn you. Damn you all. If the Ministers don't agree I'll resign.' He behaved like a spoilt child.

I thought the risk for him was substantial and he ought not to go. It could make things difficult for him politically. He would at once be accused of interfering with the generals. But he was going to the Middle East and that was that. He was tested for high flying and apparently he was physically all right.

On Saturday afternoon, 1st August, the day after this rumpus, I had to go to No. 10. While waiting to see the P.M.

he came out to the private office where the Secretaries were gathered. He was wearing a red false beard and giggling like a girl. This was to disguise him for the journey to the Middle East. He made me put it on to show how it would look. It was an absurd scene.

Fortunately the incident killed any intention of Winston going disguised. If his plane had been shot down or he was taken prisoner it would have been ludicrous. When I went into the Cabinet Room to say good-bye he asked, 'Where is the beard?' He said he didn't mind the critics. He was above all that.

As to interfering with the generals, he had every intention of doing so. Things couldn't be worse than they were then as we were in a serious position in the Middle East. He said, 'I am going.' He wasn't going to take me as there was no room. He would, however, give me a 'show' some other time and said I deserved it for all my hard work for which, he said, he was grateful and wished to thank me. He then shook hands with me and so we parted, he to his greatest gamble and me for a bath. He expected to be away for a month.

The next day Attlee announced to the House in Secret Session that the P.M. had gone to Egypt and hoped to see Stalin. In the evening, as Clemmie was alone, I asked her to dine with me at Claridges with Gil and Edna Lloyd George and General Sir Frederick and Lady Pile.

Clemmie was most indiscreet and was scathing in her criticism of some of the Ministers, e.g. Shakes Morrison. She said he was just a Tory edition of Ramsay MacDonald, Anthony Eden was a weak, ineffectual but lucky man, Jim Thomas she had no use for, Geoffrey Lloyd she thought dull and conceited and Mr. Attlee a funny little mouse of a man. I thought it was rather bad taste to criticise her husband's Ministers at a mixed party like this. Apart from her comments on Geoffrey Lloyd, her views were shared by me.

On the day Parliament adjourned for the Summer Recess in 1942 I had a long talk with Randolph Churchill. He had had an accident and looked ill. He told me of his experience with his parachute jump. He said the worst moments were just before you jumped and then about twenty feet from the ground, when it suddenly seemed to leap up at you. Thank goodness I didn't have to drop by parachute. I suppose if it were a matter of life or death—one would jump.

When the P.M. got back from the Middle East the Cabinet gave him a lunch at the Admiralty. Afterwards he made a brief speech about his travels and especially his Russian visit. He said that Stalin had a great sense of humour and they got on very well. I could well imagine that he had a great sense of very wide humour, rather like his own. The P.M. also dealt with what he called the terrible state of the army in the Middle East. It required revitalising. General Alexander was the man for the job.

As usual, on his return from a trip the P.M. addressed the House on the up-to-date war situation. It was not one of his best speeches. He seemed somewhat lifeless, no doubt because of the stresses and strains of his visit to our army and to the Russians. Stafford Cripps made a stupid mistake in lecturing the House about attendance. The House was furious. Cripps was like a schoolmaster. Aneurin Bevan made a vicious attack on the Prime Minister the next day. I had to go to No. 10 to see the P.M. We met in the cloak-room and wash place. We were both washing our hands and I was talking to him when he suddenly turned and walked out. I had to follow, throwing my towel away, and finish drying my hands on my handkerchief.

We went into the Cabinet Room. He walked up and down talking about Cripps's stupidity and then went out on to the verandah leading to the garden. I thought the interview had ceased. Then I heard his voice say, 'Come on.' I hurried back but, before I got out to the verandah, he was stamping his feet and half shouting 'Come on, can't you?' We sat down on a garden seat for a bit then walked round the garden for about half an hour. He had suddenly become friendly again and gave me a cigar. He again criticised Cripps as Leader of the House. Conversing with Winston tête-à-tête was not easy. It was difficult to know if an audience was ended or even begun. He stopped talking to admire two butterflies and a red flower. He said it was the colour of pigeon's blood, and my audience came to an end as we walked back into No. 10.

There was never a restful moment in politics at No. 10. It may be more leisurely in peace-time and with a less highly strung Prime Minister, but in wartime with a dynamo as a Prime Minister and everyone jockeying for position it was very difficult. I had never seen much of this kind of back-biting on such a large scale. There was always someone on the mat, often because the critic wanted a job. This proved a good education for me and stood me in good stead in my post-war activities.

The latest victim was P. J. Grigg, a top Civil Servant before he joined the Government as Secretary of State for War. Duncan Sandys appeared to be making things unpleasant for Grigg, and, as the son-in-law of the P.M., he was in a fairly strong position. He had a tremendous lust for power. He was not, however, very popular in the House.

It was at this time that I was involved in an extraordinary libel action. I had gone on leave to Scotland in the second half of August 1942 to stay with my family; while I was away, a storm had burst in certain sections of the Press about a speech I was alleged to have made at a garden party in my constituency in the village of Petersham. (I hadn't been to Petersham at all at that time.) I was reported to have said our shipping losses were more severe than the public had been led to know. Was it really wise for Churchill's Secretary to hint at things the newspapers are not supposed to print? This was in the *Daily Herald* of 12th August by Hannen Swaffer, often called the Pope of Fleet Street. This libel was repeated and even made worse in allegations by 'Cameronian' in *Reynolds News*. In the *Daily Herald* Swaffer wrote, 'Addressing the local Conservatives, amid the lovely and spacious grounds of Montrose House, Petersham, he sneered at the advocates of a Second Front by saying they had never distinguished themselves by any great desire to shoulder arms.

'In asking how we could get a million men across the Channel, Watt said, "Our shipping losses are far more severe than we have been led to know so far as the public press is concerned." Is it really wise for Churchill's Secretary in the hour of Russia's agony to denounce as violent political propaganda the Aid for Russia demonstrations which more than anything have proved to Moscow the great goodwill felt by the masses towards our comrades in the Soviet Army?'

Mr. G. O. Slade, my counsel in the subsequent law suit, said 'The case affords an illustration of the harmful consequences flowing from the publication of inaccurate statements.' The German radio seized the opportunity of broadcasting to the world that Colonel Harvie-Watt's statements had given rise to stormy comments in London.

In *Reynolds News* 'Cameronian' wrote, 'Let's leave mumbo jumbo and take a look at the political mice nibbling industriously at the national morale. For example, Col. Harvie-Watt, in a recent speech, commented that advocates of a Second Front had never distinguished themselves by any great desire to shoulder arms, thus sneering at Ernest Bevin, the Minister responsible for deciding who shall and who shall not bear arms in a conscript country. When Harvie-Watt became Parliamentary Secretary to the Prime Minister, I regretted that a political illiterate should occupy so important a post. So will Winston if he does not sack him.'

Mr. Slade said it was only fair to the defendants to say that the moment they realised their mistake they became only too anxious to put matters right. They were indemnifying the plaintiff (me) in respect of the costs. Col. Harvie-Watt would not dream of making any personal profit out of the action and he accepted the defendants' apologies. I was damned generous. I could have had heavy damages. The case was settled before Mr. Justice Birkett in the King's Bench Division.

Valentine Holmes appeared for all the defendants and said that as soon as the very grievous mistake was brought to the attention of the newspaper the editor of each immediately tendered an apology to Harvie-Watt, the plaintiff. They desired to recognise his magnanimity in the matter and to repeat the apology.

It was one of the most disgraceful libel actions I have ever known. I was very upset about the false allegations in the Press. Before I brought the action, I naturally had talks with the Prime Minister and the Law Officers of the Crown. I remember one day we sat in the gardens at No. 10 and occasionally walked up and down discussing what I should say. Donald Summerville, the Attotney-General, said I would certainly get heavy damages, for the statements were most damaging to me. David Maxwell-Fyfe, the Solicitor-General, agreed that the damages might be as much as £12,000 to £15,000. I thought they ought to be £30,000, for they were disgraceful attacks on my honour and integrity.

Churchill, who was walking up and down with us or sitting on a garden seat considering what we should do, said I ought to go for heavy damages and then I could give them to Clemmie's Aid to Russia Fund. For me the balloon burst. The Press had been full of the libel, an extraordinary libel, and I thought their attacks had been scurrilous. In cases of this kind I have no doubt some mud would stick, despite apologies. On the other hand as a Scot I could see no point in getting damages and giving them away as a gift. I accepted the apology. That was the end of the matter.

I often saw Hannen Swaffer in the Lobby of the House. He did apologise and said he could not understand how he came to use my name in connection with the speech at Petersham, which village of course was in my constituency. He said he must have dreamed about the speech and associated me with it as the M.P. It was a silly thing to say, but that was the end of this Pope of Fleet Street for me. So far as 'Cameronian' in *Reynolds News* was concerned, I never found out who he was or his name, and he hadn't the courtesy to write or even make a point of speaking to me. He hid under his pseudonym; he may have been an embittered Scotsman.

After the strain of the libel action, which worried me a lot, I was glad my wife came south from Scotland for a brief change. The Churchills were most friendly and we were invited to lunch at No. 10. The party consisted of the P.M. and Clemmie, Mary Churchill and Sir Charles and Lady Portal. He was the Chief of the Air Staff. There were also the Dean of Westminster and his wife.

It was one of the usual weekly luncheons. The P.M. was somewhat depressed. He was in his customary boiler suit. Clemmie was cheery and pleasant and vivacious but I thought a little nervous and tense. Portal I liked very much. He was quiet and efficient. Mary I liked tremendously. She exuded friendliness and I should have thought she was a great help to her father when she was on leave. She was serving in the A.T.S.

After lunch I had to see the Chief Whip. Apparently the Speaker was going to retire from the Chair, although the Prime Minister did not want that to happen yet. Cripps was apparently making himself difficult. He considered that he and the P.M. had drifted considerably apart and that he was not taken into the P.M's confidence enough. The other Minister for whom the P.M. had a coolness was P. J. Grigg. This was apparently blowing over, but the P.M. still showed some asperity in his notes to the War Secretary. It was extraordinary how often these little clashes occurred but it was understandable with so many prima donnas.

The P.M., when not abroad, spent a lot of time at the House. He had been a Member for so many years that it was a second home to him and he liked the gossip of the Smoke Room. There was to be a Debate on India shortly and when I was leaving the Smoke Room Stafford Cripps, who was going to the P.M's room, put his arm through mine and we walked together discussing the business for the following week. Talking about the Indian Debate, I asked, 'Do you think the P.M. should open it?' He said he did not think so since he was liable to put both feet in it instead of one, as he did recently on an announcement about India; also it would lead to an open split in the House and that he, Cripps, would probably have to leave the Government. I duly took all this in so that I could relay it to the P.M., for whose ears it was probably meant.

Edinburgh had been pressing Winston to go up to Scotland to receive the freedom of the capital city. The day was fixed for 12th October. The P.M's party travelled up on the Thursday night and the P.M. was going to stay the week-end at Dalmeny with Lord Rosebery and his wife. We left King's Cross at 6.45 pm. in the special train. Others in the party were Stafford Cripps, Jack Churchill, Randolph Churchill, James Stuart and John Martin.

This was just about the time when the Germans were manacling our prisoners after the Dieppe raid. They seemingly thought this might act as a deterrent. The newspapers had headlines about it and were calling out for retaliation, and the newsboys were shouting this news as we got to King's Cross. Our party were reading all about it in the saloon before we even left the station.

Suddenly Winston shouted across the saloon to me and asked what I thought about retaliation. Why me—why not Stafford Cripps or any of the others? Actually I hadn't thought very much about it, but I had to think quickly as he was scowling across at me. I expressed the view that reprisals were dangerous. All that could happen would be that they would escalate. In the present circumstances, the Germans held more prisoners than we did. Their prison camps were full of British troops after the fall of France and the disasters in the Middle East. It would be our chaps who would suffer most.

There was a stony silence when I was giving my views on this matter. Winston growled and was very angry. I quickly sat back, put up my newspaper and pretended to read. I knew he did not like to be contradicted. The others of the party were all silent. Shortly afterwards he shouted, 'Harvie,' and said, 'What you have said worries me.' He had obviously not thought of that aspect of the problem.

We sat in the saloon and talked generally until dinner-time. Later Cripps and James Stuart said I was dead right but they thought I had jumped into trouble with both feet. After a drink and when we were ushered into the dining car Winston was back to normal. We had an excellent dinner. The P.M., in spite of his slight cold, was in first-class form. We talked about what we should do with Hitler after the war. It was no good having a trial and the old 'Hang the Kaiser' stuff. We should put them all on an island—perhaps one of the Aleutian Islands—and allow them no intercourse with the outside world and only books to read and no papers. Hitler could take his favourite boyfriend.

James Stuart suggested that he might be put in a barrel, like the notorious Rector of Stiffkey. Winston by this time was like an impish boy. He played with the celluloid cases of the cigars, put them together and hit his brother Jack over the head. The two brothers were very fond of each other. Cripps talked very learnedly about China. He unbent with difficulty. He thawed a good deal and became very charming. We sat and talked for some time after dinner before going to bed.

The next day my wife met us in Edinburgh. It was a delight to have a couple of free days, to see my parents at Armadale and to be with my own family. On the Monday morning we drove back to Edinburgh. I collected James Stuart at the New Club and went down to Waverley Station where we were joined by Lord and Lady Rosebery; Tom Johnston, the Secretary of State for Scotland; Ernest Brown; the Chief Constable of Edinburgh; Mr. Winant the United States Ambassador, and the Lord Provost of Edinburgh and his wife. The Prime Minister arrived at 10 o'clock. A fellow guest at Dalmeny had been Harry Lauder, the Scottish comedian and singer, whom Winston greatly admired. He had discussed with Harry Lauder the question of striking up, with organ accompaniment, his favourite song, *Keep Right On To The End Of The Road*—a good swinging tune with the right sentiments for this great wartime occasion. He had to come on as soon as Winston got to the end of his peroration.

There was quite a large crowd at the station who gave him a warm reception. We drove along Princes Street through cheering crowds, though not as many people as I would have expected. The P.M. inspected the A.R.P. services on the esplanade at Edinburgh Castle, then he drove to the Usher Hall. It was crowded with cheering and clapping people.

The P.M's entrance on the stage was the work of an actor and artist. His head was up and he marched on, almost like Hitler. His speech was excellent and he got a great ovation. He had, as I have said, arranged with Harry Lauder that the organ would crash out and he would then sing *Keep Right On To The End Of The Road*. Winston was right, Harry Lauder was right, but the organist didn't make the best of starts. There should have been a rehearsal. However, in the end it was magnificent and the audience rose and sang with gusto.

We then drove to Waverley Station and travelled by special train to London.

Chapter 12

'The Fateful Year'

After an exciting week I had to have an interview with the Archduke Robert of Austria. He was tall, rather Germanic-looking and a little dull, like an overgrown schoolboy. He was most anxious to raise a Free Austrian Army even if it only consisted of fifty men to form a rallying point for all Austrians when we invaded the Continent. I was afraid there was not much hope of that, but he was a pertinacious man and we had many meetings during the war, I'm afraid more social than business. The Poles were also a pertinacious people. They had a large army which was growing every day. One of the most interesting Polish leaders I met was Count Lipski. He told me the story of his escape from France after being taken prisoner by the Germans. He said if ever I was in the same predicament I should always go against the tide and not with it; he thought that in that way you had a much better chance of getting away. He added that in France the poorer people were more helpful.

Field Marshal Smuts was in the United Kingdom at that time and we had an historic function in the Royal Gallery when Smuts addressed both Houses of Parliament. Lloyd George was in the Chair and the Prime Minister moved a vote of thanks. It was a most impressive gathering—one of the greatest I have ever attended. James Stuart, the Chief Whip, and I went with the Prime Minister to Palace Yard where Smuts inspected a Guard of Honour of the Palace of Westminster Home Guard. He jumped out of his car like a five-year-old. I'd never seen a man with such energy and agility inspecting the ranks. We then took him to the P.M's room. From there we had a stately procession headed by the Sergeant-at-Arms down to the Royal Gallery where Smuts received a standing ovation. He was one of the most impressive figures I met in the war.

That evening at the P.M's behest Randolph Churchill, Tom

Dugdale, the Chairman of the party, and Harold Mitchell, the Deputy Chairman, dined with me at the Carlton Grill. Randolph was an amusing bon viveur but a bit noisy. He said he didn't like the Tory party but was prepared to make use of it—a pretty poor attitude.

Later Winston thanked me for having Randolph to dinner to meet the party bosses and said Randolph must not be a rebel all the time. While I was talking to him about a Cabinet dinner the P.M. continued to read the newspapers. He scarcely looked up. It was most disconcerting to carry on a conversation like that. All one-sided. However, I got used to it in time and I knew he was listening, for on one occasion I thought he had lost all interest in what I was saying and I got up to go. I felt bloody minded. He at once said, 'No, go on. I am listening to what you have to say.'

On 10th November I went with Churchill to the Mansion House for the Lord Mayor's Banquet. In peace-time this was normally held in the evening, but in wartime it was held during the day. The P.M. and Mrs. Churchill drove in an open car. I followed with John Martin in a closed car. An hour beforehand loudspeakers had announced to the City the route the P.M. would take. He got a marvellous reception. 'Good old Winnie' was the general cry. The V sign was much in evidence and the crowds were huge. The offices had emptied. The P.M. made an inspiring speech. There was not much difference between this wartime banquet and one in peace-time, though there were not so many courses and not so much to drink.

It was a hectic day as Winston had to attend the Government Eve of Session Dinner which was the revival of an old custom. The P.M. and Smuts both made brilliant speeches. It was an historic occasion and I was very pleased to be present. The P.M. received the guests. The doors were then shut and the Chief Whip faced the door to prevent strangers from entering. The P.M. then read the 'Speech from the Throne' which the Monarch would make on the morrow in the House of Lords.

The next day we heard the Germans had walked into unoccupied France. This was a new move, but not unexpected, and which could bring the whole of France into the war willynilly. It was a curious situation. Before the House sat, as it was

'The Fateful Year'

Armistice Day I laid a wreath on the Cenotaph on behalf of the Prime Minister. It was a very foggy morning and you could scarcely see the Cenotaph from the door of the Home Office.

In the afternoon the P.M. made an excellent speech in the House. I don't know how he did it. He had made three or four major speeches in the last few days—one would have been enough for me. He was congratulated by many of his critics—Shinwell, Hore-Belisha and Clement Davies—on his remarks on the situation in France. Admiral Darlan, as Winston said, had 'dishonoured the name of Rat'. The plot was thickening. Winston had played for this. He hoped now that all France would be opposed to Germany. Mrs. Churchill, who was down at the House, went out of her way to thank me cordially for looking after Winston so well. This was most gracious of her and naturally I was very pleased. There were more knocks than compliments in the House. Winston had also been most affable.

More Government changes were in the offing. James Stuart discussed this matter with me and at the end of our talks he said the P.M. and he, James, would be prepared to recommend me for a Governorship or a place in the Government. It was not an easy decision for me to come to.

I would naturally be flattered to be made a Governor, although that would mean exile for me for five years at least from this country and what would I come back to? I would have given up all my interests—the House, the Bar, the City. Before giving a final answer I discussed it with my wife and she took the sensible view that we had a young family, although no doubt they could go with us, but I would have to give up all my jobs and would be out of work when we returned home, and what would I do for a living? It was the old story—I suffered from lack of a private income. No doubt I would get high honours and live like a monarch when away but with the children to educate we both thought it wasn't on.

The appointment was certainly imminent as Brendan Bracken asked me how I would like to be a Bombay Duck and hoped I would think about it seriously. Winston had discussed it with him. Brendan said, 'I think you would do that job well.' However, after my talks with my wife I decided to say 'No'.

I was then asked by Brendan what I would like. It was felt that I might like to get ministerial experience. In all these discussions Brendan Bracken was speaking for the Prime Minister. I replied the only thing I wanted was to continue with the Prime Minister for the duration of the war unless he himself would like a change. There it was left and I stayed with the P.M. until after the war had ended. I have often wondered about Bombay.

On that Sunday in November I read the Lessons at St. Columba's Church of Scotland, Pont Street. It was St. Andrew's Day and the Prime Minister's birthday. In the evening we had a St. Andrew's Night Dinner at the Annexe at No. 10. The reason for this celebration was that there were quite a number of Scots close to the Prime Minister at that time. James Stuart, the Chief Whip, John Martin, the Principal Private Secretary, Sir Andrew Duncan, a close friend of mine who was a senior Minister, and Leslie Rowan, another Private Secretary, were present. We also had one of the most popular of M.Ps, James Maxton, one of the Clydeside Socialists and a delightful man.

The Prime Minister had had his own birthday dinner downstairs in the same part of the Annexe but had promised me he would come up for a short time to our Mess and have a drink with us. This he did and he brought Brendan Bracken and his brother Jack Churchill with him, also General Ismay (Pug). I proposed Winston's health and gave him our birthday greetings. Winston proposed the Toast of Scotland and included Maxton as one of the greatest gentlemen in the House of Commons.

We had a merry evening which continued long after Winston departed. The 'crack' was good as were the whisky and the haggis. The only thing missing was a piper. Curiously enough, this was the beginning of a St. Andrew's Night Dinner Club which continues to meet on 30th November. I am the sole surviving member of the party that originated the club on that first night at No. 10 Annexe in 1942. As someone falls out of the club another well-known Scot is elected but we confine the number to twenty. We take it in turn to act as Chairman. Churchill is toasted as well as St. Andrew, because he was present at the first dinner.

On 7th December I went with the Prime Minister to dine with the Lord Chancellor. Others present were Jay Llewellin, A. V. Alexander, Lord Portal, Lord Woolton, Ben Smith, Lord Leathers, Oliver Lyttelton and Archie Sinclair. It was a farewell party to Jay Llewellin before leaving for America.

Winston was in great form and spoke a great deal about the Englishman's love of freedom. He didn't want to get mixed up with this bureaucracy. He wanted to live his own life. We ought to see that no political party did anything to destroy that traditional freedom, and he hoped we could work together after the war. A dinner party comprising top representatives of all the parties did a great deal of good and Winston was an admirable host with humour of a high order.

The next day Richard Stokes, a Socialist Member, was asking a question about the manacling of British prisoners, so Winston went down to the House to answer him. He hoped to make a full statement before the House rose for the Christmas Recess. He was very grumpy and bad-tempered and went straight back to No. 10. Fortunately he didn't want to see me again that day.

Later I had a change from politics when I lunched at Niblett Hall at the Inner Temple, the first time I had been there since I was mobilised. I had long talks with Boyd Merriman, the President of the Probate Division and Admiralty Division of the High Court, Mr. Justice Bucknill, and Willie Spens, the new Chief Justice of India. I much enjoyed being back in legal circles again.

I had, however, to return to the House for an important meeting of the Conservative Party Committee. Usually when I went into the Committee Rooms I was greeted with a good-natured 'Sh Sh Sh. Here comes the Gestapo.'

Leo Amery addressed the Committee on Parliamentary Reform. It was an interesting speech dealing with the principles of the Conservative Party in relation to the state of the world at the present time. He said that Parliament must be built up and its reputation enhanced in the country. He dealt with such matters as House of Lords Reform, recommending life peerages, selection of candidates, election expenses, method of election, and also suggesting that, so far as procedure in the House was concerned, there should be more Committee work upstairs and that the time of the House should not be taken up with detailed matters as much as it was. He also suggested that proceedings in Parliament should be broadcast on a separate wave-length so that people could tune in at any time they wished. He felt that in this way Parliament and its Members could more successfully get across to the country. He considered this was difficult in modern times as the Press no longer gave full reports of the parliamentary proceedings.

On one of the days I went to see Winston in the Cabinet Room he had just had all his published books done in a new binding and they were laid out on a side table. It was an impressive sight. He was delighted with their appearance. He pointed his finger along the books and said to me, 'You see, I have not been idle during the years. This might have been one man's life work, yet think what I have done in Government on top of all this writing.' He was looking as pleased as Punch.

Later he gave me some of his books suitably inscribed, but not on this occasion. He said he would like to give me a little keepsake and asked me to sit at the Cabinet table beside him. There was a pile of correspondence and other papers on the table and from this he drew out a photograph of himself. While autographing it for me he said, 'This is the fateful year'—it was 1942—'Things are at their worst but they are going to get better.' I was delighted to get this autographed photograph and it now hangs, and has done since the war, at my home in Scotland.

Before going on leave on 18th December I had rather an anxious moment in the Smoke Room. The P.M. and I were having a Bristol Cream together—I can't say I liked it very much. I suddenly saw Sir William Brass coming towards us. He had previously told me he had written to the P.M. The P.M. had duly received his letter but was unimpressed with the subject matter which had something to do with bombing targets.

I could see what was going to happen and it did. Brass asked the P.M. if he had got his letter and, knowing that he had forgotten all about it, I gave him a kick under the table to alert him.

However, the P.M. was in one of his impish moods and he said, 'What are you kicking me for?' I had to fuss round like a nanny and say, 'You know, the letter you had from Billy Brass. It was about bombing and you commented on it at the time.' I almost clucked like a hen.

The P.M., of course, saw I was in difficulties and came to my rescue by thanking Brass very much for bringing the question to his notice, but he hadn't the least idea what it was all about. Brass, of course, was suspicious but between the P.M. and myself we assured him that the matter he had raised would certainly receive his close attention. He was in a funny mood.

When a moment later I saw two new Members come into the Smoke Room I thought it would be a good idea to introduce them so I said to the P.M. that these were two new Members and asked if he would like to meet them. In a lower voice I told him they were both Independents. He asked, 'What's that you are saying? Stop whispering.' So I had to repeat the names, spoiling the effect of the introductions. He could be like a small mischievous boy at times, for on occasions like those he would pull my leg afterwards.

We then walked back to his room. I had told him my wife was expecting an addition to the family. He wished me a Happy Christmas and a boy or a girl, whichever I had ordered.

The new member of my family, a boy, arrived on Christmas Eve 1942. Winston and Clemmie sent us a very nice telegram of congratulations. We called him Euan, after Euan Wallace whose Parliamentary Private Secretary I had been.

I was glad to be at home for my father was very ill. When I got back from Edinburgh on Christmas Day I went in to see him. He looked up and I told him my wife had had another boy and we were going to call him Euan. He smiled and said, 'That's good.' Those were his last words. He remained in a coma till he died in the first hour of New Year's Day 1943.

When I returned to London after the funeral the Prime Minister asked to see me. He expressed his deepest sympathy on the death of my father and asked news about Bettie and the two children. I was very much touched by his interest in my private affairs. He then told me about his projected trip to North Africa to meet the President. He also talked about some recent Government appointments and Tory politics in general.

He could not have been more friendly and patted me on the shoulder when I left the Cabinet Room.

It was not all hard work in Downing Street. There was also a lot of fun because Winston had a great sense of humour. Early in January 1943 I received a letter from the Duke of Devonshire, who was then at the Colonial Office. 'My dear Harvie-Watt, I have been asked by the Council of the Zoo, of which I am a member, to approach you about the following rather trivial matter. One of the Fellows has on several occasions suggested to the Council that it would be a graceful act if the Zoo were to present the Prime Minister with a lion. The idea did not particularly commend itself to the Council and we hoped that the matter would be allowed to drop. Yesterday, however, we had a further letter from this Fellow in which he made it clear that he did not intend to allow the matter to drop and that he would raise it at the monthly meeting of Fellows, which is open to the Press, unless we took some action. This might lead to some undesirable publicity, so I have been asked to find out whether the gift of a lion would in fact be acceptable to the Prime Minister. If he accepted it he will presumably deposit it at the Zoo, for I scarcely imagine he wants a lion, either in Downing Street or at Chequers, and no deplacement of the lion would take place, but it would be his lion and would be officially described as such and as having been deposited by him with the Society. It would undoubtedly become an animal greatly loved and revered by the populace.

'We have got a suitable lion, handsome and docile, and should be very glad to give it to the Prime Minister if he would like to be the owner of a lion.

'If on the other hand the idea does not commend itself to him we would convey the information to the Fellow concerned who would then, I suppose, be satisfied.

'I am sorry to worry you with so unimportant a matter but we have had a lot of trouble in the Zoo Council lately and do not want either to be pilloried for churlishly withholding the lion or on the other hand to embarrass the Prime Minister with an unwanted gift. Yours ever, Eddy Devonshire.

'P.S. The Zoo of course pays for the keep of any animal deposited with it, so it would not be a present wot eats.'

In due course I handed Eddie Devonshire's letter to the P.M. I was sure he would be amused and tell me to send a suitable reply. However, he decided to acknowledge the letter himself.

'My dear Eddie, I shall have much pleasure in becoming the possessor of the lion on the condition that I do not have to feed it or take care of it and that the Zoo makes sure that it doesn't get loose.

'You are quite right in your assumption that I do not want the lion at the moment, either at Downing Street or at Chequers, owing to the Ministerial calm which prevails there. But the Zoo is not far away and situations may arise in which I shall have great need of it.

'I hope to come to see the lion sometime when the weather is better, also my black swans.

'I consider you personally bound to receive the lion at Chatsworth should all else fail. Yours ever, Winston.'

Note from the Prime Minister to Harvie-Watt.

'As my Parliamentary Private Secretary you are clearly the recipient of the lion. I place it wholeheartedly in your care and I hope will see, unless anything goes wrong, that full thanks are returned to the Duke of Devonshire and to the Zoo for their kindness. I do not mind what you do with the lion so long as I am not held responsible in any way for his fortunes or his conduct, W.S.C.'

Dr. Rettinger came to see me. He had just returned from America with General Sikorski. Apparently, according to him, British propaganda in the USA was very bad and American opinion was very much against us. Lord Halifax, according to Rettinger, was not a success. This information I naturally passed on to the appropriate authority as I always did. I seemed to have become a kind of liaison officer between emigré governments and our Ministers. They, of course, had lots of sources of information but I might just pass on occasionally something that was useful.

Early in 1943 I was asked to lunch at the Mansion House by the Lord Mayor to meet General de Gaulle, who had just arrived back from Africa and from his discussions with General Giraud. I had quite a long talk with him, for I had met him before on several occasions. He was so tall that I felt like a small boy. He wore only one medal and that was the Cross of Lorraine. Winston, much later, with a lot of experience of de Gaulle, said that the worst cross he had to bear was the Cross of Lorraine. I sat between André Philip and the ex-Secretary of State Georges Mandel. It was really a most interesting lunch. I must say that, although de Gaulle was a difficult man to like, I had the greatest admiration for him as a soldier and a French statesman.

On 3rd February Lord Cherwell and I lunched with the Polish Ambassador at the Embassy. The guests on this occasion were Sir William and Lady Jowitt, Lord and Lady Dawson of Penn, also the Norwegian Ambassador and his wife.

I always found these contacts fascinating and helpful and I suppose they did some good for the war effort. They were certainly a great help to me when I had to have talks with the emigrés on points that might interest the Prime Minister. I know I found my talks with Dr. Rettinger of Poland especially valuable.

One of the most amazing incidents, and the funniest, in my dealings with the Poles was when I was asked one day to meet a Pole who had escaped from Poland to England. I had to try find out from him what conditions were like and the feelings of his countrymen under domination. I at once wondered, of course, how he was going to communicate with me. I couldn't speak Polish and I didn't suppose he spoke much English. However, this difficulty was swept aside as there would be an interpreter in attendance.

In due course there was a meeting in my room at No. 10. The introductions were made and I asked who was the interpreter. The Poles looked a little surprised and said the Polish visitor could speak good English. I was indeed relieved and began my cross-examination. When the Pole answered my first question I thought there was something odd about his voice and accent. I realised he was speaking English all right but with a broad Glasgow accent. Naturally I was intrigued and asked him who had taught him English and where he had learned it. Had he been out of Poland? The answer was no, but that he had been taught English by a soldier from the 51st Highland Division who had been captured at St. Valery.

He and two other soldiers of the division had escaped by getting into civilian clothes. When questioned they replied in Gaelic. In that way they had managed to escape to the East. This particular Scot quickly learned Polish and was used to teach the Poles English. Poor chaps. They must have found it difficult to communicate.

I told the P.M. about this experience. He was most interested and said, 'I hope you won't break into Gaelic.' He wondered how far the Russians would fall back as there were some signs of a crack in the German Army. This was encouraging news. The Russian retreat seemed to have been endless.

In February 1943 the Beveridge Report was debated in the House. There was a stormy scene after John Anderson had spoken for the Government. There seemed some prospects of a political crisis and in the afternoon there was another rumpus in the House following a speech by Kingsley Wood.

I had to go over to No. 10 to report to the P.M., who was ill in bed. He did not look very well but was anxious to know how the Debate was going and what were the likely results. He said that the Government had gone farther with Beveridge than he would have gone himself. He said Beveridge was an awful windbag and a dreamer. The Beveridge Report Debate continued to rouse the House and on one of the days allotted there was a big Socialist revolt against the Government's Beveridge proposals. Herbert Morrison made a brilliant speech.

Again, I had to report back to the P.M. He was still in bed and, if anything, worse. He kept on saying the room was cold, although I was nearly boiling. He had a fresh hot water bottle put in his bed and a great pad of Thermogene on his chest. He lay back with his eyes shut most of the time I was with him. I was talking too long. The P.M. undoubtedly had a temperature so I said I would go.

He just raised his arm. The temperature persisted and he was in bed and absent from the House for over a week. Naturally when he wanted me, and was able to listen to me, I went over for brief moments to assure him that all was well.

One of my problems was to try to avoid engagements,

especially meals, outside political circles. This was difficult to do, for I was constantly being asked by Chairmen of companies to lunch with them. I didn't know at that time that this was a regular habit of big City institutions and companies, but when later I myself was Chairman of Consolidated Gold Fields I found I had to do the same kind of thing—in other words to entertain well-known people in all walks of life so that we might keep abreast of the news outside our own company affairs.

One of the most interesting lunches I attended was with the Chairman of the Midland Bank. He was Reginald McKenna who had once been the Chancellor of the Exchequer. He was a remarkable man of eighty in 1943, spry and alert in figure and mind. He talked about personalities in politics since 1905. Little did I think then that in 1956 I would be invited to join the Board of the Midland, when Lord Harlech was Chairman. One of the directors I met in 1943 was Stanley Christopherson who subsequently became Chairman of the Midland Bank. He was also a director of Consolidated Gold Fields, and thereby hangs a tale which I will unfold at a later stage of these memoirs.

On 3rd March Mr. Speaker Fitzroy died. There was an impressive ceremony in the House. The Mace was placed under the table, the Chair was vacated and the Clerk of the House pointed to Members who wished to speak. He could not call Members by name according to the rules of the House. The Conservative Party was very much in favour of appointing Douglas Clifton-Brown, who had been in the House many years—always a back-bencher and one who did not often intervene in Debates. He had been Chairman of the House when in Committee and was experienced in the rules of Parliament.

The Prime Minister was naturally most interested in who was to be appointed and in any likely candidates that might be in the running. He sent for me so that he could be put in the picture as to what was happening. Needless to say he had his own views on this matter. He was furious with the Party for suggesting Clifton-Brown. Winston wanted Gil Lloyd-George. Despite the P.M. being still off-colour after his recent illness, he entered with vigorous advocacy into the battle on behalf of Lloyd-George. Of course, Lloyd-George's father and Winston had been close friends in Winston's Liberal days. He considered that Gil Lloyd-George would make a first-class Speaker, and I must say I agreed with him. He had the height, the dignity and the humour to add distinction to the Chair. Winston said the appointment had nothing to do with the party. It was for the House. Yes, but it was traditional for the majority party to make the appointment. I would have to put pressure on *The Times*, he said, but that was easier said than done and Members of the House would have been furious at any interference from the Press. I did not interfere with *The Times* or any other papers.

The 1922 Conservative Committee, or Conservative Party Committee as it was now called, met the next day to discuss the matter. The Chief Whip attended. Feeling was running very much in favour of Douglas Clifton-Brown. The P.M. would not be at all pleased at this selection. He was at Chequers convalescing and in consequence I had to represent the Prime Minister and Mrs. Churchill at the late Speaker's funeral service at St. Margaret's Westminster. Because of that I sat beside Attlee and the other Members of the War Cabinet. It was a most impressive ceremony. I think we must be the master of pageantry.

That evening my wife, who had just arrived for a brief visit to London, and I had dinner with Gil and Edna Lloyd-George at Manettas. This was sheer coincidence as we had arranged the party weeks ago, before Mr. Speaker Fitzroy died. We were a somewhat subdued party.

The new Speaker, Clifton-Brown, was elected the next day on the Motion of George Lambert (Liberal), seconded by Joe Tinker (Socialist). In submitting himself to the House Clifton-Brown made a good and dignified speech which much impressed most Members. It was an interesting ceremony and well done. There was no doubt that the new Speaker started with the goodwill of the whole House.

The next day, prior to the ordinary business, tributes were paid to the late Speaker by the Leader of the House and the party Leaders. Jimmy Maxton was so touched in the course of his speech that several times he failed to find words to express himself and was obviously much upset. The tributes were all of a generous and graceful character.

The Prime Minister was back in action but I didn't think he was very fit and was certainly not in good form.

The next day my wife and I attended a tea party at Buckingham Palace. It was a most interesting contrast to the pre-war receptions. We had quite a long talk with the King and Queen and the two Princesses, Elizabeth and Margaret.

I didn't have the opportunity or the time to go to my constituency very often but kept in close touch with my excellent Chairman, Colonel Bromhead, who had been one of the pioneers of Gaumont British. He and his wife lived in what used to be the Dower House to Ham House near Ham Common. It was a beautiful house. Both he and his wife were a tower of strength to me all during the war. There were, of course, no political functions but I always went down when I could to inspect Home Guard parades and public occasions of a non-party kind. My wife, when she came to London, usually fulfilled engagements in Richmond, Barnes, Sheen and Petersham. Colonel Bromhead often had dinner or lunch with me at the House or at the club. I was able to keep in touch with my constituency in that way.

An amusing incident occurred in the House at that time. During the Division on the Motion to move the new writ for a by-election in Daventry, the late Speaker's seat, the P.M. went past the Teller with his head down and his shoulders bent—a customary habit of his when striding through the Lobbies of the House. The Teller was new. He caught Winston by the shoulder and asked, 'What is your name?' The P.M. was justifiably annoyed. He gave a growl like an angry dog. The Teller looked terrified. Winston walked on. The Tellers who were used to the job usually knew all the Members by name and placed a tick against the Member's name automatically, but it was the usual custom for the Member to say, as he went through, Smith, Jones or Brown, as the Teller ticked his name off the list on large sheets before him.

On that day, as we came out of the Division Lobby, we ran into David Kirkwood, a member of the I.L.P. He was very left in his younger days but had now mellowed. Winston asked him to come to the Smoke Room and have a glass of Bristol Milk. Kirkwood was a rabid teetotaller. He said to Winston, 'I didn't know you could get a glass of milk in the Smoke Room. I thought you could only get alcohol.' When the drinks arrived and he saw it was sherry a look of consternation spread over his face and he refused to take it. I doubt if Winston had ever come face to face with a teetotaller before.

From time to time the Prime Minister had meetings for Ministers who were not in the Cabinet, and he did not see them very often. This was an excellent idea, for some of them felt right out of the picture and in the cold. These meetings were held in the Cabinet Room. Those who attended were Lord Portal, Lord Leathers, Lord Woolton, Lord Simon, Shakes Morrison, Hugh Dalton, Lloyd-George, Andrew Duncan, Lord Woolmer, Duff Cooper and Ernest Brown. He would give a résumé of what was happening on the different war fronts and the policies on the major issues.

This kept the Ministers outside the Inner Cabinet in touch with events. There were always a few intriguers and schemers who wanted either to criticise their colleagues in other Ministries or to suck up, in the hope of further promotion. I attended these meetings but I was really a comparative outsider. I found all this juggling for position rather amusing, for it had not the slightest effect on Winston.

CHAPTER 13

Scotland and Downing Street

I went up to Scotland to my home in Linlithgowshire to see the family for a brief week-end. The main purpose of my visit to Scotland, however, was to see the big football match at Hampden Park, with seats in the Royal Box issued by the Scottish F.A. We lunched at the Grosvenor Hotel. I sat at the top table with Lord McGowan, Lord Inverclyde, Lord Airlie, Sir Andrew Duncan and Jan Masaryk of Czechoslovakia, Ellen Wilkinson, a Socialist Minister, and Lord Rosebery. Ellen Wilkinson was a fire-brand in her youth and led the Jarrow marchers on their protest march on London in the early thirties when Britain's unemployment was at its worst. She, alas, committed suicide some years later. I liked her very much and we often had talks. Her heart was in the right place and I was sorry when she took her own life.

There was a Diamond Jubilee Parade of the Boys' Brigade. General Thorne, G.O.C. Scottish Command, took the salute. The football match was only incidental to the parade but the ground was packed. Lord Rosebery drove me back to Armadale as it was on his way to Dalmeny, his own home.

I got back to London and to No. 10 on the Monday morning. Previously a General McCulloch, Colonel-in-Chief of the Highland Light Infantry, had been in touch with me. Apparently a piper of the regiment had written a pipe tune called *Salute to Mr. Churchill* and the regiment was very anxious to present it to the P.M. The P.M. was intrigued. He always had a soft spot for the Scots, for he had served in the Royal Scots Fusiliers in World War I, and asked me to make arrangements for an audition.

I fixed up a suitable date and time. General McCulloch arrived with a pipe major from the Scots Guards. Admiral Kaufman of the US Navy, Admiral Sir Dudley Pound and

Scotland and Downing Street

Admiral Wake-Walker were with the P.M. in the Cabinet Room.

In due course the pipes struck up and the general and I sat in the Cabinet Room while the pipe major marched round the table—probably the first time that the pipes had ever been played in that famous room. I am a piper myself so I was particularly pleased at this interlude. The P.M. thanked the pipe major and said he liked the tune and was very happy to accept it. He then said that one of his favourite tunes was *Cock o' the North*. He asked the pipe major to play it, which he did, marching round the Cabinet table and then out to the Private Office where the Private Secretaries were all agog.

The next interesting experience I had was a few weeks later when I had to attend a dinner at Holyrood Palace in Edinburgh—a memorable evening. I was received by Lady Mary Boscawen, a daughter of the Duke of Montrose, a Lady Boyle and Miss Stirling of Glorat, the Maids of Honour to the Lord High Commissioner of the General Assembly of the Church of Scotland, the Duke of Montrose. We were lined up to meet the Duke and Duchess of Montrose, the ladies to curtsey and the men to bow. I sat beside Mary Boscawen—a most friendly and entertaining character. The toasts were the King and the Church of Scotland which, of course, was well represented and very much in the majority. The pipers, in their feather bonnets, then marched round the table of the banqueting hall the walls of which were lined with portraits of the monarchs of Scotland. It was a most impressive occasion.

There were very few young people present but we managed to get together and had a most cheerful time. We finished up dancing a reel on the lawns of Holyrood in the bright moonlight with the Duke of Montrose, the Lord High Commissioner, wearing a night cap and looking out of a window cheering us on. I also took a turn on the pipes for the dancing.

On my return to London Anthony Eden gave a dinner to about a dozen Members. He was not at all impressive and I held this view from 1931 when I first met him all through his time in Parliament until after Suez. He ought to have been a diplomat and would have been an excellent Ambassador to the United States. He always struck me as being weak and surrounded by 'yes men' in the House. He had, of course, plenty of charm but I don't think he had ever had any real contact with working people. He was like a gilded bird in a gilded cage, with a very petty temper—like a spoilt schoolboy. At this time he was a rising, if not a risen, star which he had always been since he entered Parliament. I never thought he was of the calibre of which Prime Ministers are made.

Another Member I saw a lot of at that time was Leslie Hore-Belisha, who had been Secretary of State for War at the outbreak of hostilities and fell from office when Chamberlain resigned from the Premiership. He was really a most interesting man and tremendously ambitious. He was a little late for dinner as he had made a speech in the House that day so I had to go up to his exotic black bathroom and watch him do his press-ups. He was in his underpants and looked a very tubby figure who could use press-ups.

He intended to make more speeches in the House and was gradually going to the Right. He thought he might fall into the Leadership of the Tory Party—a second Disraeli. His speech that day was excellent, on civil aviation. Meanwhile he was getting on with his dressing and had put on his green velvet dinner suit. We had an excellent dinner—champagne, punch and sherry. He did himself extremely well. We talked until 1 am. Fortunately I lived in the next street, Catherine Place, so I had not far to walk.

The next day I was a bit weary but I had to go down to my constituency to attend a Wings for Victory Week parade. I motored down with Lord Selborne, the principal guest; naturally I also had to speak and was then presented with a model Lancaster bomber to give to my eldest son James. I was delighted to be in my constituency again.

One day when I was with the P.M. at the House, after he had made an excellent speech, we went to the Smoke Room as was our regular custom. He had had a brandy before going down to the House and had a Bristol Milk with me in the Smoke Room. When I asked him if he would have another he said he could not risk it as he was lunching at the Palace and he was always dined and wined well when he went there. It would be a disgrace for him to finish up under the Royal table.

That same day I met Maisky, the Russian Ambassador, for the first time, although I had seen him many times at the House. He was a small, gesticulating man with a dark complexion, a little beard and shifty eyes—altogether a foxy-looking man and most unattractive. He said, in the course of our talk, that there was no hope for Poland having her eastern territory restored to her and that the Baltic States were Russian. He and his statements, said with relish, made me slightly sick and I thought God help Poland and any other country in the hands of the Russian Bear.

The next day, still feeling depression after my talk with Maisky, I had a meeting with King Peter of Yugoslavia, A. V. Alexander, the Lord Chancellor, and George Rendell, the British Ambassador to Yugoslavia—rather a precious man. King Peter was obviously a handful to look after. He was only nineteen but he drank and smoked cigars like Churchill. He was not a worker, but quite a pleasant person, although not helped by quarrels in the Yugoslavian Government and with little chance of getting back to his own country after the war.

I spent a week-end in June in my constituency. I dined with Colonel Bromhead at the Castle Hotel, Richmond. We then went to the Bull at East Sheen for a Conservative dance. I got an excellent reception and my speech was loudly cheered. I felt most encouraged. It was fortunate that my constituency was so close to London, otherwise it would have been impossible for me to see it at all.

I stayed the night with Colonel Bromhead and next day I lunched with the Mayor of Richmond and Air Chief Marshal Sir E. Ludlow Hewitt and Lady Hewitt. We then took the salute as the parade marched past. The speeches were made on Richmond Green. There were huge crowds of people. I had to make a speech to the gathering. I must say I got a wonderful reception. The parade consisted of the Home Guard, Air Cadets, Sea Cadets and Army Cadets. It was a goodly sight.

I had to see the P.M. for a short time in the morning. He was in a filthy temper, having had a bad night. No wonder, he was usually late in getting to bed, for he sat up most nights and often didn't get up in the morning until 10 o'clock or later. It depended on whether or not he had to go down to the House for Questions or to make a speech. In the hot summer days he occasionally had a walk in the No. 10 garden and quite often he and Clemmie sat out and enjoyed the sunshine. I remember, on one occasion, seeing him preparing a speech in the garden. It was for the Guildhall. On the whole he preferred to work in the Cabinet Room.

Charles Wilson, Winston's doctor, received a peerage at this time and Reggie Purbrick gave a dinner in his honour. The P.M. proposed the health of Moran, Charles Wilson's new title. Moran replied. Both made very funny speeches as was to be expected on such an occasion from doctor to patient and patient to doctor. Winant, the American Ambassador, also spoke, but his speech was lamentable. There were long gaps and silences.

I'm bound to say I never liked Charles Wilson. There was something sly about him, and immediately after the war he was a bit quick off the mark with his biography of the P.M. Others, of course, quickly followed suit. I myself received two considerable offers for my memoirs of my time with Winston. I had no hesitation in turning them down. Occasionally I have had other overtures made to me but I always felt that this was something for my old age, an opportunity to reflect on my past and not to make a quick buck for merely doing my duty.

On the occasion of the P.M's getting the freedom of the City of London I drove down to the Guildhall with him. The P.M. was in top hat and morning coat. He looked extremely well and distinguished. He started off in an open car, accompanied by Clemmie and Mary, and in a second car were Sarah, John Martin and me. This was naturally a closed car.

One of the Churchills I had not seen often was Sarah. She was an officer in the W.A.A.F.—recently commissioned. I thought she was most attractive and a charming and very friendly person. I liked her enormously. She was a delightful girl to talk to, with no side at all.

After a short distance the Churchills transferred to a closed car as it was too cold and windy. The streets were lined with cheering people. At Temple Bar the P.M., Mrs. Churchill, Mary and Sarah got into an open carriage and pair and then proceeded into the City. They got a tumultuous welcome. At the Guildhall the P.M. inspected a Guard of Honour of the Home Guard. I had to be announced at the Guildhall and walk up the steps to be received by the Lord Mayor. I felt very important.

The P.M. got a terrific reception and made an excellent speech, one of the best that he had yet made out of the House of Commons. We then went in procession to the Mansion House for lunch. We were received in a private room for drinks. The others with us were the Duke and Duchess of Marlborough and Duncan and Diana Sandys.

Normally when Winston was going down to the House I went across to No. 10 to collect him and we went together. One morning when I got to No. 10 I heard a noise like thunder and there was the P.M. yelling and shouting for his bath. His valet, Sawyer, was a small, nervous man who ran like a frightened rabbit to obey his master's commands. I met Sawyer often, of course, when I was at No. 10. He was an excellent valet and very fond of Winston.

I was at No. 10 when the news of the air disaster at Gibraltar came through. General Sikorski and his staff, including Victor Cazalet and a Brigadier Whitely, both M.Ps, were on the plane. Apparently the crash took place just after take-off and the plane dived into the sea. There seemed no doubt at the time that the accident was due to sabotage. The P.M. made a short statement in the Commons. Sikorski's death was a sad loss to the Allied cause. He was a leader of men and very pro-British. I had to represent the Prime Minister at the memorial service to Cazalet and Whitely at St. Margaret's Westminster. The congregation was large and included Queen Marie of Rumania. I did not know Whitely very well as he was a comparatively new Member, but I knew Victor Cazalet very well indeed. His sister Thelma Cazalet was also a distinguished Member of the House of Commons.

Shortly after this the Conservative Party had a lunch at the Savoy for the Prime Minister; as we were going there in his car he was reading an early edition of the *Star*. Before he got to the Savoy he said, 'Here,' handing me the *Star*. 'Have a look at that—a whole column about you. It gives you a good write-up.' I read it afterwards. Apparently it was written because I had now been with Winston two years. 'It is now 1943,' the article read; 'it has been a hard job but Members of all parties would readily agree that he has done it well. The first essential for the job is tact and diplomacy and Mr. Harvie-Watt has these qualities, with the result that he has been able to smooth over difficulties and negotiate delicate situations.' There was a great deal more but that was, and is, enough.

The Prime Minister made an excellent speech lasting about forty-five minutes, entirely off the cuff. He had some excellent phrases. Speaking of a strong France after the war, he said it was one of our major interests to have a strong buffer state between the white snows of Russia and the white cliffs of Dover.

There then followed a garden party at No. 10 for all the Ministers and their wives. My wife and I were the first arrivals and we stayed until the end. It was my duty, assisted by my wife, to keep the pot boiling, or rather the guests revolving. Winston and Clemmie were good at that kind of thing, especially Clemmie. With Winston it depended on what mood he was in. He could be like a growling bear but, on the other hand, he could be the most charming of hosts. This party was a great success. There had been very few of those functions which was rather a pity, since there was little chance in the ordinary course of events for many Ministers, especially the junior ones, and their wives even to meet the Prime Minister.

The House adjourned on 5th August for the Summer Recess. P. J. Grigg, the Secretary of State for War, Tom Dugdale, Chairman of the Conservative Party, Shakes Morrison, Malcolm McCorquodale and I had an hilarious end-of-term lunch together at the House. I also had a talk with Lord Kemsley and his son Lionel Berry, who had just taken his seat in the House as the new Member for Buckingham. He seemed really a nice chap, despite Winston's criticisms of a return to Munich. Winston had difficulty in forgetting the Men of Munich, although most of his Government were Members who voted with Chamberlain at that time.

Kemsley invited me to lunch with him in his private dining

room at his newspaper office. Off the dining room there were many photos of party leaders and Ministers. I had my photograph taken to hang on the wall of this distinguished 'Gallery of Celebrities' as it was called. I never went back so I never saw my photo on the wall with the others.

The Prime Minister had been in America and Canada during most of the 1943 Summer Recess and I went to Euston on his return. The usual Ministers and their relations were present on the platform to greet him. While waiting for the train to arrive I had talks with John Anderson, Attlee, Bevin, Duncan Sandys, Mary and Sarah. The usual crowd of journalists and photographers were also present. When the train steamed in there were great lights put on the engine. It was always most impressive.

Diana, Sarah and Mr. Attlee went into the coach to greet the P.M. When he appeared he was smoking his usual cigar and gave the V sign. He was followed by Clemmie and Mary. He greeted us all and asked me, 'How are you my dear Harvie?' Afterwards photographs were taken, then we got into the cars and went back to No. 10 where we all chatted for quite a while before dispersing.

In the morning I had to see Winston about Lord Louis Mountbatten. Apparently he had asked Frank Owen, a rabid left wing journalist, to be his Public Relations Officer. P. J. Grigg had asked me to speak to the P.M. about this. Why couldn't he do it himself? After all, he was a Cabinet Minister. So many Ministers, and top ones at that, seemed very much afraid that they would blot their copy books. Winston was furious and nearly spat out his cigar in his rage. He was in bed. He was usually pleased with Mountbatten and always had a soft spot for him. As I left he said, 'It might not be a bad idea to get rid of Mountbatten.'

It was with sadness that we heard the news of the sudden death of Kingsley Wood, who had played a considerable part in the House of Commons, holding many Cabinet posts including that of Chancellor of the Exchequer. The Prime Minister was very upset. Kingsley was a likeable man, although he also bore the stigma of a Man of Munich, but then so did the vast majority of Conservatives and some of other parties.

The Prime Minister paid a tribute to Kingsley Wood. He did it extremely well. I was with him most of the morning. He talked about the changes resulting from Kingsley's death. He said Oliver Stanley was no good, and Leo Amery was impossible, although he was not a Man of Munich. It looked, he said, as if it must be either Oliver Lyttelton or John Anderson. He had no time for the Men of Munich. I was getting tired of that crack, for most of Churchill's Government and enthusiastic supporters were Men of Munich. I felt that one by one we would be dropped overboard. However, instead of the sack he offered me a drink—we were in the Smoke Room at the House.

I asked him if he would like a Drambuie but he said he had never heard of it and when I said it had a whisky base he replied that he preferred his whisky neat so that you could really get the taste of that most heartening drink. So we had our whiskies. Winston then asked me to represent him at the memorial service to Kingsley Wood. For that kind of duty I used the office top hat and a dark coat. Some of us fitted them better than others but, at the worst, you could always carry the top hat if you had a big head or a very small head. Otherwise you looked not like a mourner but a comedian or conjurer.

That evening was quite a contrast. I had to dine at the Hotel Russell with Lord Alness, one of the senior Scottish Judges, and the top twenty representatives of the Scottish, English and Welsh Football Associations. I had to make a speech. Afterwards I was presented by the Scottish contingent with one of the original lithographs of Burns's portrait to whom, according to the Scots present, I had a very strong resemblance. It must have been a very good dinner. They sang *For he's a Jolly Good Fellow*. Altogether a maudlin, or a Mauchline, evening as Burns might have said.

Unfortunately I had a very busy morning after the party and I knew all the time that I had had an excellent dinner the night before. I was paying for it now. I bucked up about lunchtime and drink-time. I was lunching with Jack Churchill and Pamela, Randolph's wife. She was a most attractive girl and I enjoyed this social ocasion very much.

I also met Mrs. Euan Wallace and had a long reminiscent

talk with her because my first step in politics was as her late husband's P.P.S. when he was at the Board of Trade. She was a remarkable woman, able and charming in spite of her great loss in the war of five out of six sons. She subsequently married Herbert Agar and our paths diverged completely.

I then had to have a long talk with the Chief Whip, James Stuart, about some proposed Government changes, especially regarding Lord Beaverbrook. Winston was anxious to have him back in the Government where he might be less of a nuisance with his endless intrigues.

This appointment was severely criticised. Also, the appointments of Dick Law and Jim Thomas gave the impression that the glamour boys were the only ones going to be recognised by the Prime Minister. The P.M. sent for me to tell him what the reactions to the appointments had been. Naturally they were mixed. Beaverbrook was not popular, although most people admired his driving energy; but it was the 'glamour boys', or rather the Anthony Eden circle, who attracted criticism. It was considered that they had no experience to offer the Government because most of them had never needed to earn a penny. They all seemed to be men of wealth.

Erskine-Hill wanted an interview with the P.M. He always wanted interviews on major issues. The P.M. agreed most reluctantly because he couldn't stand Erskine-Hill but he said he agreed since I had asked for interviews for him before and he would give in for my sake. Not very gracious. Erskine-Hill turned up but he was twelve minutes late. Winston was fuming and Erskine-Hill was sweating.

The interview started off very stickily—not a word, only glares from the Prime Minister. Poor Alex had to battle his way alone. I'm bound to say he did quite well considering, although there was no need for him to have seen the P.M. at all. He was merely being important.

He mentioned the Beaverbrook appointment. Winston at once said, 'I though you were a friend of his.' This stumped Alex for he always tried to keep on the right side of Beaverbrook, despite criticism, when Beaverbrook was in office or with the prospect of a new job in the offing. 'Yes,' he said, 'I am friendly to Beaverbrook,' but he was very sheepish when making this statement. He continued, 'Don't think I object to his appointment but I felt it was my duty to inform you of the reactions in the Party.' James Stuart and I were doing this contantly, that was part of our jobs, so the P.M. was already well in the picture.

The P.M. said if Max Beaverbrook's appointment had been voted on at the Cabinet he would not have been picked, but that was not how we did things in this country. I subsequently dined with Alex at the Dorchester and tried to smooth his ruffled feathers. His visit to No. 10 was a useless exercise. However, he could always go back to the Party Committee and tell them that he had forwarded their representations to the Prime Minister.

In the autumn of 1943 we were getting another series of air raids over London, the first we had had for some months. We had them on six successive nights and they were all noisy ones with masses of AA fire and the thump and explosion of bombs. When there was a long spell without bombing you began to forget what they were like, but once they started again you were a bit jumpy to begin with. On the first raid of this series I was alone at Catherine Place, where I lived for most of the year. I was stirred from a deep sleep by noises like a thunderstorm and then I soon realised what it was. I got up and went downstairs to see that everything was all right, or as right as I could make them. Then I looked out of the front door. It was dark but the long fingers of the searchlights were probing the skies and the AA fire was very noisy. Suddenly I thought there was a thunderstorm with hail and there was a rattling all down the street. I quickly realised it was not hail but shrapnel and I got inside and away from the front to the centre of the house, like a scalded cat.

Fortunately a period of thick fog spread over the south of England and London and we had another respite from the bombing. One of those nights I had been dining with David Margesson, who had been Chief Whip when I was in the Whips' Office. He was just suited to that job and had been a great success. The fog was so dense that we lost our way at Hyde Park Corner on our way home. It was so foggy we walked into a one-way street and took some time to extricate ourselves. David, who had just been elevated to the House of Lords, was missing the Commons very much. He loved being Chief Whip and was a real dictator, but very fair at all times.

The fog continued the next day when I had to meet Lord Linlithgow, on behalf of the Prime Minister, at Victoria Station. He was returning from his stint in India. He looked very well, as did his family. It must have been quite a come-down after living so long in the limelight as Viceroy of India. His home, Hopetoun House, is in my native County of Linlithgow. On this occasion he asked me to come and see him any time I was at home, which I promised to do. In fact it was not very long before I did see him; however, it was not at Hopetoun House but in the Dower House. The front door was open but I rang the bell, I got no reply and I had to ring it several times before I saw a door open at the far end of the narrow hall and a tall figure coming along to the door. At first I didn't recognise Linlithgow. He was without a jacket and was wearing a green baize apron and had a brush in his hand. I will not bore my readers with the essentially local chat we had but, for me, the astonishing thing was the contrast between a Viceroy of India with glittering pageantry surrounding him, and the same man having to do his own housework in the small Dower House.

My stay in Scotland was brief and I was soon back in my now very familiar surroundings at No. 10. On the day I got back I had to take the P.M. to dinner at the Savoy Hotel. A police officer had to walk in front of the car all the way with a torch. The fog had returned again. As a result, the P.M. got quite tetchy and he said I was killing him and then he slapped me on the back and said, 'And, by God, Harvie, you will bloody well walk in my funeral procession.' He was in rather a hilarious mood and went down very well with the new Members who were to meet him that evening.

For some time I had been sitting for my portrait. The artist was Maurice Codner—a great character and first-class painter, who became the President of the Royal Society of Portrait Painters. My portrait was hung in their gallery and I went to the private view. He subsequently painted my wife. When my painting was sent to my home in Scotland and unpacked, it was leant against the dining room table. My old dog came in, stopped and stared and then walked over and kissed my hand, wagging its tail. My mother was very touched and so was I when she told me about the incident.

Not long afterwards I dined at No. 10 at a dinner in honour of the Marquess of Linlithgow—the third time I had met him since he returned from India. The War Cabinet and the Chiefs of Staff were present. Ernest Bevin was also there and twice he brought out his false teeth, the lower plate with his tongue, fingered it and put it back in again. I was fascinated.

During the evening the Prime Minister told us a very good story about a British agent who had to be dropped in Tunis; at the spot where he was to land he would find a car waiting for him. He was to wear three parachutes in case of accident. When he dropped from the plane he had to pull the first cord and if nothing happened he had to pull the second cord, and if still nothing happened he had to pull the third cord. He did all this and when he was hurtling to the ground he said to himself, 'I bet they have forgotten the bloody car.' This was typical of the P.M's sense of humour.

In the next breath the P.M. gave me a raspberry for telling him that Aneurin Bevan had taken the place of Shinwell on the Socialist Executive. I had got the information from Hector McNeil, a Labour P.P.S., but apparently it was wrong and I had made a big boob, for the P.M. had mentioned it at the Cabinet and the Socialist Ministers were indignant at the suggestion and told him his informant was mistaken.

After that little contretemps my wife and I lunched with the P.M. and Mrs. Churchill at No. 10. The other people present were J. L. Garvin, editor of the *Observer*, and his wife. They were rather an odd couple and I didn't take to them. He was very conceited. Sir Edward Bridges, Secretary to the Cabinet, and Hugh Dalton were also present. Winston was not feeling very well and said he had a headache as he had just been inoculated against paratyphoid in preparation for his next journey. Dalton drove me back to the House and informed me that he thought Bracken and Beaverbrook were both gunning for him.

In the evening I had dinner with Randolph Churchill and

Lady Dudley. It was his last evening before leaving for abroad. He was going to be parachuted into Yugoslavia.

It was shortly before this that Winston suggested to me that I should take Randolph under my wing. I could never imagine my being able to do that. Winston wanted me to introduce him to the party bosses, for he was very apt to be a rebel. I agreed to have a little dinner party at the Carlton Grill. I invited James Stuart, Chief Whip, Tom Dugdale, Chairman of the party, and Harold Mitchell, Deputy Chairman of the party. We met there at the arranged time, just after 7 pm. By 7.30 Randolph hadn't turned up, nor at 7.45 and at 8 o'clock I decided we would start dinner and to hell with Randolph.

We were in the middle of the first course when the head waiter came to me and said I was wanted on the 'phone by 10 Downing street. When I picked up the receiver it was Mrs. Churchill's voice. She sounded upset and apologised for Randolph's being late. He had just left No. 10. She was afraid he was very late but there had been a bit of a family row and she hoped my friends and I would not be too put out by his delay. I replied that it was all right, although really my friends and I were fuming, as the party was specially for Randolph.

I rejoined my table and no sooner had I done so than Randolph stormed in, obviously in a bad temper and with much alcohol consumed. During our wait we had taken a fair amount of alcohol ourselves and we weren't in a very good temper either. Randolph tended to shout instead of talk and criticised the party bosses and the running of the party. It was a most uncomfortable evening and I had to bring it to an early close as the other customers were all agog.

Chapter 14

Bombs and By-elections

There was a very considerable reaction in the Commons to the release of Sir Oswald Mosley from detention. The House, and particularly the Socialist Members, were much worked up over this subject and the tenseness of the atmosphere was apparent when Herbert Morrison rose to make his statement. Morrison made out a strong case for Mosley's release. He handled the situation extremely well. There were many questions and a demand for a Debate from Shinwell and Bevan. Crowds of some hundreds of people waited outside Parliament Buildings and even in the Central Lobby. The bulk of them were young men and women. Members were lobbied by them.

The Socialist Opposition appeared to be quietened by Morrison's statement but during the day a strong feeling developed, largely due to the pressure brought to bear on the Socialists by the various Socialist organisations outside the House, such as the National Council of Labour, the Trade Union Congress and the Co-operative Union. Most of the criticism which came from the different quarters of the House was directed not so much at the release of Mosley as at the timing of the announcement and the nature of the announcement itself. It was generally felt that if all reasons had been given in the original statement to the public, much of the criticism would not have arisen. The House was then prorogued.

Mrs. Churchill was very anxious to know how the Debate went and she asked me to go over to No. 10 and have a talk with her. I was with Mrs. Churchill for over an hour. She had a lot of questions to ask. She always liked to be kept in the picture. She was a very knowledgeable person about politics and political personalities. She had likes and dislikes. One of the Members she couldn't stand was Hore-Belisha. She would

Bombs and By-elections

rather have Shinwell than Hore-Belisha in the Government and wondered how he would do for the Ministry of Mines.

This was undoubtedly an outstanding week in Parliamentary circles, for on the Thursday there was a crowded meeting of the Empire Parliamentary Association Committee in Room 14, the House's largest Committee Room. Lord Cranborne was in the Chair. Field Marshal Smuts gave an address entitled *Thoughts on the New World.* When he entered the Committee Room and when he rose to speak he received a tumultuous ovation. In the course of his speech he said there were two dangers facing us—the danger of over-simplification in a world where problems were so complex, and the danger of following catchwords and so missing the real problems of the world.

Dealing with the first, he said that if we over-simplified we were lost and that was what happened in 1919. If we followed that course after this war, it would lead to a greater disaster than ever before. The problems of a new Europe and a new world were so great that Smuts doubted very much if there would ever be a Peace Conference at the end of hostilities. He felt that there should be a comprehensive armistice dealing with the matters concerning the ending of the war, and the vaster problems should be left to a long series of talks and conferences. Stressing this matter of simplification, he said that one of the big problems of the world and of the Empire was that of race and colour. He said simplification tended to mean falsification.

With regard to the second danger, he said that today we heard a great deal about freedom and democracy. These words tended to become clichés which, in the end, would not lead us very far. Our enemies were also led astray by catchwords and tended to fall into the same trap, though with different ideas. They concentrated on the idea of the Fuhrer or leadership. Smuts felt that we must have a mixture of freedom and democracy on the one hand and leadership on the other. Without freedom, leadership would not help us. We had to have, not only freedom, but discipline. After the Great War in 1919 we had thought that the balance of power concept had been abolished and that universality was established by the League of Nations.

Idealism was not enough. Universality was not a solution. We must also face the problem of power and that was what all this war was about. In arranging for a new world organisation we would have to provide not only freedom and democracy but also leadership and power. Leadership would have to remain in the hands of Great Britain, Russia and the United States. These nations would have to be responsible for the preservation of peace and for world security. Field Marshal Smuts considered that the world was completely changing and that the old Europe, as we knew it, had gone for good.

After this struggle there would only remain perhaps two out of the five great European powers. France would have disappeared and it would be hard for her to emerge again. Italy might never rise again. Germany would disappear, perhaps never to emerge again in the old Bismarckian form. We were, therefore, left with Great Britain and Russia. The changes in that country during the last twenty-five years were one of the greatest phenomena in history and her new power would be one of the facts of the world. Britain would come out of the war with glory, honour and prestige such as perhaps no nation had ever before enjoyed in history. From the material point of view she would be a poor country. America, with wealth and resources and potentialities beyond measure, would be the third member of the trinity.

Smuts said that some people attached too great an importance to Anglo-American collaboration which seemed to be one of the greatest hopes of mankind, but as an axis it would not do. It would be too one-sided. Russia must also be included. Britain would, therefore, tend to be an unequal partner in resources with Russia and the United States. She might, however, strengthen her European position by closer working and organisation with many of the smaller democracies in Western Europe. We must cease to be an island. Our experiences of the working of our Commonwealth had already opened the door to such a development. With regard to the colonies, Smuts felt that it would be a good thing to abolish many of the small administrations thus saving expenditure on the maintenance of administrative units which were frequently uneconomical. There should be a grouping together of some of the smaller colonies. It would be better to de-centralise more and more from London and to ask the Dominions near to those colonial spheres to take a more active interest in their welfare. Such a move would tend to strengthen the ties which bound the Dominions to the home country.

I have reported at length on this great speech of Smuts. I felt it was so outstanding at the time that I took as close a note as I could, using my own kind of shorthand which I had devised early in my days at No. 10, so that I could give as accurate an account as possible. Smuts has been proved wrong in some ways since November 1943, but, on the whole, it was a remarkably sound, statesman-like speech. Winston wrote at the top of my report on this subject, 'Thank you. Very good,' in red ink, and one of the Private Secretaries wrote in pencil, 'Go up tops.'

In the evening I dined at the flat of Duncan Sandys. Others present were Mr. and Mrs. Amery, Lady Hinchinbrooke and Sir Alfred Beit. It was an exceedingly pleasant evening. Amery told a very interesting story of the Boer War. When he and Winston were out as war correspondents they were sharing a tent on the veldt. It was a very wet morning and they didn't think the Commando train would go, so they turned over for another nap; Amery asked Winston to wake him up if it went, and he fell into a very deep sleep. When he finally wakened Winston had gone and so had the train. He heard firing some distance away—if he had gone with Winston he would have been taken prisoner too.

Winston had also told me of the ambush and how he had tried to escape up a high banking. When he got to the top he he saw a Boer officer on horseback and, although he might have got away by killing the officer, the Boers were surging forward and he realised the odds against him were overwhelming so he was forced to surrender. He told Smuts that story some years later and said he had always regretted not shooting the Boer officer, for he was sure he would have got away. However, Smuts said, 'It was a good thing you didn't, for that officer, Botha, was a first-class shot. You would have been killed and you wouldn't have been here to tell the story.'

The P.M. did not seem very well. I didn't like the news of

him nor the tone of the communiqué that was issued and particularly a mention of his heart. Everyone was rather worried. He was abroad at that time meeting Roosevelt. Mrs. Churchill had told me she was going to fly to the Prime Minister. She was naturally very anxious. Attlee read a bulletin to the House. The news came as a profound shock as his illness had not previously been announced. However, he was now on the mend and the very next day, 18th December 1943, further good news about his health arrived. The worst was over and he would soon be back in action.

At the beginning of 1944 I went to Paddington with Jack Churchill and Mary Churchill. Only the Cabinet and the family were present, together with the high-up railway officials. Winston looked pretty well as he came out of the train but Clemmie looked very tired indeed. I then drove to the House with Diana, Mrs. Duncan Sandys, to get tickets for the family for the House.

I went down to the Commons with the P.M. He had a drink of water before leaving No. 10 and had sat down to drink it, looking a bit tired and much older now that I was close to him. Going up the stairs from the House of Lords entrance, he walked very slowly like a very old man. He had certainly had a considerable shake. He told me he thought the conference had gone well and the stay at Marrakesh was most pleasant and restful. He had gone out for picnics nearly every day.

He got an excellent reception from the House. Members stood up and cheered, as did the members of the public in the Public Galleries. I had never seen that happen before. After the proceedings in the House I went with the P.M. to the Smoke Room where he held court to many Members anxious to shake hands with him. I'd never seen him getting such a warm welcome from Members before. They were greatly delighted to see him back in his old Parliamentary haunts again. He said to me he was paying a great compliment to Members by going straight to the House from the station after his trials and tribulations. It was all well timed and dramatic. He had a great sense of the theatre.

When I got back to No. 10 Downing Street James Stuart, the Chief Whip, wanted to have a talk with me because Winston,

Bombs and By-elections

or the Boss as he was often called at this stage, had spoken to him about the Chairmanship of the party. He wanted a change, although it was not so long ago since Tommy Dugdale had been appointed to that post after a good deal of pressure from the Chief Whip and the other party bosses.

Apparently the P.M. wanted to appoint Lord Margesson to that post because he felt he would be the ideal man. James was naturally trying to defend Tommy. A crisis was likely to blow up soon. There was always too much jockeying for position by a few pushing Members with ambitions for themselves. It wasn't so long ago that the P.M. said that he would like me to be the Chairman of the party and I could keep on being his P.P.S. as well. I had said, 'No.' I didn't want any changes unless he himself wanted me to take on another appointment. However, Tommy Dugdale remained as Chairman of Central Office and that, in my view, was a good thing, for he was doing an excellent job. He subsequently received a peerage.

Tom Johnston, one of the leading Scottish M.Ps on the Socialist side, wanted to see the P.M. because he was anxious that George Mathers, M.P. for my native constituency of Linlithgow, should be appointed Lord High Commissioner to the General Assembly of the Church of Scotland. Apparently the Moderator of the Kirk was enthusiastic. I was not so sure that Winston would welcome this appointment. I saw Winston on that matter, for I thought Mathers would be a successful High Commissioner instead of one of the usual hereditary peers of Scotland jobbed into the position.

I didn't like the look of the P.M. He seemed to have aged a great deal. He was in his siren suit and a ragged old dressing gown, and looked miserable. He didn't seem to have the old fire. He was enthusiastic about the new Allied landing in Italy. He thought the Allies should soon roll the Germans out of Italy. Alas, it was not to be so easy. There was still a long way to go.

The P.M. talked with me about the pending by-elections. If they continued to go badly we would have to have a General Election. His messages to candidates were getting stronger and stronger and I sensed a desire to have a more dictatorial regime.

We were in the midst of what became known as the Little

Blitz. The bombing was pretty bad. One evening I was in the Carlton Club having dinner with James Stuart and other friends. I thought it was getting late so off I went. I walked down St. James's Street. The guns were barking and the bombs were coming closer and closer. I got to the Mall and went into St. James's Park when the next thing I knew was I was being tossed about like a leaf by the blast of a bomb which had landed at the bottom of St. James's Street. I got up and went as quickly as I could to the No. 10 Annexe and to my 'dug-out' bed.

The next day James Stuart tried to find me everywhere, for he and my other friends at the club had thought that I had walked out straight into the bomb attack and had been killed. They had tried 12 Catherine Place but I wasn't there. They never thought I had gone to the Annexe where I rarely used my bedroom unless I was working late. My walk from the Carlton Club to the No. 10 Annexe was not at all a pleasant one. Fortunately the bombers didn't follow me but went the other way to the west and north of London.

The P.M. was furious at the newspaper talk of his message to Brighton for the by-election. He said, 'Before I am done I will make the message a damn sight stronger.' He was very touchy about almost anything just now. However, I was so used to his moods by this time that I could take them in my stride. The one thing Members mustn't show was a jumpiness or uneasiness at his displays of temper, for it only made him worse.

Winston had been having correspondence with James Stuart, Tommy Dugdale, Beaverbrook and Bracken on the Conservative Party organisation. Why he should discuss the party organisation with Max Beaverbrook and Brendan Bracken I couldn't think, for neither of them had ever been close friends of the Conservative Party, and indeed had been mostly critical of it and how it was run. The P.M. was very depressed and distressed as the result of the Derby by-election which had been won by an anti-coalition candidate who had resigned from the Labour Party in order to stand. He looked very glum and to Beaverbrook, Bracken and me he suggested an appeal to the country. Of course, he was listened to carefully by the two

Bs, who were critics of the party anyway. My comment was that he would be taking a step which would be most unpopular in the country as a whole and that such an appeal could split the country.

We were still getting frequent air raids. There was a particularly bad one on the night of the 18th–19th February. 12 Catherine Place shivered and shook several times with falling bombs, and the noise was tremendous. Whitehall was a sorry sight. A bomb had gone down through the Treasury. Two others had landed in the Horse Guards. Downing Street was a shambles and even the Cabinet Room and No. 10 were badly damaged. All its windows were blown out. My room was the least damaged of the lot. Nothing was disturbed but the window was shattered. It was bitterly cold February weather. The structure of No. 10 was not too badly damaged, so Winston ordered that the Cabinet would be held there as usual. The Chief Whip's room at No. 12 was a mess. The furniture was hurled about all over the place. Lord Portal, the Minister of Works, got gangs of men working on No. 10 and especially on the Cabinet Room. It was completed and the Cabinet was held as usual—a remarkable feat by Lord Portal and his men.

There was a Debate on the war situation in the House, which was packed to hear the P.M. make his first big statement for months. It was a great success, although there were the usual snarling critics. Many people came to see me to try to get seats but, of course, it was a hopeless task.

Winston had a word with me afterwards. I think he had been brooding about the by-election and his talks with Beaverbrook and Bracken, and he suggested to me that he would like me to take on the vetting of the Tory candidates to see that we got the right kind. He said he had great faith in my judgement on all House of Commons matters and it would be of assistance to him if I would do so.

Naturally I agreed but it wouldn't be an easy task. Harold Mitchell, who was Deputy Chairman of the party and who at present looked after candidates, was rather upset and, as we stayed together, he could have been difficult; but he said he would be only too glad to help me, and so it went on to the end of the war.

I attended a very interesting dinner party at the Dorchester. The host was Jay Llewellin. The principal guest was Walter Nash from New Zealand. At that time he was the Finance Minister. He later became Prime Minister. In the years to come I met him many times at various Commonwealth Conferences. The others present were Stanley Bruce, the Australian Prime Minister with whom I also became friendly over the next few years, and A. P. Herbert. It was a change to discuss Commonwealth matters instead of Poland, Austria or Greece. We felt at that time we were all of one family. A. P. Herbert was in cracking form and as he bid us good-night he said 'You have heard of people and met them who were going to dine with Borgias that night but never met people who had dined with them last night. Well, I hope I shall see you all in the House tomorrow.'

I spent the night at the Annexe as there was another noisy air raid. The P.M. took Clemmie down to the shelter. He had to be carried upstairs and downstairs by marines as the steps were very steep. Throughout the war the marines did duty at the Annexe. I had dined at the Carlton Club. When I left the sirens began their wailing. It was a good thing I took shelter, for a bomb hit the main pillar of Marlborough House. I had passed within fifteen yards of it only fifteen minutes before, otherwise I would most certainly never have lived to tell the tale. I reached the Annexe by the time the explosion took place and, despite the iron shuttering, double windows and blackout, the curtains blew into the room.

The next night there was another air raid. James Stuart and I went to the Annexe and we talked with the Prime Minister until 2 am. His stamina was really quite remarkable.

The next night I again went to the Annexe where Brendan Bracken and I sat and talked until 1 am. He was a great conversationalist and a truly remarkable man, especially as no one really knew anything about his background. The story was—according to him—that he came from Australia with a little money and managed to get into Sedbergh School in Yorkshire, where he only stayed a year, possibly a little longer. His life was then a bit of a mystery until he emerged a few years later as a great friend of Lord Beaverbrook and later also of Churchill. He got into Parliament at an early age. How he made this jump from obscurity to fame remains a mystery. After the war he was a great newspaper personality, but only a few years elapsed before he died suddenly. There were even rumours of suicide. He had burned all his public and private papers, which was a great pity, for he had much to recount of British history and personalities over the war and post-war years.

There was some feeling among Members of the House, notably Quintin Hogg, afterwards Lord Hailsham, about what he called Counsels of the Bed Chamber and not the Counsel Chamber. He thought that Beaverbrook, Bracken and Lord Cherwell were an evil influence on the Prime Minister and were doing him irreparable damage. Apparently he was annoyed because this led to a lot of ill-feeling among the members of the Cabinet who were not in the inner circle.

I slept again at the Annexe, for I was working late and I didn't want to be disturbed. The atmosphere was either too hot or too cold and I slept badly. You could hear the guns and bombs through the air ventilators.

Shortly afterwards, I went down to the House with the P.M. He was taking his Questions and then I went on with him to the Savoy for the lunch of the Royal College of Physicians. The P.M. was very fed up at having let himself in for a speech. Actually he made a very good after-lunch speech. There were about three hundred doctors present and they certainly enjoyed his visit. It was always easy to accept all kinds of invitations to speak at a variety of functions when they were fixed for some time ahead, but when the day approached you wondered why you had ever let yourself in for another boring function. This one was not a bore.

The weather was bitterly cold and I had a beastly cold as a result of my windows being blown out at No. 10. I couldn't get rid of it. As a matter of fact it developed into a very bad chest cold and I had to remain in bed for several days and then had a few days' recuperation in Scotland.

The P.M. seemed genuinely pleased to see me and patted me on the knee as he drove me to the Annexe and then he suddenly saw a cat out of the window as we drove up to the door. I had heard he was very fond of cats but I had never actually seen one with him before. He made a great fuss of it as it rubbed itself against his legs. This was a nice tailor-made black cat. He bent down and fondled it. He looked up from the cat to me and said, 'They are lovely friendly creatures. I much prefer them to dogs.' I just grunted—a grunt that could have meant anything—for I much preferred dogs and couldn't stand cats.

On Friday 18th March the House went into Secret Session for a Tank Debate. Sir Andrew Duncan opened the Debate with a very good sound business-like speech. He traced the history of the tank position since the loss of the tanks in the Battle of France, discussed the production of the Lee and Grant tanks and said that by 1942 it was clear that the Sherman and Churchill tanks were necessary. He maintained that the Valentine was a stout and reliable tank and that 2,300 had gone to Russia, where they had been much appreciated. They were not apparently suitable for the desert. There had been disappointments and mistakes but it had not been easy and results must be based on experience. The Americans, and even the Germans, had had their worries also. The Tank Board consisted of every type of expert. It was an excellent speech, though it did not satisfy the House. Nevertheless it helped to calm the somewhat explosive atmosphere. Andrew Duncan was popular with all Members.

On that same day the Government was defeated on the Education Bill—great consternation. I made a terrible boob, for I thought that the Division would be later and had dashed back to Catherine Place where we had a Division Bell and it was possible to get back to the House for a Division. I decided to have a bath and change, for I still felt a little delicate after my 'flu. I had just got to the door when I met Harold Mitchell. He asked, 'Have you missed the Division?' I replied, 'Surely it has not taken place yet.' He said it had and the Government had been defeated.

To make matters worse Rab Butler was coming to dine with me that evening along with Gil Lloyd-George and James Stuart. I was in a pickle, for I gathered from Harold Mitchell that

Rab Butler had threatened to resign. However, our evening passed off successfully, for Rab said that Winston was going to treat the defeat on the Education Bill as a Vote of Confidence. The House was suspended until 2.15 pm. the next day. The Debate was then resumed. At that time I spoke to the P.M. on the 'phone and told him what was happening, so he came over to the House at once. Anthony Eden did not want him to come into the Chamber lest it exaggerate the importance of the Debate. I mentioned Anthony's idea to Winston when I met him. He was furious and asked if he had been barred from the Chamber. He said, 'I am a Member, am I not? I never heard of such a suggestion,' and strode past me into the Chamber. He glared at Anthony and asked, 'Why do you have to send me a message that I have not to come into the House?' Anthony whispered to me, 'He really must leave me with something to do and let me do it.'

The P.M. had a long talk with Jimmy Maxton. He was very fond of him. He called him the Raven because he had long black hair which hung over his face and which he constantly had to brush back with his hand. Maxton said to Winston and me that the mistake the P.M. made was in not recognising the I.L.P. He said several times to Winston that they should be the official Opposition. The P.M. replied and said, 'Jimmy, I have either to McGovern [McGovern was one of the other I.L.P. members] or get out.'

The Labour Party had a meeting to decide what to do in the Division. Attlee beat the big drum and told the Socialist Members that if they didn't support the Government it could burst the truce and the Socialist Ministers would have to come out of the Government. That did the trick, although many abstained from the actual Vote. The Debate was a flop, owing to a narrow ruling from the Chair, and even Winston didn't get his speech delivered. This didn't improve his temper but he was pleased at the Vote. He thought that I should send a two-page telegram to the King. However, I found that the Vice-Chamberlain had already reported, so the proposal came to nothing.

I walked back to his room at the House behind the Speaker's Chair. The P.M. walked up and down for a bit then stopped and stared at me and then said, 'Do you remember when Disraeli was Prime Minister he used to send a letter to Queen Victoria every day the House was sitting?' I said, 'Yes, I remember reading about that in my history classes at university.' Winston said, 'I think it is a very good idea. What do you think about it?' Before I had a chance to say anything, the P.M. said, 'I think that the practice should be resumed.' I replied that the days of Disraeli were not hectic like they were at the present time. 'With the burden that you are carrying you couldn't possibly undertake this additional chore.' He stopped tramping up and down and stood and looked at me. 'I'm glad you like the idea,' he said, 'and I'm glad you think it would be too much to add this to my other duties. I'm not going to do it but I think that you should do it. I'm sure the Monarch would be most appreciative.' I realised I had been properly caught. He said, 'You can send a weekly letter. I have always enjoyed your weekly reports to me. They have kept me in the centre of the Parliamentary picture and,' Winston added explosively, 'if on any vital days you can get off an evening message to the King, that would be much appreciated.'

From that moment I sent a Parliamentary Report to the Monarch. I heard nothing from him but some months later Sir Alan Lascelles, who was the King's Secretary and whom I knew quite well, told me that the King asked him to thank me. As a result of these reports he had stopped reading the political news in the Press and all he read was my report and 'Toby M.P.' in *Punch*. That column was written by Guy Eden, a first-class, amusing political writer whom I knew very well. We had a good laugh at the Monarch's comments about our respective columns.

After that morning talk with the P.M. I went to lunch at the Dorchester with Lord Rushcliffe, a former Conservative Minister, Lord Milne and Harry Methven, a Director of the Dorchester. Ernest Bevin was the guest and he held court all through lunch—talk, talk, talk. There would be 300,000 vehicles for the invasion. We would have been better to have gone through Portugal but it would mean longer lines of communications. Bevin said the frontal assault on France would be a bloody business and would not give room for the deployment of our vehicles.

It staggered me that a Minister should talk freely about those things, even if it was to a very confined group. Bevin said to me that the Government was proposing to take in Shinwell and if that were so he couldn't remain in the Government. This was at least the second time he had said that to me. If it happened Bevin would leave the Government and would leave politics altogether. I doubted that. He liked power too much to give it up lightly.

About the end of May 1944 there was a meeting of the All-Party Committee with Lord Winterton in the Chair. About 150 members were present, to hear Sir Samuel Hoare, then our Ambassador to Spain. He got a warm reception when he rose to speak. His theme was the British success in keeping Spain out of the war on the Axis side, and specific points he mentioned were:

1. Getting Spain to agree—despite strong German pressure—to withdraw the 'Blue Division' of Spanish troops from the Russian front.
2. Curtailing, if not completely halting, German sabotage and espionage activities centred on Tangier and the Straits of Gibraltar.
3. Cutting down the export from Spain of such crucial materials as wolfram, which Germany desperately needed.

These three prongs of the offensive in Spain had hit the Germans hard. Sir Samuel Hoare made a far better speech than on an earlier occasion when he had addressed the Committee, and it created a most favourable impression.

The next day I went down to the House with the P.M. to hear Shinwell make an imperialist speech in the Dominion Affairs Debate. After it I suggested to Winston that he should make Shinwell Vice-President of the Primrose League. He was quite amused at that idea. He thought it was a pity that Shinwell was not more popular in the House and in his own party. I had known Shinwell for many years. I had heckled him when he was fighting as a Socialist candidate in my home constituency of Linlithgowshire in 1924 and in 1929.

When I went down to the House with the P.M. for

Questions the next day, he was looking very bad and at one point I thought he was going to collapse. He went to the lavatory when he arrived at the House and stayed an inordinately long time. Members thought he was about to have a stroke. Those near him at No. 10 found this very disquieting.

His instinct was remarkable. He knew he had created a bad impression and in the afternoon he went down to the House again to be seen in the Lobbies, the Smoke Room and the Chamber. A few of his intimate friends had a conference to decide whether he should speak in the Budget Resolutions Debate on that Thursday. I argued against it and suggested the Finance Bill later. He wanted to warn the country where it was going, with all this vast expenditure of money. It had been a gloomy day.

Sir John Anderson, the Chancellor of the Exchequer, wound up the Budget Resolutions Debate. He was a very pompous man but very nice and pleasant to talk to. His stock in the House had risen tremendously. I recollect an occasion before the war when I was an Assistant Government Whip and I was on the Front Government Bench as Whip on duty. It was during the dinner hour. The House was very quiet and I was sitting doodling on my Order Paper and looking round the Chamber from time to time. Most Members were in a somewhat similar condition, except the few who wanted to catch the Speaker's eye. Idly I glanced along the Front Government Bench to see who was there. Suddenly I was struck by the fact that there were only five of us on the Government Bench and we all came from the same school, George Watson's College, Edinburgh. They were John Anderson, the Chancellor of the Exchequer and later Viscount Waverley; Shakes Morrison, afterwards Speaker of the House of Commons and later Viscount Dunrossil and Governor-General of Australia; Tommy Cooper, the Lord Advocate for Scotland; David Maxwell-Fyfe, later Viscount Kilmuir and Lord Chancellor, and myself. Although the school had five Ministers in the Government in 1918–1922, never before had a Scottish school attained this record and I don't think it has been repeated.

Chapter 15

Dominion Visitors

At that time I had many hectic days starting at 8 am. and finishing at midnight or later. It wasn't like slogging at a desk or in a workshop. It was all variety, and mostly of an exciting nature—meeting people, interviews, the House, taking notes, writing reports, lunches and dinners, and occasional drink parties, attending memorial services on behalf of the P.M., meeting people arriving in this country at stations and occasionally off planes at small aerodromes—no Heathrows in those days—visits to my constituency and speeches. Our hours were pretty erratic. Often we went to each other's flats—James Stuart, Charles Waterhouse and others. Charles was the better cook. On one occasion I had to leave a lovely picnic meal at James's to go down to Croydon to meet Mr. Curtin, the Australian Prime Minister.

It was an impressive sight. The plane looked large, but it was tiny compared with the usual planes today. It was escorted in to land by six fighters which roared round the aerodrome until the civilian plane had landed safely. I was there to meet Mr. Curtin on behalf of the Prime Minister. Curtin looked exhausted. There was a great battery of cameras and hosts of Press men. He made a very good speech of brief duration. I thought at first it was extempore but I noticed that the script was handed back to one of his entourage.

I had not been at home in Scotland for some time but I went for a long week-end at Easter 1944. It was a tremendous change from the bustle of London and all the late nights. It was all so quiet. There had been a few raids in the West of Scotland—very bad ones indeed—and in Edinburgh, but only the odd bomb had dropped in our area of Linlithgowshire and very little damage had been done.

I travelled back to London on the sleeper—Harold Mitchell

and Bob Boothby were also on the train and we sat and talked in Harold's berth until Berwick.

The next day I spent in the City. I attended the Freedom Ceremony in the Guildhall for Curtin and Frazer, the New Zealand premier, and had to endure the ordeal of having my name announced and having to walk up the centre aisle to be introduced to the Lord Mayor and Lady Mayoress. There was the usual distinguished gathering on the dais and in the hall. Both speeches were good but far too long. Curtin was excellent. When his name was called he walked sturdily forward to the microphone and proceeded to speak for twenty-five minutes without a note. He was quite an orator and I could understand his influence on the Australians. Frazer had a few notes but didn't consult them much. He too was first class and they both got rousing cheers from the large and distinguished audience.

On the following day there was another great occasion in Parliament. This was the McKenzie King ceremony in the Royal Gallery. I met Winston at the Ladies Gallery entrance and then, headed by the Sergeant-at-Arms, we proceeded down the Lobbies—the two Prime Ministers, then James Stuart and me. There was a big turn-out of Members of both Houses. The speech from McKenzie King was dull and commonplace. Winston, on the other hand, was in wonderful form and got a rousing reception. But the best reception of all was given to the Speaker, who was most popular. Gradually the procession returned to the Commons and then dispersed.

In the evening I dined at the Savoy to honour Tom Levy, a Tory M.P. who was celebrating his seventieth birthday. There were about twenty M.Ps present and I had to make the speech. I was never asked or warned that I would have to do so. This kind of thing annoyed me. Everybody seemed to think that I could get up at a moment's notice to say the right thing. You did have successes like this but you could also make a terrible flop. Fortunately my speech seemed to go down all right and the rest of the party went well. I then returned with Brendan Bracken and we sat talking until 2 am.

The next day I went to Paddington Station where I met Geoffrey Lloyd. We had a reserved compartment to Birmingham. We were going to attend the Freedom of the City

Ceremony to Field Marshal Smuts. Geoffrey gave a dinner party that evening to about fifty people in the Midland Hotel. Local government, industry, the Press and Parliament were represented. Smuts made an excellent speech and offered to answer questions, which he did for an hour.

The Freedom Ceremony took place in a crowded Town Hall. Smuts got a terrific reception everywhere. The arrangements were not too good and Leo Amery walked out before it was over. I thought it was a bad show, but he said to me afterwards that he was a very small man and he had been placed at the back of the Hall. I couldn't think why he was placed in such a position as he was a most distinguished Cabinet Minister and Parliamentarian. It was an insult to one of His Majesty's Secretaries of State.

I sat with the Earl and Countess of Dudley. We had tea in the Mayor's Parlour and then said good-bye to Smuts—probably the greatest man I have ever met. He generated more warmth and affection than did Winston, and Winston took a lot of beating. Geoffrey Lloyd and I returned to London together. I sat and brooded over some of the things Smuts had said to me, such as, 'The British Empire is the greatest romance, the greatest adventure and the greatest Odyssey of human history.'

I then went to Bovingdon aerodrome, which had been taken over by the Americans, to see McKenzie King off to Canada. He went in a converted Liberator. There was quite a crowd of Canadian notabilities to see him off, including General Crerar, the G.O.C. of the Canadian Army. I had a long talk with McKenzie King while waiting for take-off. He was most friendly and hoped I could visit him in Canda. He spoke about Winston's health and the affection he had for him. I was quite impressed by McKenzie King after I had met him several times but he took a lot of knowing. There is no doubt he was a good politician.

After all this travelling I was glad to settle down quietly at Catherine Place and No. 10 for my usual chores, a change from the very hectic time I had had with the Dominions visitors.

Pat Hornsby-Smith, one of my young, very politically-minded constituents, came to see me. She was secretary to Lord Woolmer, the head of one of the Ministries. She had been one of my most enthusiastic young Conservatives in Richmond before the war. She was very keen to get into Parliament and, in fact, did so after the war, being elected for Chislehurst, Kent. I spoke for her at her various elections. She did well in the House, became a Minister, a Privy Councillor and a peeress, and is now in business. After the war I also spoke for Margaret Roberts at her first election. She made a first-class speech and dealt with the hecklers magnificently. Little did I think then that this young candidate would one day become the Prime Minister as Margaret Thatcher.

Harold Mitchell and I had dinner at Catherine Place to discuss the affairs and organisation of the Conservative Party, with special reference to the Central Office. Rab Butler, James Stuart, Ralph Assheton and Henry Brooke were also present. Harold had prepared charts and notes as a basis of discussion. I was disappointed at the calibre and ideas of some of these so-called leaders, with the exception of Rab Butler and James Stuart who were first class. Ralph Assheton and Henry Brooke I thought pretty good. It was the people down the line of whom I was critical. All the criticism I could see was against Sir Robert Topping, the head professional at Central Office. Yet, if he was so bad, why did they want to increase his salary by £700 per annum?—big deal, as the Americans would say. It was suggested that Donald McCulloch should become Publicity Officer for Central Office and Henry Brooke would be in over-all charge. The Chairman, Tom Dugdale, was never mentioned though the meeting was really about him and how Central Office was doing.

I then attended a meeting at the House. The P.M. made his speech on foreign affairs. It was not particularly startling. He turned round after fifteen minutes and asked me to get him a glass of water. His voice was not very strong. This was a rare occurrence. However, he completed his speech in his usual rather flamboyant style. I walked back with him to his room but he was in no mood for talking so I left him there.

I was walking along the Lobby later when I was stopped to

be introduced to Frances Stephens, David Lloyd-George's second wife. She had been his secretary and mistress for many years. I thought she was most charming and still a very attractive woman. She had lived with him, I understand, since the end of World War I. I gathered that Megan Lloyd-George wouldn't have anything to do with her. Well, I could understand that, but after such a lapse of time I would have thought all would have been forgiven, if not forgotten. My friend Gil Lloyd-George was much more tolerant.

I went up to Scotland for the week-end as I had to dine at Holyrood House during the General Assembly. I had drinks in the Equerries' Room with Col. Stephenson, Erskine-Hill the M.P., and Col. Murphy of the Irish Guards, then up to the Reception Room where we were met and received by Lady Victoria Wemyss. I saw many people I knew. I sat at the top table between Lady Anne Southby and J. S. McIntyre K.C., Dean of the Faculty of Advocates. The band of the Royal Scots played in the gallery during dinner. Then a piper played round the table. It was a wonderful sight. Lord Linlithgow, dressed as a Lord Lieutenant, and Lady Linlithgow, tall, fair and good-looking, were of course the hosts.

The toasts were The King, when the National Anthem was played by the band, and The Church of Scotland, and this time the band played *The Auld Hundred* and *All People that on Earth do Dwell*. The last toast was Their Graces, then Lady Linlithgow left the table followed by her ladies and each in turn, when they got to the end of the room, curtsied. I had talks with Lord Hamilton of Dalziel, Lord Linlithgow and Lady Victoria Wemyss. After the guests departed I went back again to the Equerries' Room for drinks. I then left to have a very foggy drive home to Linlithgowshire.

I drove back to Edinburgh the next day as my daughter Rachel was born on the 31st May 1944 and I was a very proud father indeed. Mrs. Churchill sent us a telegram of congratulations. I then had to go to Linlithgow, my county town, where I had lunch with Provost Wright of my native town of Bathgate, Lord Linlithgow, Lord Charles Hope and Mr. Crichton, the Convener of the County Council.

Lord Linlithgow took the salute at the march past of the

Home Guard, Scouts, Guides, V.A.D. and the other voluntary services.

On the way back to London from Edinburgh, on the station platform at Waverley I was introduced to the Princess Royal by the Chief Constable of Edinburgh, who was seeing her off after engagements in the City. I had about ten minutes' conversation with her. She was charming and when she smiled I thought her beautiful. I was sorry the meeting was so brief. The Press and the photographers had never done her justice.

Arthur Woodburn and George Mathers, two Socialist Members, sat in my sleeper and talked and talked. It was Newcastle before they said good-night and I got to bed. When I returned to Catherine Place I breakfasted with Harold Mitchell, who said that Tom Dugdale, though not fully recovered from an illness, was coming back to Central Office. Harold feared that no reorganisation would take place at Central Office after all.

That afternoon the P.M. made his first statement on the Second Front operation. The House was very full and very excited.

The P.M. was very late in getting down to the House. He hadn't finished the preparation of his statement and Questions went quickly. Naturally the House expected a statement and were impatient to hear it, so the House had to remain in suspended animation until Winston arrived. I'd never seen that kind of situation in the House before or since. However, the war seemed to be going well, despite the bad weather. The landings in Normandy had been an amazing success. Now that the landings had taken place people were already looking forward to a rapid advance up through France. The feelings of optimism seemed premature, for the most difficult part had still to come.

Arthur Henderson had complained to me about his treatment by the civil servants and soldiers at the War Office; the position of Under-Secretary of State for War seemed to be ignored. I suppose they were too busy running the active side of the war in Normandy but it must have been frustrating to be the Under-Secretary of a Department and to be told nothing. This was the lot of quite a few of the Under-Secretaries. I would certainly avoid promotion to any of those positions.

Later I had to go down to my constituency, to lunch at the Town Hall with all the local dignitaries, the Mayor and Corporation with their ladies. Lord and Lady Croft were the principal guests. I sat beside Lady Croft at lunch—rather a grand old lady of the old school. The opening ceremony of the 'Salute the Soldier' campaign on Richmond Green was a great success. Lord Croft made an excellent speech and the march past of the various organisations was very well done.

I spent the afternoon and evening with Colonel Bromhead at Petersham and discussed outstanding constituency matters but, of course, party politics were very dead, and rightly so, for national affairs had to come first.

The next day I lunched at the Dorchester with Professor George Catlin, the husband of Vera Brittain and father of Shirley Williams, recently a Socialist Minister. I thought he was a most pompous man. He wanted to go on a lecture tour of the United States and to meet Max Beaverbrook. He had a good but rather a crazy idea of a religious regeneration of the world after the war.

Malcolm MacDonald visited me at No. 10 before flying back to Canada. He would have preferred to stay here as he thought it was wrong for M.Ps to have jobs out of the country at this time. Also he wanted to get back so as to do some nursing of his constituency. He had done an excellent job in Canada and I thought he should continue in that post for the time being.

I had a working lunch—indeed most of my meals, even breakfasts, were working meals—with P. J. Grigg and Ralph Assheton. P.J. was in good form; he had a pungent and cruel wit. Apparently the campaign in France was going well so far and many prisoners were now falling into our hands. There had been some general criticism of de Gaulle. The P.M. made a statement in the middle of June to the effect that there should be no Debate then owing to the delicacy of the situation.

In a private meeting of the Conservative Members Foreign Affairs Committee a discussion took place on the question of the French National Committee. There was a strong feeling against any recognition at present. No one knew what the opinion of the French themselves would be or the kind of government they would want. De Gaulle was a military symbol but it was impossible to say if he was anything more than that. The National Committee was a self-appointed body and, therefore, was not a properly constituted government like the other Allied governments who had left their countries when invasion took place. The recognition of de Gaulle now might conceivably mean a dictatorship being thrust upon France which would be unwanted and unpopular with the French people.

In June 1944 I had lunch at the Savoy with Sir Montague Hughman, who gave a birthday party for Lord McGowan and Sir Andrew Duncan. The others present were Lord Teviot, Sir Edward Crowe and Sir Alex McColl. Harry McGowan was a very shrewd and amusing old boy. He rose literally from nowhere to become the Chairman of the Imperial Chemical Company. Those of us present that day decided to form a luncheon club called 'The Old Gang'. This club is still going strong. We confine our numbers to twenty. When one dies the remainder elect a new member.

At the time of writing I am the second oldest member of the group, not in age but in seniority. Our membership covers a wide range of interests including Members of the Government, leading business and professional people and well-known members of the community. The conversation is of a high order. Usually somebody—the host for the day—initiates a debate on a vital issue, not necessarily political, and the cut and thrust of debate is a lively entertainment for us all. That day I initiated a debate on Scottish Nationalism and Home Rule. However, this is running into the future and I must return to 1944.

We had a long-drawn-out meeting at the House on the Finance Bill and the House was late in rising. However, I had to report to the Prime Minister, who was in an extremely bad temper, on the Adjournment Debate, initiated by Cunningham Reid, on the P.M's recent visit to France. Cunningham Reid was not the P.M's favourite M.P. In fact, Cunningham Reid was the favourite of practically nobody in the House, for he apparently had spent a great deal of the war out of the country, amongst other places Honolulu. For a long time afterwards, when he rose in the House to ask a question or make a speech he was greeted by Members shouting, 'Honolulu' or 'Go back to Honolulu'.

Dominion Visitors

I was late in getting to bed and I slept badly as we had a very bad air attack. I knew we could expect the flying bombs any time soon but I couldn't believe they had started yet. I was wrong. There was a noisy and continuous air raid during the night. It was still going strong in the morning. To the general public, who knew nothing about them, it must have been an unpleasant shock. The shells and planes seemed to be overhead for hours.

I realised that this was a different kind of raid from all the others. This was the expected arrival of the flying bomb which most people dreaded. There were alerts all day. The new bomb was apparently about a ton in weight and was jet-propelled with, of course, no crew. Comparatively it had very little penetrative effect but the lateral blast was tremendous. It was an eerie object. The numbers of raids grew daily for some time and caused a lot of damage and many deaths.

It was at that time that the House of Commons changed its venue from Westminster to Church House which was supposed to be a safer building. It was sad to leave the old Palace of Westminster and somehow the majesty of Parliament went with our move. My first meeting in the new building was to attend the Executive Meeting of the Empire Parliamentary Association. I was astounded to hear that the Secretary, Howard D'Egville, had suggested he must go out to Canada again. He had already spent two years there and there was no necessity for him to go at all. Why not to Australia? It was just nonsense for our Secretary to spend any time of the war in Canada.

That evening I was so tired that I slept very soundly. Thank goodness, for it was a pretty heavy night of bombing. The flying bomb had now received the name of doodle-bug. Somehow this didn't sound or seem as bad as a bomb, but they were far worse than the ordinary kind and I could well understand the fear which the population felt for them in their flight paths from the south coast to London, and why they felt jittery, waiting for the engine sound to cut out and then the plummeting to the ground with devastating effect on houses and people. The population didn't want to stay in shelters for hours. The bombs were very bad for morale.

Life, however, went on much as usual and we all hoped the

Allied armies would advance quickly and overrun the flying bomb sites. I became quite a fatalist and, therefore, kept my cool—at any rate enough to enjoy a non-political dinner at Claridges given by Sir Herbert Morgan to Sir Alfred Munnings. Others present were Lord Camrose, the newspaper proprietor, Sir Otto Niemeyer, Anthony Devas, an up-and-coming artist who died prematurely, Gerald Kelly, Maurice Codner, Sir Walter Lamb, Sir William Reid Dick, the sculptor, and Sir Alfred Webb. We all had to make speeches. It was a fascinating evening for me since there were no politicians present and the evening became a rabelaisian affair. It was an excellent interlude.

Codner was a great friend of Munnings and, in due course, I too became very friendly with him. He was, of course, President of the Royal Academy. He had much in common with me and I with him—mainly the same sense of humour. We had many entertaining evenings together with mutual friends, political and artistic. When he wrote his autobiography in 1951 he sent me a copy, duly inscribed, with delightful drawings on the endpapers.

His name, too, crossed my desk at No. 10.

Note to Prime Minister

I met Sir Alfred Munnings, the new President of the Royal Academy, the other night. He had hoped to see you at the Other Club on Thursday. He is very anxious that two of your paintings should be shown in this year's Academy and he hoped you would agree to this suggestion. I understand that it would be the first time that any Prime Minister has ever exhibited at the Academy.   Harvie-Watt.

March 25th, 1944

'Art is no courtier to politics. Thank you. W.S.C.'

Then it was back to the chores again. The Employment Debate was a dreary, but I suppose a useful, one. It lasted for three days. Ernest Bevin, the Minister of Labour, who was in good form opened the discussion with an excellent House of Commons speech when he succeeded in maintaining the balance between the ideas of the left and the right. It was one of the first big Debates in Church House. Conservative opinion on the right wing had felt that there was too much bias towards public enterprise, while the Socialist Party had thought that the White Paper placed too much emphasis on private enterprise. Jimmy Maxton made his usual amusing and critical speech suggesting that the White Paper could well have stopped after the first sentence; the rest might have been published as 'some murmurings and meanderings by a Cambridge or Edinburgh undergraduate'. He added that 'the early stages of the war against Germany were not nearly as phoney as would be the Government's war on unemployment'.

Afterwards I had a walk in St. James's Park. It was a gorgeous evening, despite the doodle-bugs. I went back to the house in Catherine Place I shared with Harold Mitchell. It had undergone many changes since I left that morning. It had suffered as the result of blast from a bomb that came down near the brewery in Victoria. All our back windows were out and some of the doors were off their hinges. However, the repair squads were soon on the job.

In the midst of those activities I had to meet a deputation of the Mid Surrey Golf Club at Catherine Place. I couldn't imagine what they wanted to speak to me about and I could scarcely believe my ears when the deputation said they had come to me about their taxation position. They felt it was too high. I had to control myself or I would have burst out laughing. Here was the house I was living in a bit of a shambles and a world-wide war was on, and they had come to see me about the taxation of a golf club.

While I was still speechless another doodle-bug went off close by but fortunately not so close as the other. However, the house shook as it was already damaged. I had had enough of the golf club's taxation and they thought they had had enough of the bombs and that they had better get back to Richmond. At that moment there was another bomb, I suppose in the Victoria region, for there was a terrific crash. I was glad to say good-bye to my hurrying visitors and I promised to look into their taxation problem.

The next day I went down to the House with the Prime Minister. There were many alerts and, to make matters worse, there was a very heavy thunderstorm. I must say the P.M. took all that in his stride and seemed very cool and collected. He was like a rock and that was what he appeared to be to the British people. His strong bulldog look was an inspiration to the public.

One morning the Prime Minister summoned me to the Annexe. He was still in his dressing-gown and looked as broad as he was long. He said, 'What is all this about the people getting windy with the doodle-bugs? I want you to keep your eyes and ears open as to what the reactions are and let me know. Personally I think it is all balls.' A doodle-bug went over as we were talking, making a great noise. We had to stop speaking until it got out of earshot. We didn't hear it explode. If you were in the park or in the country you could see the flight of the bomb, but in London they seemed to arrive suddenly over the buildings. Sometimes you could see the crash but at other times you just heard the explosion.

At the House there was an interesting Debate on the Ministry of Information. Brendan Bracken, the Minister in Charge, was in bright and breezy form. Speech after speech was in praise of the Minister, who spoke brilliantly, both at the beginning and at the end of the Debate. Brendan did not have to speak often in the House, but when he did it was obvious that he was a natural House of Commons man. It was summed up by Sir Edward Grigg who characterised the opening speech as one which lacked the usual Front Bench verbiage and was a model of lucidity and direction, having at the same time a considerable fund of humour. Brendan had undoubtedly been a great success in that most difficult position.

In July 1944 I was asked by Stanley Christopherson, then Chairman of the Midland Bank, to lunch in the Chairman's private dining room to meet a Mr. Robert Annan and a Mr. Geike. Annan was Chairman of Consolidated Gold Fields—a Scot from Lanarkshire and a mining engineer. Geike was also a Scot and a mining engineer. The Chief General Manager of the Bank, Mr. Clarence Sadd, was also present.

I knew I hadn't been asked for my good looks but little did I think that this meeting was going to influence the rest of my life and change its direction. Twice during lunch we had to get under the table because of doodle-bugs. They seemed to be flying over all the time. The lunch was excellent and I suppose I must have created a favourable impression, for there was a very very important sequel for me later on.

In the evening I gave a dinner party at the Savoy and my guests were Sir Alfred Munnings, P.R.A., Sir William Reid Dick, Lord McGowan, Arthur Greig, brother of Sir Louis Greig, Maurice Codner, Geoffrey Lloyd and James Stuart. Despite the bombs we had a merry party. Reid Dick wanted to go to the loo but, instead of opening the door, he tried to get out of the window, whereupon James Stuart dashed after him and escorted him to the proper place. He then saw him to a taxi. By that time Reid Dick had thanked James Stuart and took a sixpence and a shilling out of his pocket and looked at the coins carefully. However, his Scottish instinct prevailing, he gave James a sixpence for his trouble.

At that time the Prime Minister felt it necessary to make a statement in the House about the doodle-bugs in view of the apprehension felt by people living on the south-east coast and in the area of the approach air space to London. There were many supplementary questions which made him impatient and, to crown all, the police made his car go to another entrance. He was furious. Such a thing had never happened to him before.

There were now more functions being held in the constituencies as the British armies did better on all fronts. I went to the Mayoral lunch at Barnes to the 'Salute the Soldier' Campaign. I, of course, had to speak and I got an extremely friendly welcome. The next day I told the P.M. about the march past and how a flying bomb went over, fortunately going far from us, and our large crowd, and how steady and calm the people were. He grunted and said that it was a bit late for them to do anything about it.

From the conversations I was having with the top soldiers there seemed to be a growing optimism that the war could be over by Christmas 1944. It seemed too good to be true. I did know about the plans for a battle at Arnhem. Nevertheless there was an odd optimism about and many of the soldiers were in a curiously excitable state. Alas the battle, though so nearly won, just slipped through our grip and the war continued. Those who knew something about the possibilities were very disappointed.

I accompanied the P.M. to the Dorchester for a Conservative lunch. The lunch passed off well and the P.M. spoke in good form. In the car going back to No. 10 Winston said to me he could always resign from the Leadership, but while he was Leader it was a good thing for him to meet the Tory Members. He was in another of his critical moods against the Tories and what happened at Munich. He said he might well resign before the election and criticised Baldwin because of his disastrous tactics at the 1935 election and on delay in rearmament; he was a great deal to blame for the position in 1939–41. This was very unfair criticism and I thought he ought by this time to have got over it. If Baldwin was responsible for even a modicum of rearmament in 1935 the Socialists didn't think it was anything but full-scale rearmament. In my constituency in Keighley in 1935 I lost my seat by a few hundred votes and lost on the Socialist claim in their posters that 'a vote for Watt was a vote for War'. Many Conservatives lost their seats on that issue. With that reaction Baldwin could not have been doing anything else but pushing for the rearmament of the country.

The doodle-bug was still flying. The 3rd August 1944 was one of the worst days we had. The P.M. made his big speech in the Commons on the developments in Europe. He was magnificent. It was one of his best speeches. The House then rose for the Summer Recess.

My family spent their summer holiday at a little seaside place in Fife called Elie. They had been there in 1943 and liked it so much that we bought a house there late in 1944 with entry in the Spring of 1945; it was to become our home where our family was brought up.

On my return to London my usual routine began again. This time there was a different atmosphere. Victory was in the air, although there were still some months to go. I lunched at the Reform Club. One of the senior Liberal leaders paid me a very high compliment. It was Sir Percy Harris, who said I had been a great success as P.P.S. to the Prime Minister, that I was a good mixer and that Winston could not have been better served. I was naturally pleased at these complimentary

Dominion Visitors

comments, for my job was certainly not a sinecure and was open to all to make kind and unkind comments. I couldn't please everybody.

However, as the autumn months passed, although the military news grew better, we had still to contend with the V2 bomb. If you heard them coming you were all right. If you didn't, you were dead. The first of these V2 bombs were not publicised in the Press. They were tremendously more powerful than the V1—the doodle-bug.

CHAPTER 16

The Yalta Debate

I lunched with Hugh Dalton, one of the Socialist leaders, who said to me, 'I think I ought to tell you that the Socialist Party will definitely not have a coupon or coalition Government and that they will fight on party lines, although a lot of Socialists would like a coalition to be re-formed after the election. The Socialists are very optimistic that they will gain a lot of seats but they don't think they could gain a complete Socialist victory.' In other words, they wanted it both ways.

When lunching with James Stuart, the Chief Whip, he told me that Tommy Dugdale was again ill. He didn't appear to be very robust. Harold Mitchell later in the day gave me the same information. This was a serious matter for the party. The other party bosses thought he ought to resign since a party machine could not afford to have a Chairman who was not in good health.

The Chief Whip again suggested that I should become the Chairman of the party and thought that I would make a great success of it. I didn't think I was really interested but if I was ordered to I would have to accept, although I would really rather remain as Parliamentary Private Secretary to the Prime Minister. The Chief Whip said that Winston would be delighted if I remained P.P.S. and took on the other job as well. It would be difficult, if not impossible, to do the two jobs. However, the situation did not arise, for Dugdale was better and not going to resign the Chairmanship after all.

Another important political matter we discussed at that time was the question of financing the Conservative Party through industrial resources and beginning to prepare for a General Election. At that time a General Election seemed a long time away but this was all part of the change that was taking place in the thinking of the time.

With all the rumours of the early ending of the war, my constituents were beginning to agitate for more events in the constituency. I went down to Richmond and met General and Mrs. Nation. He was in the House of Commons with me in the 1931 Parliament and she was the Chairwoman of my Party Association Women's Section. I met the members of the Women's Branch of the Party. The Nations gave a cocktail party for me to meet the leaders of the Association—a very good party and helpful.

The Debate on the war and the international situation was the best that the House had had for a long time. The House was really in good form and the speeches were on a high level. The Prime Minister made an excellent speech, although there were some criticism of the procedure of dividing a big speech into two parts.

The critics of this procedure thought that it spread out the speech too much and that it was difficult when it came to the second part for the P.M. to recapture the House. The first day's Debate tended to concentrate on the Polish-Russian problem, whereas the second day tended to deal more with the treatment of Germany after the war. Aneurin Bevan, the Socialist orator, thought the political and psychological warfare of the Government against Germany had been deplorable and it was because of this that the Germans were now fighting like tigers.

At the House I stood the P.M. and the Chancellor of the Exchequer a drink but the P.M. made Collins, the Smoke Room waiter, give me back my money and said, 'I must stand Harvie a drink,' which I accepted although he often did that and I felt I should pay my whack as well. He was a generous man in every way. He often lost his temper and cursed some of the Members, but after a short time if he was still in the House he would ask me to find the Member and bring him along to the Smoke Room for a chat and or a drink to make it up.

The P.M. was at the House for a quite exciting day on the Compensation Clauses of the Town and Country Planning Bill and intervened in the Debate. On the Socialist side it was felt that the P.M's intervention had given them a heaven-sent piece of ammunition for their party propaganda and that they could now say that the clauses were withdrawn by him under the pressure of vested interests. I had no doubt that the Socialist Party would make use of that argument to the full. On the Conservative side, feelings were somewhat mixed. Some Tory reformers thought it was a pity that he intervened at all or that the clauses were withdrawn. They were certain that the Government could have had the clauses as they stood, with only a small minority against in the Division Lobby. The general feeling of the Tory Members, however, was that the action of the Government was wise, although there was some doubt as to why the P.M. had to deal with the matter and not the Leader of the House.

I had a drink with the P.M. afterwards when he said that scenes in the House gave it prestige and standing, for it drew attention to its affairs. He personally loved to be the centre of rows, for he was so good at dealing with the hecklers.

The next day I developed a very sore throat with a croak and hoped I was not sickening for something because the P.M. was just back from his visit to Russia and wanted me to put him in the political picture as to what had happened while he was away. He seemed very vigorous and stimulated by his visit. He talked about it a lot and it appeared to have been a great success.

He also reverted to the Town and Country Planning Bill and said if some Tories voted against the Bill then he would resign the leadership. Not a very fair threat, for if he was not the Leader of the Conservative Party I couldn't see them winning the next election and he knew that. The Socialists would be returned and he certainly would have no place in their Government. At the moment I was a bit fed up with my job. Three years was a long time to work for a prima donna, no matter how brilliant and entertaining he might be.

It was felt that we should now begin to have a series of meetings in the constituency—not party meetings, while there was still a National Coalition, but rather social meetings of a non-party kind which I could attend. We certainly had to stir the electorate, for I was sure that as soon as the war was over

5   The PM on his return from one of his many overseas journeys. Behind him, Herbert Morrison; behind Mrs Churchill, Lord Woolton

6 Welcome home. Leo Amery, Herbert Morrison, Author, Anthony Eden, Oliver Lyttelton, Clement Attlee, the PM, Mrs Churchill

there would be a General Election and almost certainly on party lines.

On Sunday 5th November I attended a crowded meeting in Richmond in honour of the Home Guard. It was now felt that the Home Guard should stand down as the emergency and the danger of invasion had passed. I had to make the speech on behalf of the people of Richmond and then I took the salute at the final march past through the main street of the Borough. The pavements were crowded and the men marched like the Brigade of Guards. What a contrast to the early days when the men didn't even have rifles! Incidentally, I was touched by the generous reception I was given by the crowds, both inside the Hall and out.

I had the first of my arranged meetings in Richmond on 8th November. Colonel Bromhead was in the Chair supported by the Chairwoman of the Women's Association. There was an audience of well over three hundred, which was quite good at any time for a political meeting in Richmond. I spoke for about half an hour, the basic subject being to prepare for the General Election. It seemed to go down well. There were quite a number of questions, largely about coalition or party elections. It was too early to say anything about it. My own feeling had been that we ought to have a coalition government after the war but I knew the Socialists wouldn't want that.

After the meeting the senior office-bearers had dinner at the Castle Restaurant and it was quite a reunion. The next day I went to the mayor-making of the Borough of Barnes. Richmond and Barnes were the two Boroughs in the Richmond Parliamentary Division, each with a Mayor and Council and really two of everything, which meant lots of duplication of work for the M.P.

On the evening of 14th November the P.M. returned from a visit to France. Shortly afterwards I had a long talk with him on his recent appointments. He was sensitive to public feeling about the appointment of Duncan Sandys who had never been a popular personality in the House. He seemed aloof. To be universally popular in the House would be impossible. Duncan didn't seem to go out of his way to be friendly but I must say I always got on quite well with him. The P.M. also talked about bringing into the Government all the Members who had been decorated. It sounded a good thing to do but gallantry didn't necessarily go with a good brain and an interest in politics. It also seemed to be too much of a gimmick.

I had now re-started my At Homes in the constituency. I put an advertisement in the local paper to the effect that I would be in my constituency offices on a certain day and at a certain time. I had done this since I was first elected to Parliament, first at Keighley and then at Richmond. In my advertisement I invited anyone with problems to come and see me. Sometimes I got only a handful of people and at other times I had dozens of people with problems—housing, political questions, and personal problems. I stayed the night in the constituency with my Chairman. The next day I attended a church service with the Mayor of Barnes. I then took the salute at a march past of the local Defence Services.

I hadn't been feeling very well for some time so finally I went to see a doctor who had been recommended to me. He gave me a thorough examination and told me I had a tired heart, I had low blood pressure, I had a cold in the chest, a temperature and was suffering from depression. After all that I felt even more depressed. Next, another doctor came to see me and gave me a thorough examination but I still had to stay in bed.

Fortunately I was in the No. 10 Annexe so the Private Secretaries came to see me and helped to cheer me up. But I missed the dinner at No. 10 on the opening of the new Session of Parliament. To make matters worse my wife rang me to say that none of the family was well. They had all had bad colds. However, after a week I was able to get up and go out.

James Stuart picked me up at the Annexe to go to White's Club for drinks with Lord Rosebery. We then went on with Arthur Greig to the Dorchester to our St. Andrew's Night Dinner. The others present were Lord McGowan, Sir Andrew Duncan, Sir Alex Fleming of penicillin fame, Sir William Douglas, David Maxwell-Fyfe, Sir Andrew Agnew, Alan McDiarmid and McWhirter of the *Daily Mail*. It was a good evening and I was none the worse.

I say a good evening, but while we were having drinks my

wife 'phoned to tell me my daughter Rachel was seriously ill and that Professor McNeil of Edinburgh had been called in. I was obviously looking pretty low when I returned to the party, for Alex Fleming came over and asked me if I had had bad news and I told him the situation. He asked a few questions, then wrote on a piece of paper, handed it to me and told me to go and 'phone my wife and get her to tell me the symptoms of my daughter in answer to the questions on his paper and, if necessary, he would go to Scotland that night to see her. Of course, I did this at once.

Shortly afterwards my wife 'phoned back with the local doctor who was with her. He was an old friend of the family. Alex Fleming took the message which answered his questions and said to me that my daughter would be all right now. She was over the worst but if she was not better I had to let him know at once and he would go up to Scotland himself. I was amazed and terribly impressed by this great-hearted and sympathetic friend. Actually I had to see him in a professional capacity before many months had passed. I was glad to get to bed that night but cheered by the encouragement of so many of my Scottish friends.

I was back in No. 10 in the Mess on the Saturday night and the news from Scotland was good so I mended quickly. I continued to feel a bit groggy for a while but I was glad to be in harness again and back to the old routine of receiving visitors from all parties, learning what they had to say about this and that, about the war and Parliament and the squabbles that went on, and all the undercurrents.

But then a set-back. I visited the doctor again and he thought I should have another heart test—a bit depressing. However, I was going with the P.M. to dinner at the Dorchester for some sixteen M.Ps. The P.M. had now met nearly all his back bench Tory M.Ps and most of the Junior Ministers of all parties in this way, and some of the more prominent M.Ps more frequently. I had also introduced him to most of the Liberal and Socialist M.Ps. It was an amusing party and the P.M. enjoyed himself. He loved to reminisce on those occasions and, of course, they were enjoyed by everybody. He was most good-humoured and we didn't get away until nearly midnight. Winston smiled easily but he was easily roused to tears or bitterness, sentiment, anger and emotion.

I went down to the House with him the next morning and we had a drink together in the Smoke Room. He was rather down in the dumps that morning.

Later that day the P.M. and Mrs. Churchill received a presentation from the Conservative Members of a print of the House of Commons in 1740 and a black and white miniature of Sarah Jennings, Duchess of Marlborough. Mrs. Churchill made a charming speech, comparing her own qualities with those of Sarah Jennings. The print had come out of the old House before it was destroyed. Winston said about the print, 'There is the old gal. She started them all and will see the end of them all.'

The P.M. and I went to a dinner party at Claridges with the Liberal Nationals, Sir Frederick Hamilton, Lord Rosebery, Lord Teviot, Alec Beecham, Bill Mabane and Lord Hutchison of Montrose. This was an excellent meeting for the Liberal Nationalists, although there were not many of them in the Commons. They seemed to be neglected except, of course, for the fact that they had quite a few Members in the Government. The joke used to be that to become a Liberal Nationalist was the quickest way to the House of Lords or the Government.

Speaking of honours and promotion, I told Winston how a taxi driver who dropped me at No. 10 one day had asked, 'Why doesn't the P.M. get a reward when other people get knighthoods and other honours?' I said, 'What would you give the P.M.?' He answered, 'I would give him a knighthood.' The P.M. was most amused.

My last medical appointment of the year was in Harley Street for a medical check-up. A cardiograph of my heart was taken and also an X-ray. Thank God there was nothing organically wrong. I was delighted, for this malaise had been hanging over me for too long.

I then went down to the House with Winston for his last Question of the year. He wasn't in very good form. Afterwards we had a Christmas drink in the Smoke Room. That night I went up to Scotland for Christmas and Hogmanay. What would

1945 have in store for us? Peace later in the year, of that I was certain.

The first speech in the House by the P.M. in the New Year was thought by many to be the best he had made since 1940. The majority of the House felt that his references to Greece should put this whole question in its proper perspective and that it ought to have a sobering effect on the critics in the country. The Conservative Party and the National Liberals were behind the Government to a man on this issue, as were also most of the trade unionists in the House.

It was really what Quintin Hogg, afterwards Lord Hailsham, called the 'lunatic fringe' which produced the criticism. It was interesting to note that the same people who were critical about Greece had been critical of Winston and the Government on every big issue in the last three and a half years. Stokes and Seymour-Hicks made the most violent speeches against the Government's policy. Stokes said we went into Greece because we expected a coup by E.A.M. and we wanted to forestall it, and that we were endeavouring to prevent the Russians getting a foothold in the Mediterranean. He said it was time the Government stood up to Russia and that the situation in Greece had not been helped by the P.M's speech.

Lipson, the Independent Member for Cheltenham, made a particularly poisonous speech. He said on previous occasions that the P.M. had spoken as a great national leader but the first part of his speech this time was that of a partisan. There was a strong feeling on the Conservative side that Lipson should be opposed at the next election. I told the Prime Minister that I would be quite prepared to take this contest myself. The P.M. discussed this point with me but we decided to wait and see how things went in the next few months.

Jim Griffiths, in winding-up for the Socialists, was also critical. He said the intervention in Greece was similar to the intervention in Russia in 1920 after World War I. Aneurin Bevan made the most vitriolic speech of all. He said that he hoped the P.M. would make a conciliatory speech and not a swashbuckling one which might well result in more British lives being lost. He said we ought not to run away from our responsibilities behind this barrage about atrocities. He also said that there was nobody more capable of distorting facts than the P.M. and that there was a parallel between his speeches today and those of 1920. The P.M. wrote in red ink on my report that he wanted to speak to me about it. He also said that Mrs. Churchill wanted to see it and he wrote in red ink 'Thank you very much', initialled W.S.C. This was becoming a regular occurrence. He seemed to find my reports helpful. He often congratulated me personally on them.

At that time I was continuing my series of dinners for Junior Ministers and M.Ps who often didn't have an opportunity to meet senior Ministers on a social occasion. I entertained Lord Swinton, Sir Reginald Blair and Sir Walter Smiles. The last was a descendant of Samuel Smiles who wrote the famous *Self Help*. Unfortunately Sir Walter Smiles, who represented an Ulster seat, was drowned a few years later in a ferry boat disaster on its way to Belfast. I had walked with him through the Division Lobby that afternoon. His death in this way came as a great shock to the House and to me, for I must have been the last M.P. to speak to him.

It was now clear that the war would be over in a matter of months and there was an agitation to have consituency agents released from the services so that they could get the party machines going again in preparation for the General Election which would follow after the cessation of the fighting. Jock Colville, who was one of the Private Secretaries when I first went to No. 10 in 1941, was back again after a long spell in the Air Force. He was a first-class member of the senior staff at No. 10.

A most interesting engagement I fulfilled at that time was to spend a week-end with an excellent Member, Sir William Brass. He was an amazing man, for during practically the whole of the war he gave week-end parties to young service men from the Dominions. He would invite four or six at a time. They would go for two nights. He would feed and rest them well, then have a small gamble on the last night at which he staked them so that they didn't lose any money but could win. He would photograph them before they left on the Monday morning. Later he would write to their parents a nice friendly letter and send them a photo. He had masses of letters

The Yalta Debate

in return from the boys and from their parents. It was a unique way of keeping the home fires burning and helping the young soldiers from the Dominions and the colonies.

The P.M. had returned from the Yalta Conference. All the Cabinet and the Chiefs of Staff assembled to greet him. He was dressed as an Air Commodore. He looked very fit and sunburnt. He was most friendly and thanked me for my excellent reports. He felt he had been kept fully informed about what was happening in Parliament.

I went to the Commons with the P.M. for Questions. He was most benign. The cheering was not so loud as on previous returns from abroad, and Anthony Eden got very little except from the Tory reformers who, as one M.P. put it, looked like a lot of bitches in heat.

James Stuart, the Chief Whip, and I had several talks to discuss the mood of the House. There were a lot of little groups in all the parties, each jockeying for power and I could see this would get worse as the war came to an end. The P.M. was very shrewd. He had sensed the atmosphere and had talks with me about my reports. Every day he would come down to the House with me and go to the Smoke Room. He spoke to all sorts of Members to try to break down any criticism before next week's big Debate in the House.

The House was delighted to welcome Winston back. The general opinion was that Members had not seen him looking so well or in such obvious good spirits for some time. His visits to the Smoke Room had an excellent effect on the Tory Members, who were inclined to be critical of the Polish part of the Crimean Agreement. Much of the heated criticism had died down. Many Members, who were at first critical, had decided to support the Government. Gallacher, the Communist, thought the P.M. had done a grand job and would support him. I had spent a good deal of my time in the Smoke Room myself this week, talking to the critics in all the parties. Members thought that the decision to have a three-day Debate was a good one. It would give Members ample opportunity to express their views on what they felt was the biggest event since the war began.

At the Conservative Members Committee the Whip announced that a motion would be put down by the Government for next week's Crimea Conference Debate and that the matter would be treated as a Vote of Confidence. There was still a lot of feeling on this issue but the majority opinion was that there should be no attack on, or criticism of, the Russians. Some Members hoped very much that a motion amounting to a Vote of Confidence would not be put down, for in all the darkest hours of the war the Conservative Party formed the strongest support for the Government and it would be most unfortunate if a Division was forced now when it would tend to split the Tory Party.

On Tuesday, 27th February, the big Debate on the Yalta Conference began. The P.M. made a good speech but when Lord Dunglass interrupted to ask a question the P.M. was rather annoyed and showed it. However, he reluctantly gave way. When Andrew McLaren and other Socialists interrupted he was most gracious and gave way. He seemed amazed by the Conservative Party's opposition on the Polish proposals. It was one of the best Debates I had ever heard in the House of Commons. The speeches were all of a high standard. Victor Raikes, Dunglass, Eden and Petherick all made good speeches.

The P.M. sat talking in the Smoke Room a long time after the Debate. I had great difficulty in getting him away as he was basking in the adulation, but he was dining that evening at Buckingham Palace and he could not be late. I had to remind him several times. He gazed at me with baleful eyes.

Finally I got him away and in the Lobby he asked me why I was in such a hurry. 'I have been indiscreet, is that it?' I said, 'No, but you are to be at the Palace for dinner and the time is getting short.' He gave me his usual grunt and said he knew and he would be there on time.

During the last day of the big Debate in the House I had a long talk with the P.M., first of all in the Smoke Room and then in his own room at the House. Harry Strauss, a Conservative Junior Minister, had resigned from the Government. Winston said he was a nice fellow but events would prove him wrong.

I asked Winston if he thought Stalin had a sense of humour.

The Yalta Debate

He said, 'Yes. At Moscow I proposed the health of the Proletariat. There was a lot to drink and vodka was in generous supply. Stalin was a good drinker and during an interval he got up and proposed the health of the Carlton Club.' Winston said Stalin must have been told it was the headquarters of the Conservative Party.

During the last phases of the war there was some wordy conflict in the House about Education Officers lecturing to the troops regarding affairs at home and about the issue of pamphlets to the troops for discussion with Education Officers. When the proposal was first made by David Margesson, Secretary of State and afterwards Lord Margesson, there was a veritable outcry among Conservatives and many Liberal Members. Although Margesson was in favour of this proposal, I had a feeling he had allowed himself to be talked into it and was not very keen to bring it before the Prime Minister.

Margesson suggested that I should test the climate by sounding out the P.M's reaction. I did so, whereupon the P.M. nearly exploded. The troops were abroad to fight and win the war and not to attend lectures and discussions about home affairs. Such a thing was bound to affect their morale. I thoroughly agreed with the Prime Minister on this issue. I was certain that a lot of left wing views were being propagated in this way.

Winston was hopping mad. Margesson was sent for but he had the backing of the Socialist Members and Ministers, some Liberals and a few Conservatives. Winston finally came round to the proposal, though reluctantly, and I was certain that that decision lost him the 1945 election. In the circumstances I suppose he could not have come to any other conclusion, but he took a long time to calm down, although he muttered and scowled every time he thought of this scheme coming into operation. He was certain it would undermine the political views of the troops. He was right. The Education Officers were bringing theories and ideas from home which, up to that time, the troops had not time to be bothered with. Educational classes were always popular, for you could sit down, get off your feet, and fall into a little doze instead of pursuing the hardier military curriculum. Winston felt the election would get off to a bad start.

I was determined I was going to get off to a good start and I had been going down to Richmond and Barnes fairly frequently. I attended the Finance Committee and dined with my Chairman, who had a small party of leading constituents to meet me. The number of letters from my constituents was growing to more like its pre-war proportions. I also addressed the Rotary Club and a New Forum organised by the Kew Parish Church. I spoke on Parliamentary procedure and then answered questions for half an hour. I didn't get back to No. 10 till after 11 pm. I would have to do this kind of thing every few weeks.

I went home to Scotland for the week-end to attend my daughter's christening at St. David's Church, Bathgate, where I also was christened and worshipped with my parents for many years. My daughter was christened Rachel. A lot of my old friends in the district were present.

The next day was the Conservative Party Conference. I went with the P.M. and Mrs. Churchill. They received a stupendous reception—again rather like an election gathering. The P.M. got great cheers when he was criticising the Socialists about their attacks on the profit motive. He asked what was their alternative. 'I presume the loss motive.' This comment brought the house down.

Since the Party Conference I had been making soundings at Winston's request to find out what Members were saying about his speech. Some Members ranked it with the great orations he had made in 1940. There had been lively speculation in the Lobbies regarding the P.M's comments on what might happen after the Socialist Party left the Government and before the election, and what would happen after the election.

On the right wing of the party there was a feeling that there should be nothing said now about any coalition after the election. There was also some speculation among Socialists who wondered which of their leaders would go with the P.M. in the event of a further coalition and whether any of them had already committed themselves.

On the Army Estimates there was another scene—this time

The Yalta Debate

between P. J. Grigg, Secretary of State for War, and Aneurin Bevan. After a good deal of argument Bevan withdrew. It arose on a brief discussion regarding the necessity for a conscripted army after the war. Bevan thought that that meant we would make preparations for another war and collective security was bound to fail.

P. J. Grigg stated that the country had stood alone with not much help from Bevan. Bevan shouted out that it was a lie. It was quite a lively moment in the House but it soon died down, although it was resumed in the Smoke Room later when there were some bitter exchanges between Grigg and Bevan. For a moment it looked as if they might even come to blows. Fortunately this did not happen.

The war seemed likely to end before long and a lot of the Members were beginning to fuss around me about honours. No political honours had been granted in the war, other than peerages granted when a Minister was required in the Upper House. Since 1939 the political honours list had been pretty well extinct and, on the whole, politicians had not been recognised.

I personally thought it was wrong, for many M.Ps did yeoman service for the nation but were not recognised in the traditional way which had been accepted by the nation for many generations. James Stuart and I discussed the problem, for undoubtedly an Honours List would be published when the war was over and James Stuart, as Chief Whip, would have to play a leading part. We also discussed the question of change of Government. It looked as if we must have a party election, although there was still some talk of carrying on the coalition for a short time after the war to get reconstruction going, demobilisation settled, and other questions resolved before going to the country.

It was on that same night that we heard of the death of Roosevelt. This was a stunning blow. The next day the Prime Minister moved the Adjournment of the House as a token of respect. The death of Roosevelt shocked and stunned the House. Although it was felt that this sad loss affected us all, Members recognised that the P.M. was affected more particularly and were distressed that this personal sorrow should add to his many heavy burdens at the moment.

There were one or two dissident notes raised in the Smoke Room by Bevan, Stokes and Cove. They felt it was absurd to adjourn the House. They asked what would happen if de Gaulle or Gerbrandy or some other national leader were to die and whether we had established a precedent which might prove awkward in the future.

The question which buzzed round the Lobbies and caused more interest at this time than any other was the one of the General Election, coupled with some violent exchanges between Bracken and Bevin. Members tended to feel that the gloves were off and that party politics could again be stressed. Bevin's speech, it was felt by Conservatives, was rather lowdown and despicable in view of the many kindly references which the P.M. had made about him during the time he had been a Member of the War Cabinet.

I must stress here that Aneurin Bevan had been a steady critic of the Government all through the war, whereas Ernest Bevin had been in the War Cabinet for most of it. The Socialists were all trying to pipe down. They were afraid lest there should be an early General Election. They wanted it in the autumn, but not before; the greater the delay the more time they had to spread their poison in an endeavour to discredit the Prime Minister. They thought, and thought rightly, that Churchill was the greatest election asset. Anything that could be done to counteract this asset the better it was from their point of view.

The subject was discussed at the Conservative Members Committee when the general opinion was in favour of an early General Election and that any period of a 'Caretaker' Government should be reduced to the shortest possible time.

That same day in April a Dr. and Mrs. Stark Murray lunched with me at the House. Both were Scots and graduates of my old university, Glasgow. He was to be my Socialist opponent at Richmond when the General Election was fixed, and he was beginning now to nurse the constituency. I liked them both. Nevertheless he looked a tough customer and should be a good candidate, and I would have my hands full. This meeting might help to take the bitterness out of the election in Richmond. So far as I was concerned I had never descended to personalities and I usually got on well with my opponents.

The Yalta Debate

Somehow or other Stark Murray managed to connect his speeches with the Highland Clearances in the eighteenth century—a bit remote from the 1945 General Election.

I did other constituency engagements at the week-end. The first was going with the Mayor and Corporation of Barnes to an R.C. service in aid of Sailors' Week. After the service we went from the church to the church hall and had pints of beer with the priest. I could not imagine anything like that in the Kirk of Scotland. It seemed to me to be a very civilised habit. I then went to Barnes Sports Club and later attended a whist drive in the R.C. hall.

The next day Ralph Assheton, by now Chairman of the Party, told me the P.M. wanted me to vet candidates. The P.M. had mentioned this to me before. It was rather awkward, as I have already explained, because my friend Harold Mitchell, the Deputy Chairman of the Party, did that job. Ralph Assheton said the P.M. had told him that he thought I had very good judgement of men. That was very flattering but it was going to take a lot of time—almost a whole-time job in itself before an election. I was going to be busier than ever at No. 10. I talked it over with Harold Mitchell that evening at Catherine Place. It was a lovely evening and we sat on the flat roof until midnight. He took it all very well and I said we could always discuss the candidates together. He wasn't keen on that and I could well understand why.

On the following day the Roosevelt memorial service was held at St. Paul's Cathedral and later the P.M. paid his tribute in the House of Commons. Beforehand there was a very interesting scene in the House when the first-ever Scottish Nationalist took his seat. His name was McIntyre and he had been elected for Motherwell in Lanarkshire. He didn't look like a brawny Scot but more like a nervous schoolboy. It was an ordeal for him. The P.M. could not make his Roosevelt speech until after the swearing-in of the new Member and he was furious at the delay. However, that was the rule of the House. None the less he made a brilliant speech, as he was bound to do, for he had a great affection for the President. His reception from the House was also enthusiastic.

Each day was now getting even more hectic, because I often

had to deal with the P.M's constituents, as obviously he hadn't the time, and events were moving quickly. There was great excitement in the air, for hopes were now running high that we were nearing the end of the war and that peace was at hand.

I interviewed several possible candidates at Central Office with Harold Mitchell so that I could see the procedure. Next day I would be on my own, when I would interview them at 10 Downing Street. It would mean considerable extra work but it would be interesting. In the afternoon the P.M. asked me about the type of candidates we were getting. He said again he was very sorry that there had to be a party election, or an election at all, as he had received such loyal help from all parties. He had certainly had a comparatively easy time from the party political point of view but it couldn't go on for ever and the Socialists were determined to fight on their own.

The next day I went with the P.M. and his daughter, Diana Sandys, to the Press Gallery lunch at the House of Commons. It was a dull, long-drawn-out affair. Lady Astor made an ass of herself and Winston got very red in the face, a sure sign he was indeed angry. She told a story of how when she first got into the House of Commons she asked Winston why he was cruel to her and he had said, 'I feel as if I have been caught by a woman in the bathroom, naked and with only a sponge to protect me.' It went down at the lunch as a good joke, but Winston didn't think so. However, he recovered enough to make a fine speech and paid high tribute to the Press Gallery of the House.

There were many Members anxious to go on the delegation to see the horrors of the concentration camps. The names selected, however, did not seem to be widely approved. Probably no selection would have been universally accepted but it was felt that a stronger team could have been chosen, consisting of more Members who had some ability to sift evidence. The House, however, approved of a delegation going out. The representatives were deeply impressed and horrified by what they saw. Ernest Bevin was asked if it would not be possible for further delegations to be sent from the House, and promised to pass that suggestion to the Prime Minister.

I'm bound to say I had no desire to go and see the horrors.

I knew, in particular, two people who went—Sir Archibald Southby, who never seemed the same again, and Mavis Tate, a well-known woman M.P. of a number of years standing. Mavis, whom I knew quite well, rang me up one morning at No. 10 and asked if I could dine with her that night as she felt depressed and low after what she had seen in the horror camps. She had felt quite sick the whole time she was on the delegation. I replied that I simply couldn't get out of my other engagement. It was a political one. She seemed to be in a terrible state. She said she must speak to somebody and besought me to come. I was very sorry but there was no way in which I could manage it. I could hear her sobbing as she said good-bye. The next day I was horrified to learn she had committed suicide. I have regretted ever since that I didn't go and see her. The question of suicide never entered my mind and my mere presence might have been some comfort and prevented her from taking that fatal step.

By the last few days in April and the first few days in May there had been much suppressed excitement over the war news. People were beginning to assume that it was nearly over. There had also been a rush of prospective candidates for interview. Most of them were colonels and brigadiers, or at any rate officers, and all wanted safe seats. I used to put them through a mild cross-examination about their careers and experience in politics, if any. Usually they had no experience at all, some because they were too young to have gained political experience, but even the older applicants had little or no political work behind them.

I always asked them if they had had any local government experience. The answer was invariably no, and of course none of them had much chance to have fought local elections, let alone Parliamentary elections. I used to say to a lot of those men, 'Then as you have no political knowledge, perhaps you would like to fight Aneurin Bevan, the left-wing Socialist Member? That experience would give you a real background to what a political career and elections are all about.' However, none of them wanted hopeless seats.

They expected, with no political experience at all, to get a reasonably safe seat because they had rank or title and inherited wealth; they believed that those attributes alone would qualify them to fight and pay for a safe parliamentary seat. I'm afraid I made myself unpopular with a lot of them; many, if not in 1945, found their way into the House in the elections in 1950 and later, and of course they didn't really want to know me.

Winston frequently asked me about the type of candidate that was coming forward. He said, 'Brigadiers and colonels are all right in small doses and you were a brigadier when you became my P.P.S. in 1941.' 'Yes,' I replied, 'but I had already been fifteen years in politics and ten years in the House.' Churchill often asked if there were no decent intelligent sergeants and corporals who could become Conservative candidates. That would make them popular with their constituents and they could always shout down their critics.

I had just got back to my room when the 'phone rang. A voice I hadn't heard for years spoke. It was J. H. Thomas, who had been an important Socialist Cabinet Minister and who spilled the beans about a Budget secret on the question of a tax on tea. He got the tip on the golf course from his partner, who was also an M.P. and also in the know. He said significantly to Jimmy Thomas, 'Tee up.' He took the tip and ruined his career. I always felt sorry for him as he had come up the hard way from the humblest beginnings to Cabinet rank. His son Leslie later became a Conservative M.P.

However, to revert to the telephone call. Thomas, being a Cockney, dropped his aitches so he called me "Arvie, 'ow are you? I want to see the P.M. about the election. I'm staying at Paddington. The railways are in a bloody mess.' I told him I would tell Winston. The P.M. was in a perky mood and agreeable and I made the arrangement for the two to meet. Winston much enjoyed his talk with his old friend.

7 V.E. Day. Churchill and Author on way to House of Commons

ACK-ACK

BRITAIN'S DEFENCE AGAINST AIR ATTACK
DURING THE SECOND WORLD WAR

by

GENERAL SIR FREDERICK PILE
G.C.B. D.S.O. M.C.

*General Officer Commanding-in Chief
Anti-Aircraft Command 1939-45*

> To Brigadier Sir George Hamer-W who served in Acti Aick before and during the War and was one of its first Territorial soldier to reach the rank of Brigadier. It was due to him and his likes that this story could be written.
>
> F. A. Pile

GEORGE G. HARRAP & CO. LTD
LONDON   SYDNEY   TORONTO   BOMBAY

Title page inscription by Frederick Pile

Chapter 17

Coalition Break-up

After I had dined with the P.M. one evening in March 1945, he had spoken hopefully of early victory over Germany. I said that it looked as if his big task of winning the war was nearly over. He replied, 'Yes, but the biggest task has yet to come.'

He didn't like dissolving the coalition and going back to party politics. He was sorry there was going to be a bitter party election as he had received such loyal help and support from all parties.

That was no empty expression of opinion encouraged by the friendly atmosphere of a pleasant social occasion. The P.M. said to me that he disliked the idea of an election. 'People who have grown to love me,' he explained, 'will grow to hate me and that will hurt me.' That was a regular theme of Winston's.

Churchill dreaded more than anything else the bitterness which might follow a return to the old rivalry and bickering of the political market place. That was the topic of conversation as we drove away from the Savoy back to No. 10 Downing Street.

Our task, he said to me, was to secure a return to normal life as easily and as happily as we could. All the human strands in the complex fabric of our nation, organised for fighting, had to be unravelled and woven anew into that of a nation organised for economic production and civil process. He also insisted that the return to normality must be something more than a return to pre-war conditions.

'The social and economic problems,' he continued, 'are immensely urgent. The action needed is without parallel. Our machinery of government, however, has never had to tackle anything like it before. That is why the parties should continue to work together as they have done since 1940. We have been good colleagues and we have been happy to co-operate.

The partnership has been a successful one. Why dissolve it now?'

The normal practice after those dinner parties was for us to travel together to the Annexe. There we usually parted. Sometimes I slept in the Annexe, where I had a room, but more often I walked the half-mile to the house in Catherine Place.

'Where are you sleeping tonight, Harvie?' the P.M. asked me as we turned out of Whitehall. I replied, 'Catherine Place,' with some surprise as he had never put such a question to me before. Then, addressing the chauffeur, he ordered him to drive straight into the park. 'I'm taking the Brigadier home,' he said. There was an uneasy silence. I did not know what to make of it as we passed down Birdcage Walk. Obviously the P.M. was wrestling with some problem and perhaps he wanted to talk to me about it. Knowing him, I waited for him to speak.

'Stop,' he called to the driver, and we pulled into the side of the roadway in front of the sentry box at Wellington Barracks, near Buckingham Palace. For the next half-hour or more he thought aloud, occasionally inviting my comments. There, in the darkness of the black-out, we discussed the political future of the country. It was a strange place and an odd moment for such a purpose. We might have had the talk in the privacy and comfort of the Cabinet Room at Downing Street, or in the Annexe in Great George Street. He preferred the stillness of that quiet Spring evening in St. James's Park where there was nothing to suggest that one of the great triumvirate of World War II was consulting a humble member of his staff about an important decision which would profoundly affect the political future of Britain.

Naturally I was flattered by the attention he paid to my views, which I knew were shared by most of the Tory supporters of the Government at Westminster. Part of my duties as his Parliamentary Private Secretary was to report trends and keep him informed of reactions to policy.

'Our friends,' I began, 'think that you are mistaken in your desire to prolong the coalition.' He interrupted, 'Why?' 'Because the Socialists would let you and us down.' I went on, 'They are only paying lip service to the need for co-operation now and are working like beavers to undermine the Tory Party in the constituencies. That is why we believe that the longer an election is delayed the greater is the chance of an overwhelming defeat.' He said, 'Is that view widely held?' I replied, 'I am afraid it is.'

It was clear to me that Churchill did not appreciate the extent to which the Socialist propaganda had been directed against continued co-operation. He had been too busy winning the war to give time to such a domestic party matter.

'I've always known that there is little gratitude in politics,' he said, 'but it is shabby to treat the Tory Party like that. It has been the rock and the bastion of the war effort.' There was a pause during which he seemed to reach a decision. His voice was firmer when he resumed talking.

'The Tory Party gave me its full support when I became Prime Minister in 1940.' He added, 'I must do something for it now.' There and then he seemed to dedicate himself anew to the task of mobilising support for the party which he hoped to make the instrument for the betterment of mankind. He had recently passed the psalmist's allotted span of three score years and ten and could have retired with all the honour he had won. Instead he chose to spurn the slippered ease, for further public service.

I referred to the mistake Lloyd-George made in staying on after his great victory was completed, and pointed out that Churchill was an older man than L.G. had been at that time. 'Why should I not be Prime Minister after I am seventy?' asked Churchill. 'Gladstone was called to office when he was over eighty.'

As we talked there in the darkness he could not conceal the disappointment caused by the growing eagerness of the left for a contest in the constituencies. Several times he claimed that, even at that hour, the co-operation of the three parties within the Government itself was a complete success, so much so that a division on party lines was almost unknown in its councils.

The failure was in the constituencies where the Socialist Party machinery proved steadily intractable to coalition requirements. As long, therefore, as an appeal to the constituencies was remote the coalition was safe. Anything which brought an election nearer endangered it.

Nothing that had happened had made the Prime Minister change his view that there should be a three-year period of tranquillity from party strife after the struggle with Hitler. That would provide an opportunity for the country to settle down after the great strain of the war years. There was support for that view in other quarters. The Sinclair Liberals would have agreed if the Socialists had been willing at that time. Even Ernest Bevin had no great desire to precipitate a domestic upheaval.

The Tories were at a considerable disadvantage. Their organisation, both national and regional, had been allowed to run down. Most of the staff were on war service, while the Socialist machine had been kept together through trade union branches and was in good trim for any sudden call. In consequence, the idea of an election did not at all perturb our opponents, who appreciated the poor state of the Tory machine and hoped to profit by it.

My own views were that the Tory machine could not be efficient for some time and, in the interval, required a great deal of preparation. The Labour Party organisation could be further improved, but they were ready.

The handicap seemed so great that we could not have got over it for a long time. On balance, I thought it better to fight at once with whatever resources we had than give our opponents time in which to make the odds heavier against us.

Churchill was well aware of our unpreparedness and was anxious about it. We agreed, as we sat in the car, that the necessary steps would be taken quickly to improve the position. An election moreover must be fought on something. He was confident that his Government's record in domestic affairs and the prestige acquired in the conduct of the war would stand our party in good stead and that whenever the election came it would return stronger and safer electorally than any other combination of parties.

The nation wanted peace at home and, above all, a settlement abroad, he said. These could best be assured by the return of the Tory Party. The Socialist devotion to peace was no greater than his and the Socialist Party was a class party while ours sought to represent all that was best in the nation and its life.

How wrong his judgment was proved to be. He failed at that moment to understand the insidious form the Socialist propaganda took. It aimed at showing that the Prime Minister was out to destroy the Socialist Party by the creation of a Centre Party which, by including progressively-minded men and women, would attract from the Socialist ranks those willing to co-operate in a National Government—shades of 1931. Any such movement had to be nipped in the bud. It had taken the Socialists a long time to recover from the secession of Ramsay MacDonald and his friends, and the Transport House caucus was determined at all costs to avoid a recurrence of a further schism. It was that fear more than anything else which precipitated the break-up of the first Churchill Government.

There was no doubt, from our talk that evening, about Churchill's vision of the Britain which he desired should emerge from the war and of the part the Tories should play in its realisation. If he could not have the co-operation of the other parties then he must lead the Tories alone along the path which he saw clearly marked. Socialists have often called him a reactionary. More accurately he should be described as a practical visionary—a man who was full of ideas and then set out to give them substance.

After he had pictured the happier Britian he wanted to see and hoped the Tory Party would work for, he started asking what I thought about it. When I first became P.P.S. in 1941 I was told he was an extremely difficult man to work with and hard to please. Well, he was all that. Why shouldn't he be, with the great burden he was carrying? But he often asked my views on Parliamentary and political affairs. Sometimes he made comments and sometimes just grunted. There were a lot of grunts that night.

Our conversation ended. He told the chauffeur to drop me at my house in Catherine Place. That night I'm bound to say I got little sleep. My mind was too active. I thought of that talk with the greatest figure of the day and what might be the turning point in Britain's history and of my four years' association with him.

I was so impressed by my talk with the Prime Minister that I decided to send him a note on the forthcoming election. This was in early May. My note, which I give below, was entitled, 'General Election'.

'*Prime Minister*

The feeling in the country on this subject is largely in favour of no Election until after the War with Japan is finished. It is felt that, after all, this is the best Government we have had for many years and why should it be broken up when there are still so many problems of a complicated and difficult character to be solved. Those who think otherwise, and they are a considerable minority, mainly consist of Right Wing Tories and a majority of the Socialist Party. The latter think there is a swing to the Left in public opinion and want to take advantage of it.

'In the House of Commons it has come to be considered an irrefutable fact that Parliament cannot be extended beyond this year. It is felt that to postpone the Election beyond November would be difficult, if not impossible. I do not altogether agree with this view. If the Party Leaders could agree on a policy to continue together until after the War with Japan, I feel sure the House could be induced by a large majority to continue its own life for another year, or part of a year, whichever period would suffice to bring the Japanese War to an end.

'If such prolongation could be secured with the Government continuing as it is until the end of the War with Japan I feel sure that this would be the most popular course so far as the country is concerned. Members, however, are inclined to take a different view. They say Parliament is too old already and there could be no justification for its prolongation, and it might be very difficult for the Government to obtain any extension of this Parliament. There is left, therefore, the certainty that there will be a General Election by November. There are two schools of thought—

1. An Autumn Election. The people who favour this are those Members who are not standing again and are there-

fore indifferent to the exact date of the Dissolution, though naturally prefer it to be as late as possible. Also those Conservative Members who think our organisation can be improved in the few months that will be available. The number in this category, who desire a late Election, is dwindling. There is a feeling that the Socialist Party is playing for an Autumn Election in order to raise the necessary funds which they can do by that time, and to perfect their propaganda and organisation in the constituencies. The bulk of the Socialist Party naturally favour the late Election for they feel it is to their advantage to postpone the Dissolution as long as possible.
2. An Election as early as possible. In this group are most of the Conservatives, although there are some who disagree, Left Wing members of the Socialist Party and some Independent Members also favour an early Election. The Conservatives who disagree with this course think that our organisation in the constituencies will be better in the Autumn than in June. This is not a good argument as the Socialist organisation will also be better with each month that passes so that the disparity in organisational matters, if it exists, is likely to continue to November.

'The arguments used in favour of an early Election are—

1. Victory against Germany will be the best electioneering asset.
2. Your popularity, which it is thought is at its height today, will tend to decline from now on—a decline which will be carefully fanned by Socialist propaganda.
3. Socialist candidates are working like beavers, literally beavers, in the constituencies and whatever the Socialist Leaders may be doing and saying in the Cabinet or in talks with you there is no doubt that the electioneering campaign on the Left is in full swing in the constituencies. This makes it difficult for the sitting Conservative Members of Parliament. The seats belonging to the sitting Members are the ones we want to hold and are most likely to retain. But a Member with his parliamentary duties cannot give the same attention to the constituencies as the

Socialist or other Left Wing candidates can. This is even more marked in the cases of Ministers and the Parliamentary Private Secretaries. Delay will accentuate this difficulty.

'The majority Tory feeling is that, if the Socialist Party could be made to leave the Government as soon as possible without appearing to be pushed out, an early Election is the right course. The Socialist Party, it is thought, has already given notice that as soon as the German War is over they will quit the Government.

'This is not strictly speaking accurate. Naturally they will want to leave the Government at their own time and the Conservatives are afraid lest their "own time" will be some date in June or July when it would be too late to have an early Election. This would mean that the Conservative Party and the other people of goodwill towards you and the Party who are going to continue together will be left with a Caretaker Government for three or four months. Such a course would be disastrous. It is felt that there must surely be some way in which you can explain to the country that the authority of the Government is no longer what it should be if you are to carry out the tasks now facing the country. It is most difficult to keep the Government together if the Parties are working and speaking against each other in the constituencies, and that you can surely ask for the Vote of Confidence from the people in order to meet the problems which will arise from International Conferences, War with Japan, domestic difficulties and so forth.'

The Prime Minister thanked me very much for the above observations and at the top of my report he put in red ink, 'L.P.S. to read and return'. The Lord Privy Seal was Lord Beaverbrook. His Private Secretary wrote to Martin, the P.M's Private Secretary; all he said was, 'Lord Beaverbrook asks me to return the attached Minute by Brigadier Harvie-Watt on the General Election which the Prime Minister sent him. Lord Beaverbrook has no comments to make.' I was surprised, for this was the most vital issue at the time and he usually had many caustic comments to make.

At that stage I was seeing candidates every day and I never ceased to be amazed at the men who had such a good conceit of themselves. I felt rather depressed, for if everybody wanted a safe seat—and the so-called cream of the applicants all wanted that—I couldn't think we could do well at an election. All along I had thought it was going to be an election which might not go our way.

All the talk was now about an early election. Many Tory Members were against it. I was in favour because the longer the other side had to spread their poison the worse it would be for the Conservatives. While all this argument was going on, the news filtered through. It was peace at last. It came as something of an anti-climax. Pandemonium and disorder broke out at No. 10. It was like a bear garden, not that I've ever seen one but it was what I imagine it would be like.

On 8th May the P.M. made his historic broadcast from the Cabinet Room. All the staff crowded in the nearby rooms and on the stairs and lobbies. I'd never seen such excitement. Victory celebrations were now the order of the day. There were amazing crowds in the streets of London.

With an escort of mounted police I then drove with the Prime Minister in an open car to the House of Commons through enthusiastic cheering masses. The only open car available was a 14 h.p. Wolseley as used by the police. Two of the detectives in the entourage stood on the running boards, one on either side. Everybody wanted to touch the P.M., and at different places en route a few people tried to jump in the car to pat his back. Naturally we had to keep them off. Nearing Palace Yard a man tried to jump in the car and he landed on my hand and broke a finger. I felt no pain at the time. There was too much excitement. But for the mounted police, we would never have got through into Palace Yard and the Members' Entrance to the House of Commons. The exhilaration was terrific.

It was an impressive scene in the Chamber of the Commons. The House was crowded with cheering Members as Winston took his place behind the Despatch Box. The House then formed up two by two behind the Mace Bearer, the Speaker in full wig and gown, and the Prime Minister. We then walked in procession to St. Margaret's for a Service of Thanksgiving.

Afterwards we processed back to the Commons and slowly dispersed.

I returned with the P.M. to Downing Street and then left for my constituency to take part in a Service of Thanksgiving with the Mayor and Corporation of Richmond. Afterwards I spoke at Sheen at an Anglo-Soviet meeting which had been arranged some time before. My two political opponents were also there, Dr. Stark Murray, the Socialist, and Dr. Gordon, the Liberal. All three of us were Scots.

Next morning I drove to Westminster Hospital to get my finger seen to and put in splints. In the evening my immediate friends in the House, James Stuart, Charles Waterhouse, and Jimmy Edmondson, all of whom had been in the Government, dined at the Carlton Club to celebrate the victory, the end of the war and the four years we had worked together. We had champagne and a very good dinner. It was a grand evening. Jimmy Edmondson was going to the Lords. He well deserved his promotion for all the solid years of work he had carried out in the Whips' Office. We went back to Catherine Place, where Harold Mitchell joined us, and had more drinks. However, all the drink didn't help a toothache and suspected abscess, which I'd had for several days. What a time to have it.

All next day I was at No. 10 spending a lot of time with the P.M. on the Election. I must have looked pretty awful, for after a short time Winston looked at me in astonishment and asked what was the matter with my face, so I told him. He was all solicitude and said, 'My dear boy, you must go to the dentist. I will make arrangements with my dentist, Dr. Wilfrid Fish.' So he rang a Private Secretary and made the appointment there and then. I was most grateful to him since I really was in agony.

That evening, through the milling crowds, I drove up to Cavendish Square and saw Dr. Fish, the P.M's dentist, afterwards Sir Wilfrid Fish. There was also another doctor, who was an anaesthetist, and a nurse. It looked like an operating theatre. They examined me thoroughly then through my agony I heard Dr. Fish say, 'I think we should get Alex over.' I couldn't think who Alex could be. I was tied up with sheets and my jaws ached, and then I saw Alex come in. He was my old friend, Sir Alex Fleming of penicillin fame. At once my Scottish mind began to think of what all this was going to cost. I'd never seen so many top brass doctors or dentists before. Then I subsided under the anaesthetic thinking this was going to cost me a bonnie penny. I hated the suffocating feeling of going under. I had not had any anaesthetic since I had my tonsils out as a small boy.

After it was all over we had a good dram together then Dr. Fish drove me back to the House of Commons. I was most grateful to them all. Dr. Fish and I had another dram and a meal. That evening I caught the night sleeper to Scotland to spend the week-end with my family and returned to London on Tuesday morning. My toothache had gone and I was back to normal.

The Prime Minister wanted to talk over his Junior Ministerial appointments with me and he did also ask me about some of the senior appointments. James Stuart was with us most of the time. I had never been in on a Government-making session before. It was a fascinating experience. The P.M. tried to ring up some of his proposed Ministers but it was difficult to find many of them since they were in trains, so trains had to be stopped and prospective Ministers contacted by telling them to ring up at the next station. The train just had to wait until the P.M. had talked with the proposed appointee. For me it was all very exciting.

We were with him for some hours. Most of the time Winston lay smoking his large cigar, and James Stuart and I sat at the end of the bed. After he had got through his list, he turned to me and said, 'I haven't put you in the new Government, for I have something else in mind for you after the election.' James Stuart was continuing as Chief Whip and I was remaining as Parliamentary Private Secretary to the Prime Minister, but he knew I would like to be Chief Whip so he informed me that after the General Election James Stuart would be made Secretary of State for Scotland and I would be made Chief Whip. There was also some talk between the P.M. and James Stuart that I should be recommended for a baronetcy. At any rate it was no change until after the election. Apparently Anthony Eden had suggested me as Under-Secretary of the Ministry of Economic Warfare at the Foreign Office. I did not want such promotion or any promotion until after the election.

Meanwhile I continued with preparations for my own election at Richmond and was spending more and more time in the constituency. I was no longer vetting the candidates because that job was finished, but there was a mass of political letters coming into No. 10 which I had to cope with.

29th May was the first day of the new Government. There were some sharp exchanges between the P.M., Herbert Morrison and Aneurin Bevan. Electioneering had clearly started. I dined at the House with James Stuart to browse over the reactions and exchange views on the new situation in the House.

CHAPTER 18

The 1945 Election

My wife arrived from Scotland on 1st June. She had had a terrible journey and had to sit up all night. We were going to be staying at the Park Lane Hotel for the duration of the election. Next day she typed the draft of my election address. It wasn't bad. In the afternoon we went down to the constituency, I to attend one of my At Homes and she to open a church bazaar. So we were back together in the political swing.

This was my fourth Parliamentary election. We dined and stayed the night with my constituency Chairman and his wife, Colonel and Mrs. Bromhead. The next morning we attended church at Ham and then returned to London to complete my election address.

I had now started meetings in the constituency and was preparing my speech for the Adoption Meeting on the 14th June. This had to be a good one.

It was a packed meeting and the speech was relayed outside—one of the best meetings I've ever had in Richmond. It was obviously going to be a tough election but I was optimistic.

The next day I lunched with James Stuart, Gil Lloyd-George and Bob Grimston, another Whip. James, as Chief Whip, and I, as P.P.S., were very close in our work and in our friendship. We worked well together but that close co-operation was soon to end, for I had other paths to take. We remained close friends until his early death.

Now for a broad view of the General Election of 1945, one of the most important elections ever held in Britain. Before the war the Conservative party machine was the most efficient of its kind in the country. Its bosses had been carefully chosen and they knew every worthwhile trick in the political game. At the outbreak of war in 1939 the call for manpower was answered immediately and the staff dropped whatever they were doing and flocked to the colours or to other wartime jobs. Many Conservative and Liberal Members were in the Army, Air Force or Navy Reserves. There were over forty Tory Members serving with the Territorial Army. I was one and I was at once mobilised. The old and unfit were often absorbed in other jobs. In a short time only a skeleton staff remained at Conservative Central Office and many area offices ceased to function.

That was as it should be at a time when 'None were for the Party and all were for the State'. Nobody could have complained had the truce been kept, but it was sometimes more honoured in the breach than in the observance by a section of our Socialist opponents who, disregarding the understanding made by their leaders, contested by-elections as they occurred. Naturally the Conservatives were at a great disadvantage in those contests. Their organisation had been allowed to run down while trade union officials, through their branches, were able to maintain the nucleus of their machine which was ready to function as a Socialist party organisation at short notice.

By the late Spring of 1945 it became clear that the coalition could not long survive the end of the war. The Socialists' decision to dissolve it as soon as possible after V.E. Day was no surprise but it was nevertheless a disappointment. No one who appreciated what they stood for grudged them their right to political independence, but that right would not have been infringed if they had waited a little longer. In our view the bases for continuing an honourable and patriotic collaboration between the parties had been fairly laid. It was an abdication of common sense not to try to make the most of them. The Prime Minister desired our national unity in face of the problems of reconstruction similar to our national unity in face of the war problems, and he claimed that the coalition which surmounted the war difficulties could be more safely entrusted with the solution of the difficulties of peace than any alternative Ministry. It is always easy to be wise after the event but I was not alone in the belief that the very difficulties which subsequently arose might have been avoided by a united approach.

There were two main ideas behind the attitude of the Socialists—a personal distrust of the Prime Minister and a belief that they could win a General Election without allies and then rule the country by themselves. Despite those feelings, it was still a fact that if the Prime Minister had been chosen, like the American President, by popular vote Churchill would have been elected by an overwhelming majority. He was still the idol of the nation. Everywhere he went during the election campaign he was hailed with enthusiasm. It was not organised. It overflowed spontaneously.

However bitterly he was attacked he retained a great personal hold on the masses of the people. The man in the street saw in him a leader whose disinterested courage and unfailing resource during crisis after crisis had visibly pulled the nation through. But the public gratitude was not expressed in the ballot box.

Sir John Anderson and Clem Attlee led the Commons to the House of Lords for the Prorogation Speech read by the Lord Chancellor. Members then filed past the Speaker and shook hands with him, many for the last time. And so ended my second Parliament.

The fourth longest Parliament in history was dissolved on Friday 15th June. It was rather a mournful scene saying goodbye to many parliamentary friends who were retiring and many others who would lose their seats at the election. There was speculation also as to the result of the election and who we would see on the benches when the new Parliament reassembled in a few weeks' time. The Prime Minister did not go down to the House, which surprised me.

I spent the rest of the day in my constituency with my agent and senior office-bearers.

On the Monday morning I went to No. 10 Downing Street to see my mail and sign letters. I had a talk with Randolph Churchill, who was leaving for Preston to fight his election. I went into No. 10 most days in the morning to deal with mail and keep my finger on the pulse, for I was still doing some work for the Prime Minister. Otherwise I was in the constituency with my wife for speeches, canvassing and generally working till late at night. I had some wonderful meetings at Barnes, Sheen and Richmond. Fortunately microphones were now in use and my speeches were relayed to great masses outside the halls, which themselves were crowded.

My wife had also started her speaking campaign, mostly at Ladies' Meetings in the afternoons. Some of those I also had to attend. Richmond was very lucky to have had a candidate whose wife could speak so well and was also pretty good at answering the hecklers. We attended every other function we could manage to fit in, as well as public meetings—bowling clubs, cricket clubs, Boy Scouts and Girl Guides. There were always two or three gatherings in the evening.

I had first-class meetings, with every hall packed. There was a certain amount of heckling but that I enjoyed. I had been brought up in tough places—mining and industrial areas—and was capable of facing pretty dangerous mobs but, of course, I had none of that in Richmond or Barnes. I had three opponents—Socialist, Liberal and Commonwealth, a very left-ish group. The election was fought with goodwill and good temper.

On nomination day I received a wonderful letter from Churchill; 'My dear Harvie-Watt, I confidently appeal to the electors of Richmond and Barnes to vote for you on July 5th. You have served me faithfully and well as Parliamentary Private Secretary for four years. Your great knowledge of the life of the House of Commons, and the broad and penetrating accounts of its affairs that you have given me every week during this long struggle, have greatly helped my general work and increased my contacts with my parliamentary home. I am most anxious that I should continue to have your support in the next Parliament. Yours very sincerely, Winston S. Churchill.'

As usual I stood as a Conservative and Unionist Member. I always called myself Unionist; it was a name the Conservatives should never have dropped. After a week's campaigning in the constituency my opponents and I met at the Town Hall in Richmond for nomination on June 25th. The Mayor provided us with coffee and biscuits. We stayed until noon to see if there were any surprise nominations. There was none. We then left to go our separate ways.

In addition to my own meetings, I addressed meetings in the Spelthorne Division and also at Chiswick, where Harold Mit-

9 Arriving at PM's entrance at the House of Commons after being greeted by the crowds. Author holding broken finger—it had been jumped on.

10, Downing Street,
Whitehall.

16 August, 1945.

My dear Harvie Watt

    I was very pleased to read your name in Mr. Churchill's Resignation List. If I may say so, your honour is well deserved and will give much pleasure to your friends in all political parties.

Brigadier G.S. Harvie Watt, T.D., M.P.

10   Letter from Clement Attlee

The 1945 Election

chell was contesting the seat he had held since 1931. That was one of the rowdiest meetings I had addressed and I didn't like the atmosphere. It was not friendly to the Conservative Party or to the candidate, or for that matter to me. I had literally to fight to say what I wanted to say. This meeting gave me my second feeling of disaster. My first was at Spelthorne. I, on the other hand, was having splendid and friendly meetings in my own constituency, with the exception of a few noisy, but on the whole good-tempered, hecklers. My wife and I did a lot of canvassing and were delighted at the wonderful reception we got in working-class homes.

I had a few noisy and tough meetings in the evenings, usually caused by hecklers from outside the constituency, but after electioneering in Scotland and Yorkshire the noise didn't bother me. In fact, I much preferred that kind of meeting, for it stimulated me and I could rise to the occasion. My supporters loved it when I scored off my hecklers. By 23rd June I began to feel more optimistic. To begin with there had been a tremendous amount of apathy. The last General Election had been in 1935, the Richmond by-election early in 1937, so it took some time to work up a real election fervour.

On Saturday evening before the poll I heard that the Prime Minister was going to speak for me in Richmond Green on the following Monday. That was a hectic day and the nervous strain was terrific; altogether I addressed six full-scale meetings. I must say Winston did me proud. I don't think Richmond had ever seen anything like it before and certainly never saw the like again to my knowledge.

My wife and I drove with him through my constituency where he spoke to a gigantic crowd on Richmond Green and got a terrific reception. 'I have come,' Mr. Churchill told the electors, 'to say a few words on behalf of my friend Harvie-Watt, who has been of real assistance to me throughout the war. I am very glad to come and ask you to give Harvie-Watt your utmost support. Great matters will turn on your decisions on polling day and it is no use saying you support me if you do not support the candidates without whom I should have no influence to guide the course of affairs in the new Parliament. You have laid heavy burdens on my back but you must give me a strong, substantial and trustworthy majority in the House of Commons.' He finished by calling for three cheers for Harvie-Watt. I think that was my greatest moment.

During the election campaign I was greatly honoured to be called within the Bar by the Lord Chancellor, Lord Simon. The ceremony took place at the House of Lords. I wore my full-bottomed wig for the first time. It was a proud occasion for me. I had been called to the Bar in 1930 and now in 1945 I was a K.C. I was indeed a proud man.

The weather all during the election had been extremely hot and trying, especially on polling day when my wife and I drove through the constituency in a decorated car, calling at polling stations and party committee rooms to thank all the Conservative workers. The polling stations appeared to swarm with Socialists wearing their red colours; the Conservatives seemed nothing like them in numbers. I had twinges of apprehension about the result, recalling my experiences at Spelthorne and Chiswick which were hitherto safe Conservative seats. Could the same be happening at Richmond? I began to feel depressed but, of course, I was very tired. After it was over we had drinks and sandwiches with Harold Mitchell. All of us were depressed and not at all hopeful for a Churchill victory; but we would have to wait for the result, since the count would not take place until 26th July.

The day after the poll I felt deflated and dead tired. My wife was the opposite. She was perky and optimistic. She went to Maurice Codner for the last sitting for her portrait. I had to see an orthopaedic surgeon about my finger. Apparently there was nothing more to be done about it—it might get all right; so with that mild comfort we caught the night train for Scotland and our family home, between Bathgate and Armadale. We found my sister was giving a party to welcome us after the election and we didn't get to bed till well after midnight. So ended a long, long tiring spell.

My wife and I went on to our new home in Elie, Fife, where the family, two small boys and a daughter, were waiting excitedly for us. I had not seen much of them. They were aged five, three and just over one. Colonel and Mrs. Bromhead arrived from Richmond the next day for a rest and holiday with

The 1945 Election

us. We all needed it. I was quite exhausted. I had taken on a part-time secretary to help out with my mail which had been building up over three weeks. My wife, who usually acted as my secretary and was first class at shorthand, typing and filing, was equally tired and exhausted. She needed a long rest herself.

After nearly three weeks at home I departed for London for the election count. I was staying at Catherine Place again with Harold Mitchell. He was quite certain he had been defeated. In fact he was, by a large majority. I attended my count at the Town Hall in Richmond. Early on it became evident that I would win. Nevertheless it was a terrific strain. I was elected by a majority of 8,325, a considerable drop compared with my 1937 by-election, but a good result compared with the debacle in the country. There were very few people waiting to hear the result of the poll which, in the circumstances, I thought was quite remarkable.

A few hours after the count I was back at No. 10 Downing Street, where the Prime Minister greeted me warmly, thanked me again for my services and asked whether I would continue as his P.P.S. in Opposition. I attended his farewell meeting of Ministers before joining friends at dinner.

The next day I attended the Prime Minister's farewell meeting of the Cabinet. He spoke to us for a few minutes. He said he felt that the future was grave and grim. The attack would come from two sides—on property and on liberty at home while abroad the Russians were going to carry on an expansionist policy. How true all this has proved to be over the last thirty years and more as I write these words. We can see for ourselves what has happened to property and liberty in our own country as well as throughout the world, and we have seen the spread of Russian influence. If Winston Churchill had won the 1945 election in Britain the world everywhere would have been a better and different place in which to live.

On 1st August the Speaker was re-elected. There were amazing scenes in the Commons. Churchill got a warm and enthusiastic reception from the party, although our ranks were much depleted. We sang *For he's a jolly good fellow*. It was the first and only time I ever heard the House break into song. The

Socialists then sang *The Red Flag* but there were a lot of sheepish-looking faces, especially among the ex-coalition Ministers like Attlee, the new Prime Minister, Cripps and Ernest Bevin. The next day we took the Oath of Allegiance in the new Parliament.

The end of a big chapter in my life had come. The party had been defeated. There were no posts to fill. It was not a Churchill Government and the Socialists had a huge majority. Looking back now, it was a pity I had been one of the survivors. My ambitions must seek another outlet.

A few days later I received a letter from Winston written not from No. 10 but from his own home at 67 Westminster Gardens. The letter was dated 10th August 1945 and read— 'My dear Harvie, I have been granted the privilege of sending in my Resignation List of Honours. It is my intention to submit your name to the King for a Baronetcy and I hope you will allow me to do so. Perhaps in order to save time you will let T. L. Rowan at No. 10 Downing Street (Whitehall 4333) have your reply by telegram at the earliest moment. Your sincerely, Winston S. Churchill.'

The defeat was quite a shock to the Conservative Party and large sections of the nation. Only a few weeks ago at the final coalition cocktail party at No. 10, most people there thought it was going to be a walk-over for the Conservatives, and several Socialist Ministers said to me, 'You are bound to get back as a Party and I know you will remember me when the new Government is being formed as your Government will undoubtedly wish to include some Socialists and Liberals.' They fully believed that the coalition would be continued.

Even some Tories, who were not sure of their position, thought they might lose their jobs and that I might be in a position to help them. Alas we lost the election and some of those friends were never quite so friendly again; when the Tories did come back to power in 1951 I was no longer so close to the sources of patronage and it was interesting to see how friendships, warm all through the war, soon cooled off.

What interested me even more, however, was the number of Socialist Cabinet Ministers who thought the Tories would win and who made no bones about suggesting that I might keep them in mind when the new Government was being formed.

As their party won, they were in the Socialist Government and likewise their warm friendship for me soon withered away. This was an aspect of politics I had never thought about, but I realised from that moment it was each man for himself. It was one reason, although a minor one, why I began to lose interest in politics. Men whom I had helped, and helped a lot, in their ambitions drifted out of my life. It was interesting that when I became Chairman and Managing Director of one of Britain's largest public companies, I was rediscovered by some of my wartime friends, who felt that, because they had been in Government, they would be an asset in the City and did I remember the old days? Yes, I did remember the old days!

I then said good-bye to the staff at No. 10. It was a sad occasion after a very hectic four years. I would miss my contacts with John Martin, Anthony Bevir, Leslie Rowan, John Peck, John Colville—all first-rate people with distinguished careers to come—and all the other Secretaries and Messengers who had been so good to me at all times.

On 14th August my baronetcy appeared in the Private Office List—'G. S. Harvie-Watt KC, M.P. for Keighley Division of Yorkshire 1931–35 and for Richmond since 1937, Parliamentary Private Secretary to the Prime Minister, Mr. Churchill, 1941–45.'

On 26th October I was back in my old place behind Winston in the House of Commons for his speech on demobilisation. This time we were on the Opposition benches. He again said he wanted me to go on 'mothering him' in the Commons. I would do so but it was not the thing I could do for long, only for the time being. A full-time 'shadow' job in Opposition would never suit me now that I had to look after a substantial family. The Socialists had a vast majority and could certainly govern for five years. I couldn't see myself as being a party hack for that long. I would have to make better use of my time. There was really nothing much I could do in Opposition. Although I held one or two directorships, I had to have a career—either a return to the Bar, which did not now attract me since I had been so long away, or a career in the City. It was not just directorships I wanted but a full-time executive position.

Meanwhile I carried on as P.P.S. to the Leader of the Opposition.

After the election our close relationship continued, mainly on personal rather than official business. I felt very honoured when Winston asked me to sit at the ex-Ministers' table in the Members' Dining Room at the House. One political journalist wrote that he hoped that I would be released for more active work in the House. The wartime Parliament knew me for my great service in the war to Churchill, for my tact and discretion, for my geniality and my capacity for friendship. 'They are in danger of forgetting that before his appointment as a Whip in 1938 this shrewd, sandy-haired Scotsman was an eloquent speaker and a formidable debater.'

I was elected joint Honorary Treasurer, with Sir Stafford Cripps the Chancellor of the Exchequer, of the Empire Parliamentary Association. This was to be one of my main political interests for the next six years and was to take me to Canada, the United States, Australia and New Zealand.

Early in December the Opposition moved a Vote of Censure. Winston spoke. I thought the Vote of Censure was ill-timed. We could have had one on demobilisation but four months of a new Parliament was not long enough for a Vote of Censure. The Government had had little time to do anything. I thought the tactics were wrong and said so, but my views were not popular.

One evening about that time (late 1945) I accompanied Winston to a dinner with a party of Conservative Members at the House. He was in a foul temper. I was now used to this but he nearly bit the head off Lord John Hope for criticising the leadership of the Party. Winston said the people versus Socialism should be the great rallying cry. He drove me home and, as in the old days, ordered the chauffeur to pull in to the side of Birdcage Walk. We sat for a long time. Winston said he was sick of the Conservative Party and wondered whether he should resign the leadership. He said the new Members were just a woolly lot of pinks. This was not the way to combat

Socialism, which he said had a terrible grip on the country. We missed a Division. It was a late night and I was very weary so I was glad to hear him say, 'I'm going to bed. I'm tired and fed up.'

All the talk in parliamentary circles was the proposed American Loan. I was not happy about the party decision on this matter. They had decided not to vote on the American Loan Agreement. This was ridiculous. The money was urgently required for our post-war purposes. If there was no loan then the standard of living in this country would go down. What I was afraid of was that the money would be thrown down the drain of Socialism, and it was.

The House then rose for the Christmas Recess and the end of 1945, surely one of the most momentous years in British history. What the House and the nation owed to Winston Churchill can never be fully appreciated. It was also, in a minor way, a memorable year for me. The sun shone on me. Before the election one paper had written 'politicians of all parties have been wishing good luck to Brigadier Harvie-Watt in his election campaign and though he is a Conservative his personality is such that few members of other parties will not welcome him back to the House. His Raeburnesque features rarely carry other than a pleasant smile and he is the most approachable of men.' But as the battle went on I was not the pleasing young man but just the fighter.

Parliament was still my number one interest at that time and I asked to be put on the Committee which was to examine the Transport Bill which was intended to nationalise railways. As a director of the Great Western Railway I took an active part in the Committee stage of that Bill and spoke many times. I was never a supporter of railway nationalisation, I have seen not improvement in services but the reverse. It was the same with the other industries that were nationalised. In the House I asked many questions and spoke on Army Estimates Debates.

At this stage of the 1945 Parliament I was still interested in the work of the House and played quite an active part, in addition to acting as P.P.S. to Winston as Leader of the Opposition. I was still politically interested and hopeful that when the next election came round in 1950 I would have worked my way again into the Ministerial orbit.

I have already mentioned that, before the war, I had been invited to join the Boards of some gold mining companies, the Globe & Phoenix Group. They were small companies and, like M.Ps' salaries during the war and indeed after, the fees were low. None the less they enabled me to keep body and soul together when I had no other income. I had been brought up in a coal mining area of Scotland and had been down nearly every mine in the district. I had been associated with miners from my early days and it was a great and useful experience. In the T.A., when I was serving with the 52nd Lowland Scottish Division Royal Engineers, many of the men were miners from Lanarkshire. They were first-class soldiers and tough.

My interest in mining was given a boost when, just at the end of the war, I was asked by Consolidated Gold Fields of South Africa to join the Board as an outside director. My name had been mentioned by Stanley Christopherson, Chairman of the Midland Bank, and I recollected that during the doodle-bug period he had invited me to lunch in his private dining room at the bank to meet Robert Annan, Chairman of Gold Fields. I had thought nothing of it at the time. Annan was a Scot and a mining engineer and he obviously had been pondering the matter for some months.

That was the greatest business and personal decision I ever made, for when the war ended I began to take an active interest. In due course I became Managing Director, Chief Executive and Chairman of this great company, founded by Cecil Rhodes.

Now that the Conservatives were in Opposition, my duties were less onerous, and I was able to take a fuller interest in Consolidated Gold Fields, together with the Globe & Phoenix group of companies. I had also been elected to the Board of the Monotype Corporation, a renowned maker of typecasting machinery. This was going to prove one of the most interesting of my company associations.

I also found time to go back to soldiering. Towards the end of December 1946 General Browning sent for me to see him at the War Office regarding the command of a T.A. AA brigade. He wanted me to take on the job as I had been so long associated with the Territorial Army. I was surprised and pleased by this offer. He also asked a lot of rather personal questions, I didn't think much about this at the time. I was more intrigued when, in the course of the talk, he joked about the high taxation he had to suffer. His wife, Daphne du Maurier, had an income from writing of some £30,000 per annum, and he made only a few thousands as a general. Yet he was responsible for the payment of his wife's tax.

I would be only too happy to go back to the T.A. I gave up command of the 6th AA Brigade in July 1941 to go to the Prime Minister. So here, after just over six years, I was back with my absorbing hobby. Shortly after that interesting talk with General Browning I became conscious of more discreet enquiries being made about me from different sources. Soon afterwards I was appointed an A.D.C. to King George VI. Hence all the enquiries. I remained an A.D.C. to the Queen on her accession to the throne until 1958, when my tour of duty came to an end. Shortly after my talk with General Browning, I lunched with General Lund, G.O.C. AA Command. He wished to discuss the brigade with me and informed me I would be appointed Brigade Commander of the 63rd North London AA Brigade. This suited me very well, for I could carry on my other activities—Parliament and the City especially—without having much travelling to do. I spent most of that day at AA Command so that I could put myself in the picture.

On 1st March 1947 I reported for duty to command the 63rd AA Brigade. Our H.Q. was near Victoria Station, at 20 Grosvenor Gardens. So it was back to the army again. I was medically examined at Chelsea Barracks and next morning I went to my new H.Q. and waded through a mass of paper work to catch up on the present situation in the brigade. My routine was now changing. Each morning I went to my Brigade H.Q. and did the administrative work, which was considerable. That I enjoyed. I visited the regimental H.Qs at Tottenham, Finchley and Willesden in the evening when I could get away from the House of Commons. The three regiments in my brigade were the 486 Regt, 490 Regt and the 669 Regt.

During that period the Army Estimates came before the

House. I listened to much of the Debate and suddenly I decided to speak and rose and caught the Speaker's eye. So I spoke in the House without a note and it wasn't too bad, but I had a feeling that my interest in the House was on the wane. I had command of a T.A. brigade, I was a director of some major companies and my activities were moving more to the City. They had already moved from the Temple and now it looked as if they were on the move from Westminster.

For the remainder of that Parliament I was in great demand as a speaker at by-elections and I travelled all over England, and sometimes in Scotland. I was always asked to address the tough, industrial and working-class meetings. I felt en rapport with those people. My meetings were sometimes rowdy, with lots of booing and shouting and first-class heckling. They were good politicians. I often ended up by having a drink with some of the noisiest interrupters. Sometimes I was even cheered. They were not, of course, going to vote Conservative. The many Conservative garden parties I had to address in the summer months were a different kind of meeting altogether. There was no heckling, and questions were not usually encouraged. None the less those garden parties were invaluable, for they were usually held in the dead political season and they helped to keep the party workers together.

My other continuing interest in the Commons was the Empire Parliamentary Association. I was re-elected Hon. Treasurer, and continued in that office during the whole time of the post-war Socialist Parliament until the beginning of 1950. I was always a Joint Honorary Treasurer with the Socialist Chancellors of the Exchequer, Mr. Hugh Dalton and Sir Stafford Cripps. It was a most valuable interest, for we entertained at meetings and lunches visiting Empire statesmen from all over the world. The Secretary was still Sir Howard D'Egville, a most experienced imperialist.

I had a further spate of public meetings at by-elections and other constituency functions. I spoke at Croydon and at Scunthorpe in the Brigg by-election. Then to Yorkshire; I had high tea with Lord Scarborough and then set off for Rotherham where I addressed meetings at Wentworth, Rother Valley and Rotherham itself. The halls were crowded. One of the Conservative candidates didn't turn up because his wife had just had a baby. God help politics if this was an excuse not to come to a vital constituency meeting.

The Rotherham meeting was one of the toughest I had ever addressed. The hall was crowded and noisy. When I got up to speak I had only said, 'Mr. Chairman, Ladies and Gentlemen', when I was greeted with great shouts of 'you're a bloody liar'. I realised at once this would be no kid glove affair. I refused to be shouted down and managed to get one or two funny cracks in. The crowd, though noisy, was a sporting one and gradually they quietened down a bit and I managed to get a few arguments across. Many of them afterwards came up to speak to me and finally I got away with an exchange of some good-humoured cracks and a few drinks.

In this round of meetings I spoke at Finchley and at Keighley, my old constituency which I won in 1931 and lost in 1935. I got a tremendous reception everywhere I went especially in Keighley where it was a crowded and enthusiastic meeting. Then I spoke in other towns and villages in the constituency. It was a reunion of old friends and I was greatly touched. I finished this tour of meetings in Oban on behalf of the sitting Member, Major McCallum. I was glad to get back to London, for it had been a strenuous tour.

CHAPTER 19

South Africa and Canada

I had been in South Africa when the war began, on a visit to the Globe & Phoenix and the Phoenix Prince Mines. In 1947 the companies again wanted me to visit the mines and report on them. No director had been out since I went there in 1939.

My wife and I decided to go by ship; flying was then not a very common way of civilian transport overseas. We sailed from Liverpool in the 15,000-ton *Corinthic* of the Shaw Savill Line. Most of the passengers on board appeared to be emigrants to South Africa, Australia and New Zealand. Our companions on board were Mr. and Mrs. Joe Davis, Joe Davis of course being the well-known snooker champion who had been undefeated for twenty years. We remained friends until his death in 1977. They often stayed with us in our home in Scotland. We soon slipped down the Mersey from Liverpool and Birkenhead where the ship had been built by Cammell Laird; it was her maiden voyage. We arrived in Cape Town on 19th April.

We were met by representatives of the Globe & Phoenix Gold Mining Company, the Monotype Corporation, Consolidated Gold Fields, and also of the Chamber of Mines. I was now in a real mining community and I felt much at home.

I lunched at the House with the President of the Senate, Senator Brook. He had been in the commando which took Winston Churchill prisoner during the Boer War. He told me that once when he was on a flag of truce to the British lines the British officers were playing cricket and asked him if he could play. He said he did and apparently put up a very good show with fast bowling and batting. The British officers then asked him what his commando was most short of. He replied, '·303 ammunition, army biscuits and sardines.' When the British officers left him, having seen him through the lines, he examined his saddle bags and found them packed with plenty of ammo, biscuits and sardines. He added, with a smile, that the ammo was used very successfully a few days later against the British soldiers. What a war!

We then went up country to Johannesburg, where we were met by Colonel Fleischer, the head of Gold Fields in South Africa. We drove round the mining area outside the city and visited several mines. That was the first of many visits to the gold areas of South Africa.

On that visit there was one place I felt I must visit and that was Pretoria, not because of the Parliament Buildings, not because of Paul Kruger's house, not to visit the Voortrekkers' Memorial erected in 1933 after a wave of nationalist feeling (although I did all those things), but to visit the school where British officers were prisoners of war during the Boer War.

It was from that school that Winston escaped and managed to make his way back to England. I had to ask many people where the school was. Of course, Pretoria was very Nationalist and nobody seemed to know, or pretended they didn't. At last a schoolgirl was able to guide me. It was, of course, an ordinary little school and there was no plaque or any distinguishing mark of any kind to say it had been a prisoner-of-war camp.

The only gold mine I went down on the Rand on that visit was one of the oldest mines in South Africa, Robinson Deep, which at that time had sixty-three levels. The mine used the old method of crushing, a 200-stamp battery. Some of the other goldfields mines I visited with well-known names were Sub Nigel, Vogels, Vlakfontein and Simmer and Jack. Other and newer mines we visited on that occasion bore famous names—Libanon, Doornfontein and West Driefontein which became the largest gold producer in the world. The latter two mines were in the early stages of development.

My next stop was Que Que where the Globe & Phoenix mine is situated. We were met there by a Mr. Watt, a Scot who had been at George Watson's. Next day I was introduced to the mine management staff and went down the mine in a cage to the twenty-first level of the vertical shaft, then to the twenty-ninth level in the skip. I spent two weeks at the Globe & Phoenix then went up to Salisbury, the capital of Rhodesia, and motored on fifty-seven miles to Bindura to visit the Phoenix Prince mine. I stayed at Bindura a week and made a thorough examination of that mine.

When we reached Salisbury I had to go to the House of Commons. It was, of course, a smallish building but the Chamber was exactly the same as the British House of Commons. There were portraits of the King and Queen behind the Speaker's chair. The membership was small—more like the Kensington Borough Council. The speaking was also more like that of a Borough Council than a Parliament. I had tea with the Prime Minister, the Speaker and his wife.

The P.M. was Sir Godfrey Huggins, whom I had met in London several times during the war; he and I talked for an hour afterwards. I then called upon the Governor, Sir John Kennedy, whom I had known for some time.

I had to address the Joint Parliament and got a very warm reception. Huggins asked to see me later. I was most surprised at what he had to say. He wondered whether I would consider settling in Rhodesia. They were very short of people with any experience in political life. He said he could arrange for me to get a seat in Parliament and would like to put me in his Government. It was an interesting proposition but I'm afraid it had no attractions for me. So I said 'no'. The next day I flew from Bulawayo to Durban via Johannesburg. I met my wife at the Marine Hotel, where we were to stay a day or two before sailing for home.

There was no doubt that there were great prospects of success in the Union and in Southern Rhodesia. There was tremendous optimism in both countries. Of course they had their problems, not looming large at that time, but it would not be long before some of them became of prime importance. I thought it was a great pity that the Afrikaaner section of the community was forcing the Union to become bi-lingual. Everything, even notices and names of streets, were in English and Afrikaans. This could only widen the gap between the Boers and the English which would be a drawback to a great progressive country which was building up its secondary industries and hoping to trade with the other Dominions and with the United States. I couldn't believe any other country was going to learn

Afrikaans for the sake of doing business in South Africa. There was a lot of feeling between the Dutch and the English.

The Boer War still dominated relationships. There were various estimates as to the percentages of Boers and Britons but it appeared to be accepted that there were 60% Boers and 40% British. That, however, was only a small part of the population as there were some ten million natives. And the number was constantly growing.

Communist agitation was rife among the natives and their labour unions and some day there could be a real battle between the blacks and the whites. It was silly, therefore, for the Dutch and the British to cut their own throats because of incidents alleged to have happened in the Boer War. 'Despite all the problems, South Africa was an attractive place to live in and the prospects for a middle-aged man were magnificent, but for a young man I would have said doubtful.' That I wrote in 1947, but now the prospects in Southern Africa are grim.

On my return to England I was soon back in the London whirl and I had a short chat with Winston. He looked very well indeed after a hernia operation. He thought that he would be laid up for three months for a thing like that, but he was well ahead of schedule. He was most friendly. We didn't see each other so often by then, partly because I had been away so much, and likely to be more so in the future. My P.P.S. partnership now ceased, although it was understood that if he wanted my help I would always be available. As I had suspected many months ago, my political interests were waning, although I felt it my duty to fight the next election which, in the ordinary course of events, should be in 1950. I must at least take my place in the first charge against the Socialist Government.

At the Conference of the Empire Parliamentary Association held in London in the autumn of 1948 it was decided, on the proposition of the Canadian delegation, to set up a General Secretariat and Council. The idea was that this new organisation should be superimposed upon the branches of the existing set-up of the Empire Parliamentary Association. The offices of the Secretariat were to be situated in London and the General Council would meet in a different part of the Empire each year, the first being arranged for Ottawa in the Spring of 1949. That meeting would be required to draft the rules and constitution for the new body.

At a meeting of the General Executive of the United Kingdom branch of the Association held on 9th February 1949 it was decided that the delegates to the first meeting should be the Rt Hon. John Wilmot, ex-Socialist Minister of Supply, and myself to represent the Conservative Party. I was very pleased to have been selected for this delegation. Sir Howard d'Egville, Secretary of the United Kingdom branch, would also go to Ottawa as he was to be proposed as the first General Secretary. It was settled that we would leave Liverpool on 16th April. Wives were not included, but as I had relations in nearly every great city in Canada I knew there would be no difficulty with dollars and my wife could spend time with some relative or another while I was on duty.

We left Liverpool in the Cunard White Star *Media*. It was a small ship and the crossing of the Atlantic to New York took seven-and-a-half days. Our first view of New York was out of this world. I had often seen photographs but the real thing was breathtaking.

We were met by Scottish friends called McColl who had emigrated years ago. Mr. McColl had collected about thirty eminent businessmen for lunch in a private room at the Metropolitan Club, and Mrs. McColl gave a ladies' lunch for my wife in another private room. I had to speak at my lunch and answer questions about Churchill and conditions in the U.K. It was an exceedingly friendly gathering. Mr. McColl was one of the top people of the American Locomotive Company. One of the guests was General Doolittle whom I had met often in London with Churchill and Eisenhower.

We left New York on 27th April from Grand Central Station which was one of the finest railway stations I had ever seen, New York being one of the finest cities. We arrived in Ottawa at about 10.30 pm. It had been a long but fascinating day viewing the American countryside for the first time. In Ottawa we stayed in the Chateau Laurier Hotel—a most luxurious place. I don't think I have ever seen anything like it—including the spittoon between our beds.

11 The Author as a piper

12 The Harvie Watt shaft at the Libanon mine

13 Signpost to the township of Glenharvie (Kloof Gold Mine).

South Africa and Canada

On 28th April the Conference of the General Council of the Commonwealth (no longer Empire) Parliamentary Association held its first meeting in the Canadian House of Commons. Representatives were present from the U.K., Canada, Australia, South Africa, New Zealand, Pakistan, Malta, Bermuda and the Gold Coast. There were a great many introductory speeches. Two Committees were formed, one to consider the constitution and the other finance. I had been appointed to the Finance Committee.

We had lunch at the House of Commons. The dining room was large and pleasant and at the top of the building. The Parliament buildings as a whole were magnificent. In the evening the Speaker gave a cocktail party for the visiting delegates to meet Members of the Canadian Parliament.

Later we went back to the House of Commons to hear a Debate. The speeches seemed to be read. Members sat at small desks—two desks together. They often banged the lids of the desks to show their displeasure. Several small page-boys ran about the Chamber taking messages.

We were afterwards introduced to George Drew, the Leader of the Conservative Party, and his Deputy, Gordon Graydon. I was not particularly impressed by Drew, although he had a tall, fine presence and seemed to have lots of go. He appeared to be most popular with his party and his nickname was 'Gorgeous George'—a fatal name for a political leader.

The Financial Committee's deliberations were most exhaustive and exhausting as the Pakistanis were great talkers on points with little or no real substance in them. On 2nd May the General Council discussed the reports of the Finance Committee and the Constitutional Committee, which took all day.

In the evening we had a cocktail party arranged for us at Government House by the Governor-General, Field Marshal Lord Alexander. Only the members of the delegation were present, together with the members of the Governor-General's staff and one or two leading Senators. We were received very formally by the Governor-General and the Prime Minister, Mr. St. Laurent. I used to meet Alexander a lot during the war so we had a long talk together. Apparently Churchill had cabled him to say that Sarah was coming out to Canada for a new film and asked if she could come and stay at Government House for a while. Alexander was very fond of painting and had presented some of his paintings to different organisations in Canada. He was a first-class British representative and a great credit to the United Kingdom.

At the last meeting of the General Council we discussed, among other things, the arrangements for the next Council meeting and Commonwealth Parliamentary Association Conference. It was to be held in New Zealand in October or November 1950.

The Canadian Club then gave a luncheon party in honour of the delegation. There were two hundred guests and there were only two speeches, one a brief speech of welcome by the President of the Club and the other a long speech by Mr. Khan, the representative of Pakistan. He spoke for nearly an hour. It was a great pity, for the first ten minutes were excellent.

The General Council then adjourned to meet again in New Zealand.

Our last engagement in Toronto was for drinks and dinner at the Royal York Hotel, our host being Mr. Speaker Cooke-Davis. I had to make the speech. In the course of it I said, 'If the spirit shown by the Commonwealth during the war could be recaptured, there was no problem those countries could not solve. We wanted to encourage that spirit from the point of view of facing the problems of peace. The battles of North Africa and other areas were not just incidents in the war but were milestones in the history of Australia, New Zealand, South Africa, Canada and Pakistan.' I spoke for much longer but I will quote no more. I was described, however, in the Toronto *Globe and Mail*, as 'In appearance a younger edition of Winston Churchill [who] spoke with an eloquence reminiscent of Britain's wartime Prime Minister.' Well, well. I don't think Winston would have thought that comparison very complimentary to him although it was to me.

On 8th May we left Toronto and flew to Washington, where we were welcomed by various Congressmen, including Senator Kefauver. With him was his wife Nancy and her father, Sir John Piggott of John Brown & Company, the famous shipbuilders on the Clyde. I knew him quite well since he frequently came to Elie for his holidays. Mrs. Kefauver said she often longed for the Elie beach as she was practically brought up on it. Senator Kefauver stood twice for the Presidency of the United States but was beaten both times. I was most impressed by Washington. It is a beautiful city. I have never seen so many fine public buildings anywhere. I went to the Capitol for a lunch party with Senator Connally, the Chairman of the Foreign Relations Committee, in the Chair.

We were then taken to the Senate Chamber. I had my first experience of filibustering when I saw Senator Johnson of Arkansas in action. He had been speaking since noon. By this time it was 3 pm. and he had given notice that he would speak until 6 pm. I could see no point in this.

The Senate had a recess of ten minutes to enable Senators to meet members of our delegation; during it we were introduced to the Vice-President of the United States, Alben Barkley. We were allowed on the floor of the House and after the Debate had resumed we were allowed to sit at desks belonging to Senators. We were later shown some of the Senators' rooms—we saw over the suite of Senator Thomas of Utah. He had five rooms and fourteen secretaries. He was a delightful and charming man, at that time Chairman of the Labour Committee of the Senate. I then visited the Lincoln Memorial and other magnificent memorials and statues.

On 10th May our delegation assembled at the White House. There we were introduced to the President, Harry Truman. He looked a much stronger character than I had thought from his photograph. He had rather thin tight lips but was very charming. He shook hands with us and then we talked, at least he did most of the talking and we did the listening. He had obviously been informed as to who we were and what we had been doing. He said that he hoped the world would be able to solve its problems in the same way as the British Commonwealth solved theirs. The Commonwealth was a great experiment. There was a globe of the world in his room given to him by General Eisenhower. He pointed out that it was made in London. He marked the trouble spots in the world. Russia was well marked by a strip of material. When we came away he shook hands with us all again and asked me to give his regards to Churchill and asked Van Breda from South Africa to give his regards to Smuts. They were two great men, the President told us. He hoped that there would be conversations on a Parliamentary level with us so as to stress the points in common. The future, he said, lay with the English-speaking peoples. We had our photographs taken on the steps of the White House.

I thought the White House was very attractive, both inside and outside. It seemed that the President had to be much more approachable than our own Prime Minister or the Monarch.

We also spent some time in the Supreme Court and in the House, and in the evening we went to a cocktail party given at the British Embassy by Sir Oliver and Lady Franks. They were a delightful couple. He had been Professor of Moral Philosophy at Glasgow University before the War. She also came from Glasgow. The Embassy is a lovely house with a perfect garden. The Capitol was floodlit, as were the Lincoln and Jefferson Memorials. I have never seen a finer city.

From Washington we returned to Toronto and went from there to Vancouver on 14th May. We had various stops on the way west as I had engagements to fulfil. On 16th May I had to speak in Winnipeg at an Empire Club lunch. It was very difficult to make a speech there in the middle of the day. There were no cocktails and not even a glass of beer for the meal. It is difficult to make a speech on a glass of water. Before lunch the audience sang *Oh Canada*. It was the first time I had heard that anthem sung. The King's health was drunk in water and *God Save the King* was sung at the end. We drove round Winnipeg and visited the Parliament buildings and Government offices.

We continued our way westward on 17th May, across the great prairie land of Canada to Regina, and the Rocky Mountains to Vancouver, very impressive with its beautiful scenery round the River Front and its masses of hills, islands and rivers. I had the usual interviews to give to the Press and there were photographs to be taken.

We had many relatives in Vancouver so we were well looked after. It was just as well, for our hotel was very expensive and, in order to save dollars, we had to breakfast in a little cafe called the White Spot. When there one morning we looked across to the hotel and saw Harold Wilson coming out with Barbara

South Africa and Canada

Castle. He was smoking his pipe and looking very friendly. He was then Parliamentary Secretary to the Board of Trade and Barbara Castle was his P.P.S. They were out on Government business.

We had several days in Vancouver then we sailed across to Vancouver Island, again with magnificent scenery. The next morning at breakfast I met the Chief Justice of British Columbia, who invited me to sit on the Bench with him for a manslaughter case. After he took his seat on the Bench he announced to the Court who I was and the Counsel for the Crown and the Counsel for the Defence both welcomed me. It was a very interesting experience for me. The proceedings were similar to ours at home, but the absence of wigs took away some of the dignity of the proceedings.

We returned to Vancouver on 26th May, for I had to speak at a dinner at the Vancouver Club, not only speak but answer questions. Then my wife had to speak and answer questions. We fully paid for that dinner. There were about forty people present—Trade Commissioners, members of the Bench and Bar, Members of Parliament, and all with their wives.

I also went to a lunch of the Conservative Action Committee. Present were Tom McDonald K.C., all the candidates for the different Ridings (constituencies) of Vancouver, Cecil Merrit V.C., and a pretty large crowd. I was asked a lot of questions afterwards. The impression I was left with was that throughout Canada they were much more interested in their own political affairs than those of the wider world outside. We left Vancouver on 3rd June on our way back across Canada to Quebec.

We left Canada on 14th June and we reached the Clyde on 22nd June and left by car immediately for Fife and our home at Elie. We were delighted to be back. That same night I returned by train to London. My first duty was to give a series of speeches in my constituency on my experiences in Canada and the United States. I also had to speak at a by-election in Leeds. I must have spoken at nearly every by-election in that Parliament.

Chapter 20

Australia and New Zealand

It was clear that the present Parliament was drifting to its end and early in the New Year it was announced that the General Election would be held on 23rd February. I had some doubts as to whether I should stand for re-election as my main interests seemed to be shifting to the City; on the other hand, I felt that I certainly ought to fight that 1950 election because it was necessary to defeat the Socialist Party. I had strong feelings that this could be done, for in the course of all of my by-election speeches and the innumerable constituency speeches I had made it seemed to me that the political current was flowing once more towards the Conservative Party.

I again had a three-cornered contest. My Liberal opponent was David Ennals, who not long after the election joined the Socialist Party and in due course became a Socialist Minister. My Socialist opponent was called Karl Westwood. He was very much to the left of the Socialists. I would have said he was on the way to communism. *The Red Flag* was the favourite song of his supporters. I had noticed in my elections at Richmond that my opponents were always demanding joint election meetings. It sounded a good idea, but only for my opponents. They thought they would get better meetings since I drew packed houses everywhere I went. However, I was not as simple as that. Usually my opponents were inexperienced candidates and unknown, so why should I give them an audience on a plate?

It was a good stirring election. 'Back to Freedom' was my slogan. I was convinced that the electors were getting fed up with the first bites into Socialism. The Socialist manifesto, among many things, claimed that their Government had ensured full employment. That was a travesty of the facts. At least 1½ million people were at work then thanks to the assistance we had had and were still receiving from the USA by way of loan and Marshall Aid—a figure given by the Socialists themselves. In addition to that we had to remember that there was also conscription, which swallowed up 350,000 of our young men. About another 500,000 were off the labour market because of the extension of the school leaving age, and another substantial number of more than 600,000 were in work because of vast increases in the staffs of local government and the Civil Service. Disillusionment had set in. There were many people who were prepared to try Socialism once. They had tried it and it was not what they wanted.

My election result was excellent. My vote was 30,907, compared with 1945 when I polled 24,085, and my by-election vote in 1937 of 20,546. My majorities were 13,669 in 1950, 8,325 in 1945 and 12,837 at the by-election in 1937.

In the country generally there was a large swing to the Conservative Party, but not big enough to gain a majority in Parliament. The Socialist majority had shrunk to six. It was going to be a difficult Parliament for the Conservatives, and there would be difficulty in the arrangement of pairs for lengthy absences.

Meanwhile I continued speaking in different parts of the country and giving more day time to the City. I was becoming more and more involved with Consolidated Gold Fields. Alas, my army connection had come to an end and in a very curious way. One day before the 1950 General Election I was in my Brigade H.Q. when my Brigade Major handed me an A.C.I. (an Army Council Instruction) to the effect that no Territorial officer over the rank of Lieut. Colonel could sit in Parliament unless he gave up his army appointment. This was an A.C.I. that seemed to apply only to me, for there were no other M.P. Brigade Commanders. I was really in a spot. My Divisional Commander had recently told me he wished to recommend me to command a Territorial Division and I was exhilarated at the thought. He said he had discussed the matter with G.O.C. AA Command who said he would be delighted to approve my promotion. I felt, however, I could not resign from Parliament at that stage when the Government had such a small majority, and the A.C.I. made it plain I couldn't do both jobs. Looking back, it would have suited me much better to resign from Parliament.

Another curious thing which I didn't learn about until later was that I had been recommended for a C.B.E. in recognition of my services to the T.A. My General said it had been approved at all army levels. What about political levels and the above-mentioned A.C.I.? I have often wondered what happened. I cannot believe that a Socialist Secretary of State could have intervened. It would have been too petty a thing to do, but the circumstances were odd.

Before every overseas visit there was a fear that some event would intervene to prevent it. Never had there been such uncertainty about our departure as was the case when I was about to leave for Australia and the Commonwealth Conference in New Zealand. The recall of Parliament for 12th September to discuss defence and foreign affairs in relation to the Korean situation depressed me very much. It seemed inevitable that our sailing should be postponed. I had visions of my wife going in the ship from Tilbury and my flying out later to join her at Port Said.

On the Tuesday, however, Mr. Churchill announced in the House that the Opposition would not vote against the Government's military proposals. The coast was clear.

The 14th September was the day of sailing. I was plunged into gloom and indecision again as a result of the contents of the morning's newspapers. A new political crisis had arisen over the export of machine tools to Russia and the Government's decision to proceed with the nationalisation of iron and steel. This might mean a three-line Whip for Monday or Tuesday, 18th or 19th September respectively. There was nothing definite announced and I thought I would risk it rather than wait behind for a possible non-event.

Joe Davis lent us his car to take us to Tilbury, which was more comfortable than the boat train. We sailed in the *Stratheden*, a P. & O. ship. Later that night I heard on the radio about an upset in the House of Commons and the announcement by Churchill that the Opposition was moving a Vote of Censure on the Government on Tuesday night. That annoucement plunged me into difficulties. During the night of the 15th—

16th September I gave a great deal of thought to the question of returning and decided to cable to London. I was assisted in my decision when the Captain told me he could easily stop the ship at Gibraltar on the Sunday. I could then fly home in time for the Division on Tuesday. I got a cable from the Chief Whip that Churchill thought it best that I should return and thanked me warmly for proposing to do so.

Arrangements had been made for me to fly home from Gibraltar and fly back again to Cairo to catch the ship at Port Said on 22nd September. The Captain had been most helpful in all those arrangements. On Sunday morning we went through the Straits of Gibraltar. Word had got round the ship that someone was being put ashore. Gossip travels quickly anywhere but especially in a ship. Unfortunately there were eighteen reporters on board with the M.C.C. cricket team and they all wanted a story. I naturally kept my mouth shut. The ship's decks were crowded with passengers to see me going down the companion-way to a launch and shove off.

Next morning, Monday 18th September, was a lovely sunny day so the weather was all right for flying. I was back in the Caledonian Club by 6 pm. The newspapers were all full of the diversion of the *Stratheden* to Gibraltar and my trip home. The highlight of the visit home was that on Tuesday evening Mr. Churchill sent for me. I wondered what he was going to say—whether there were any rockets going around. However, he greeted me most affably, shook me warmly by the hand and thanked me profusely for coming back for the Division. He said I had performed a great public service and had shown a wonderful example. Alas, we lost the Vote, but he hoped that I still thought my return had been worth while. It had, even if it had only been to see my old chief again.

On 20th September I started my return journey back to the ship. After a long delay at Rome, the plane arrived at Cairo very late, and it was 3 am. before I got to bed, quite exhausted. I awoke early, had a taxi ride to all the places of interest and then caught my train for Port Said. I slept badly as I was over-tired and I saw the *Stratheden* sail in at 5.15 am. I was back on board at 8 am. It was a tremendous relief to be on my way again to Australia.

We arrived at Colombo early in the morning of 1st October.

Although the ship was only there for a day, we saw something of the country because the Governor, Lord Soulbury, put a car and driver at our disposal. He was an old friend of mine from House of Common days, and I had a long Parliamentary reminiscence with him over dinner before we returned to the *Stratheden* in the Governor's launch. The harbour was a magnificent sight at night, with its illuminations.

We landed in Australia at Fremantle, and were very cordially welcomed there and at Perth by officials and members of the Legislative Assembly of Western Australia. I have seen some odd things in the various Parliaments I have visited, but at the Parliament House there I saw something unique—a very pleasant billiard room outside the library.

After a conducted tour of Perth, we boarded the train for the east after dinner. At Coolgardie we entered the gold mining area, and it was not long before we stopped at Kalgoorlie, a very rich gold mining district indeed. We were met by the manager of the Kalgoorlie Mines who gave us a quick run round the town. There are some famous gold mines there—Wiluna, Great Boulder and the Lake View and Star. The last was one of Gold Fields' interests, and was reputed to be the wealthiest and finest mine in Australia. We lunched at the Railway Hotel, which, with its swing doors, could have come out of a cowboy film; some of the customers also looked as though they came from the Wild West and might draw a gun at any moment.

In Adelaide, an impressive and beautiful city, and subsequently in Melbourne we again enjoyed the hospitality of State Premiers and members of the legislature. In Melbourne I was particularly struck by the library of the Parliament House—quite the finest library I had seen in any of the Dominion Parliaments I had visited. Here Sir Clifden Eager, President of the Council, showed us the journals of the first voyage to Botany Bay, which included a list of convicts, their sentences and where they had been convicted, from Chester to Winchester.

From Melbourne we crossed the Bass Straits to Tasmania, one of the stormiest passages in the world as we discovered on the return journey. Our only official engagement was a reception at Parliament House given by the Premier and the Government, so we had an opportunity to see something of Tasmania. It is a lovely island, on one side exactly like the shires of England and on the other very mountainous and resembling Scotland.

From Melbourne to Sydney by air, and on to New Zealand by steamer, a four-day trip. We reached Auckland on 6th November; I had to give several press conferences and then went to the Grand Hotel for a meeting of the General Council of the Commonwealth Parliamentary Association. I got a very warm welcome from several old friends—Senator Roebuck of Canada, Lord Wilmot of the U.K., Clifton Webb and Harry Coombs of New Zealand, Dr. Malik of Pakistan, Howard d'Egville and many others who had been at the last conference in Ottawa.

We worked very hard for the next day and a half on preparatory work for the Conference, although of course a lot of the spade work had already been done. The delegation had been split, one half which included Shakes Morrison and Jay Llewellin was touring the South Island, while our half was to tour the North Island; we were to join up at Wellington on 24th November for the Conference proper. Leading our part of the U.K. delegation was Lord Alexander of Hillsborough, perhaps better known as A. V. Alexander, a former Socialist Minister. One evening I was sitting in the lounge of the hotel with him and Howard d'Egville when Alexander told a most incredible story about Winston. He said that in May 1940 he, Alexander, had been called to the Admiralty by Winston, who was reputed to have said, 'I hear you are going to wind up the Debate on the Motion of Censure on the Chamberlain Government. Be a sport Albert and let me see your speech.' A. V. Alexander told Winston his main points, which were critical of the Admiralty. Winston then said he would make no reply to the criticisms but deal only with the broad challenge against the Government. That was the Debate, of course, which brought about the downfall of the Chamberlain Government. Winston was most vulnerable, as First Lord of the Admiralty, on the conduct of the Norwegian campaign. There was a great deal of criticism of Winston at the time, soon swamped by larger events. I just couldn't believe that Winston would have made such an overture.

That same evening, Alexander heard from the local newspaper office that the Government at home had been defeated by twelve votes. That news put us all in a fluster. Would we have to fly home? Would there be a General Election immediately? The excitement was terrific. It wasn't until nearly midnight that we learned that it was the Government that had got a majority of twelve. We breathed again, but it was an exciting evening. During it we attended a reception given for us by the Lord Mayor of Auckland.

On 8th November we were up early to start our tour of North Island in a luxurious motor coach. This is not a guide book so I will not trace the route we took or describe the towns or the beauties of the countryside, except to say we went down the Waikato Valley, following the river of that name, until we got to Rotorua. There are a great many Maoris in this area. Traditional Maori songs, hakas, chants and dances greeted us; it was fascinating. I had never seen such a spectacle before. During the evening Lord Alexander, Sir Francis Molamure from Ceylon and I all had to make speeches. We got wonderful receptions. One of the Maori girls I talked to was a Miss McPherson Douglas. The chief was a Mr. Mitchell, whose father hailed from Scotland. How he became a Maori chief I couldn't imagine.

We moved on 20th November to Wanganui. The next day two N.Z. Scots came to see me after dinner and invited me down to the local pipe band practice. I was delighted to go. As a piper, I had been to many pipe band practices in Scotland. The band played for my benefit a tune called *My Ain Highland Hame* and then asked me to join them. We played *All the Blue Bonnets are over the Border*, marching up and down the hall. I stayed with the band for supper. It was a grand evening. I was played off to *Auld Lang Syne* with a tear in my eye.

Next day we set off for Wellington, where on 24th November I was awakened by a howling gale. I was told that Wellington is famous for its gales.

The meeting that day was a business one to adopt the Annual Report and Accounts and also the draft Constitution which three of us in General Council had prepared at Ottawa in 1949. Over forty Parliaments were represented by about ninety delegates, including those from New Zealand. Senator Roebuck of Canada was in the Chair. The members of the General Council were on the platform. The meeting lasted all day, with a break for lunch. The speeches were long and very repetitive.

After the Conference adjourned the members of the U.K. Delegation met at the English High Commissioner's office to discuss the agenda and speeches for next week. It had been arranged that I would make the U.K. speech on defence. Every day, indeed every moment, was filled in and after the meeting we had a cocktail party at Parliament House. Mr. Speaker Oram of New Zealand received the guests.

All week-end we had howling gales—very unpleasant. The four Scots of the delegation, Shakes Morrison, Gomme-Duncan, Gilbert McAlister and I attended the service at St. Andrew's Presbyterian Church.

On 27th November the Conference proper was opened by Senator Roebuck in the Chair. Prime Minister Holland of New Zealand gave the first address in a good downright speech. He was full of common sense, though not a brilliant politician. Thereafter Lord Wilmot took the Chair and Walter Nash, Leader of the New Zealand Opposition, opened the discussion on economic affairs.

In the afternoon the Debate was resumed by Lord Llewellin in a good speech, not too pompous as he was sometimes inclined to be. The Debate was wound up by Lord Alexander and Walter Nash, the latter making a very Socialistic speech which irritated me and most of the others.

The Conference next day was on Parliamentary Government. Sir Francis Molamure, Speaker of the Ceylon Parliament, was in the Chair. The opening speaker was Mr. John Diefenbaker of Canada. He made a first-class speech in somewhat old-fashioned Gladstonian style; indeed he was a descendant of Gladstone. He later became Prime Minister of Canada. The U.K. speaker was David Jones, M.P. for the Hartlepools.

Dr. Malik of Pakistan opened the discussion in the afternoon. He was most thoughtful but, as he didn't speak English too well, he was a bit trying to listen to. He had some searching things to say about Parliamentary representatives—they were too often selected for their gift of the gab and not for their character, principles and experience.

The Debate next morning was on defence, with Mr. Speaker Oram in the Chair. It was opened by Lord Alexander, who read every word of his speech, and it was not a very good one either. I also took part in the Debate as the U.K. speaker. I was in good form and many people said it was the best speech of the Conference. It certainly wasn't that, but it was satisfactory to know that it was well thought of and there was a flattering sequel to it. A few days later I was asked by the Prime Minister, Mr. Holland, to lunch. There were other Ministers present, including the Minister of Defence, Mr. McDonald. After a few preliminaries, the Prime Minister told me they had been much impressed by my speech at the Conference and the Minister of Defence wondered if I could stay on a further month and address meetings on defence in the main cities of New Zealand. I was naturally pleased but my schedule was a tight one and I couldn't see how I could possibly fit it in, so regretfully I had to say 'No'.

There was a State Luncheon at the House of Commons, with the Prime Minister in the Chair. It was a most impressive occasion and the singing of the National Anthem by 250 Parliamentary representatives, representing forty-two Parliaments, was something I shall never forget. The majority were of course New Zealanders. The speeches afterwards were all too long.

On St. Andrew's Night the Scottish members of the British delegation were invited to the Town Hall for a Scots National Concert to celebrate the great day. It was packed. At least a hundred pipers and drummers were on the platform. The crowd was most enthusiastic. The Chairman announced our presence in the front row. There was a deafening roar of applause when the Chairman told them we were all Scots and afterwards many of the audience crowded round us to know where we came from, many with tears in their eyes. We Scots are a sentimental lot.

This was the last day of Conference. The Debate was in secret, on foreign affairs, but it could easily have been in open discussion, for there was nothing secret about it. By that time my wife, who had been on a tour of New Zealand by herself, joined me in Wellington and on 4th December we had a night voyage from Wellington to Christchurch. We then toured the South Island, visiting Mount Cook which is over 12,000 ft high. The scenery was magnificent. Then to Queenstown and Dunedin, the Edinburgh of the South.

We returned to Wellington on 19th December and stayed at the Waterloo Hotel until we boarded the *Rangitoto* for the voyage home to England. The ship sailed in the late evening of the 22nd with pipers playing *The Skye Boat Song* as we glided away from the wharf. Our fellow passengers included the Archbishop of Canterbury and Mrs. Fisher, and the Speaker of the New Zealand Parliament, Mr. Oram, and his wife. They were delightful people and we became great friends. They stayed with us in Scotland several times and we also stayed with them again in New Zealand. From Pitcairn Island, where we lay-to off the shore, we went through the Panama Canal, stopped at Curacao, then sailed across the Atlantic. We entered the English Channel on the morning of 21st January. The voyage was over. It had been a long absence from the U.K. and a pretty hectic one.

It did not occur to me that my travelling days were just beginning and that in the years to come I was to visit Australia, America, Mexico, Canada, New Zealand and South Africa, not to mention the Soviet Union and other European countries.

CHAPTER 21

Politics, Monotype and Gold

I was soon right back in the Parliamentary swing again. I was also busy in the constituency as I had a feeling there would soon be a General Election. I asked a lot of questions in the House right up to the Summer Recess. It looked then as if the election would be in the autumn. It was, and our preparations were in full swing.

The Conservative Party was most optimistic. The Socialists only held office by a slender majority and it was felt that, with a hefty push by the Tories, the Socialists could be put out of office. The election was held in October 1951. In Richmond I was returned with a majority of 14,036. The Liberal candidate lost his deposit. That was the largest majority I had yet had in Richmond. The Conservative Party was back in power.

I had realised for some time, and had said so to the powers-that-be in the party, that I would not be available for a full-time job. My children were now twelve, ten and eight—all of them at prep schools, and there were heavy educational expenses ahead of me. Inevitably my main interests would increasingly lie outside the House of Commons.

One of my major interests apart from Gold Fields was the Monotype Corporation. That was a fascinating company. When I was first invited on the Board Sir Geoffrey Ellis, M.P., was Chairman, and Sir Eugene Ramsden, M.P., Deputy Chairman. I became Chairman in 1953.

Monotype had always a number of politicians on the Board, and in my time we had Harold Macmillan, before he became Prime Minister, and then his son Maurice until he too left the Board to join the Government. Ramsden and Geoffrey Ellis had been in the House of Commons and from the other House was Gavin Astor, who succeeded his father, Lord Astor of Hever. When I became Chairman, John Spencer-Wills, afterwards Sir

Politics, Monotype and Gold

John, became Deputy Chairman, a partnership which continued until 1970.

After the war we were very lucky to have an up-and-coming young Secretary, not long demobilised from the army. He was a chartered accountant, but more than that a first-class business executive who later became Managing Director. He was Jack Matson, a lad of parts as we say in Scotland. He became well known in the printing machinery world and in the printing world generally. He and his wife became our good friends and they frequently stayed with us in Scotland.

Connected with the company was a Monotype Users Association with branches in different parts of the United Kingdom. We had annual lunches at all those centres but the principal one and the most important was in London. We had an annual lunch at the Connaught Rooms when I took the Chair. It was a common thing to have over 300 Monotype users at these lunches. I think they had a tremendous influence in stimulating the successes of the Corporation. We were still struggling for some years after the war but from 1955 we began to get back into a more agreeable stride.

In March 1958 the 50th Annual General Meeting of the Corporation was held. Our main problem was the oppressive burden of taxation. For every £1 paid to shareholders the Government was having to claim £2:15s. for the Chancellor of the Exchequer. The share the Government takes nowadays is disproportionately large. But it will get larger and larger.

At the Annual Meeting that year I had an excellent story to tell regarding the Monotype Corporation. The income and profits for 1957–8 were most satisfactory. The net profits stood at £215,565, which was £93,000 more than the previous year. It was certainly a sharp recovery.

The previous year I was President of the Printers Pension Corporation on the 130th anniversary of its foundation and I was able to announce that during the year of my office a total of £66,000 was subscribed to its annual appeal for funds. A dinner was held at the Connaught Rooms at which I presided; I wore full Highland dress for the occasion. I mentioned, in the course of my speech, that the Duke of Wellington in 1857 had collected £503, and in 1907 Lord Northcliffe reached

£8,700. My old friend Sir William Mabane proposed the vote of thanks in most generous terms and then I announced as my successor another old friend, Sir James Waterlow.

In 1961 the *Investors Chronicle* announced that for the third year in succession the Monotype Corporation had shown a substantial rise in profits and an increase in the dividend. The reliability of its product and the natural expansion in demand had helped sales to move steadily upwards. In 1961 our trading profit was nearly £1 million. The company, of course, is a world-wide undertaking and undoubtedly had a great potential for future expansion in the developing countries of the world. Indeed a feature of 1961 had been the heavy demands for our products which had outstripped output, so the directors decided we should erect an ancillary manufacturing factory at Dunfermline in Scotland. That year exports formed 69% of the total sales; the Corporation exhibited widely at trade fairs abroad, including Barcelona, Poznan and Brno. Over the past seven years our export turnover had increased by almost 130%, while our home sales rose by over 70%. These were results of which we could be justly proud.

I officially opened the new factory in Dunfermline in August 1961 and already fifty new jobs had been created in manufacturing component parts for Monotype machines. We then transported the parts south for assembly at the Corporation's main factory at Salfords, Redhill, Surrey, where at that time some 1,300 people were employed. The factory at Dunfermline cost £125,000.

In opening the factory I told the employees, and the large number of people who came to see the opening, something about the company's history. It was essential that the new employees in Fife should know something about the organisation as a whole so that they would feel part of the operation. I told them that the word 'Monotype' was the Corporation's registered trade mark and was stamped on all our products, the chief of which were the type-setting and type-casting machines. Every day you read printed matter in some form. Much of it was composed on equipment manufactured by the Corporation. Books, advertisements, magazines, television, calendars, bills and receipts, comic papers, time-tables, Bibles

Politics, Monotype and Gold

and even race cards were probably all set in this way. This book that you are reading was composed by Monophoto equipment.

The first Monotype installation was made in London in the year 1900. For 450 years before that all type was set by hand with separate pieces of metal for every letter, punctuation mark, figure, space etc. It was a slow and laborious process and many inventors in the nineteenth century tried to find ways to mechanise it. Two men were ultimately successful, one of whom was Lanson with the single type Monotype machine. Lanson was American. His invention has certainly had an enormous impact in this century.

In July 1963 the International Printing Exhibition was held in London. Monotype had a very well-equipped stand and attracted many potential customers. At the time of the Exhibition we had our annual Monotype Users Association lunch at the Connaught Rooms; over 600 attended. That was a record and I paid a warm tribute to the organisers of IPEX. It was the best of its kind ever held in the United Kingdom. There was no doubt that it helped the Corporation a great deal.

A new system, which does not use conventional methods of type-setting with hot metal, was rapidly gaining ground, and had enormous potential in the future. The latest instalment of this Monophoto film-setting equipment was handed over at Tonbridge by me, as Chairman of Monotype, to Sir Denis Truscott, Chairman of Brown Knight and Truscott of Dowgate Works, Tonbridge. This machine has revolutionised the printing industry but at that time there were very few in this country.

This was a significant step forward in the development of printing technique in an industry which for 500 years had used basically the same method of reproduction. The machine eliminates the difficulties of handling and storing metal type and its output is very much faster than the old method. Sir Denis Truscott, after receiving the film-setter, said that, having taken many orders from me when in my brigade, he was very glad now to be able to give this order to Sir George.

By now there are Monophoto film-setters in operation all over the world, their product ranging from telephone directories in Persian to newspapers in Urdu.

In June 1966 the Monotype Corporation received the Queen's Award for Industry, one out of only eighteen of the 115 companies put forward. The Award to Monotype was made for both export achievement and technological innovation in film-setting and type-setting. This Award had been won by the hard work of everyone. Success was due to the meticulous standard maintained by the staff at Salfords and at Dunfermline, and by the constant research which had kept their equipment in the forefront of type-setting machinery. Monotype then employed 2,000 at Salfords and 250 at Dunfermline. A further expansion of the Monotype Works was now under way. The Monotype Corporation was one of the few companies in the country to obtain the Queen's Award on both counts.

During the war the Monotype offices in Fetter Lane were destroyed in the bombing of London, and the company moved to Lincoln's Inn Fields. It was our earnest determination to rebuild at the earliest moment after the war but, of course, a lot of London had been destroyed and we had to take our turn. As a result, it was not until 1955 that Monotype House, the new headquarters of the Corporation, was officially opened by me, on the Monday in May which was the anniversary of the blitz of the former building fourteen years before, in a brief ceremony when I unveiled a plaque commemorating the event in the entrance hall of 43 Fetter Lane. The building occupies an island site facing the Record Office at the point where Fetter Lane is diverted through to Holborn Circus. On the first floor is the Board Room, a splendid room, and there is a Directors' Dining Room at the top of the building where we entertained customers to lunch.

We had, of course, our ups and downs—fortunately mostly ups. When speaking at the Monotype Users Association in April 1969, I stated that orders for hot metal composing machines were still coming in, despite the advances being made on photo composition. I could report that the Corporation had recently sold its 300th Monophoto film-setter to the United States—a good achievement in a difficult market—and that sales of the new electric perforator in this country were very encouraging. These successful lines indicated that the Corporation was making the sort of equipment that customers wanted.

Politics, Monotype and Gold

In September of 1969 I made a bright half-yearly report on the firm's trading. Sales were 10% up at around £3.3 million, and profits too were correspondingly up and we looked like having a good year.

Changes, however, were taking place. The Monotype Corporation, because of the value of its new head offices in Fetter Lane and the many acres of ground near our factory, soon began to attract the 'take-over boys'. This was at the time when take-overs were the quick way to make personal fortunes. According to some newspapers it had long been a take-over prospect. A company called Grendon Trust and its associates acquired from B.E.T., whose Chairman was Deputy Chairman of Monotype, some 30% of the Monotype shares. They had already acquired a substantial number of shares. An attractive offer was made to Monotype shareholders and Grendon took over this famous Corporation.

They asked me to continue as Chairman for the time being, which I was glad to do to look after the interests of the Monotype staff as far as I could. I retired later that year and was made President of the Company in view of my long service to it of nearly thirty years.

As an outside director of Consolidated Gold Fields, I found myself being more and more attracted to its fortunes. This was helped by my visits to the USA in 1949, when I first met the Gold Fields' American staff in New York, and to Lake View and Star gold mine in Western Australia in 1950. I had also met many of Gold Fields' personnel and seen something of their mines during my visit to South Africa in 1947. I was being drawn closer to Gold Fields itself. It was not, however, until about 1950 that I felt that was where my future lay.

Mr. Robert Annan, Chairman, and Mr. Malcolm Maclachlan, a Managing Director with wide financial experience, asked me to dine on several occasions and suggested that I should become a full-time director of the company. I was attracted by the idea but I was not sure that office hours were what I wanted. I had never really had to clock in and clock out. I asked time to consider their proposition. I pondered the proposal and then Annan and Maclachlan asked me to dinner again. I mentioned one or two reservations I had. However, in course of the discussion, I found myself agreeing. I had the greatest respect for Annan. He had a good brain and was an expert mining man, and I felt that, with my wide experience and capacity for hard work, I might be able to add something to the running of the company.

In 1951 I became Managing Director of the company, in 1954 its Deputy Chairman and six months later Chief Executive as well. I have had my leg pulled on what was called my meteoric rise. I took the Chair at the Managing Director's meetings and from that time Gold Fields was my main interest in life. Indeed it had been so when I was made Managing Director in 1951.

Shortly after my appointment as Chief Executive my wife and I sailed in the *City of Exeter* for South Africa. Soon after I arrived I opened the seventh uranium plant to be started in South Africa. This was at Luipards Vlei mine near Krugersdorp. In opening the plant I said that the South African uranium production programme had been not only spectacular but also an impressive example of the ability of the free nations to work together amicably for the common good. The cost of the project was not far short of £3 million and a distance of more than thirteen miles had been advanced in underground development to open up the Bird Reef since the work began three years before. On this occasion we had a very wide view of Gold Fields' interests in South Africa.

On my return to England about the end of February I realised that I would soon have another election on my hands. This was the very thing I had wanted to avoid, for since I became Chief Executive of Gold Fields I had really made up my mind to retire from Parliament and give my whole attention to Gold Fields and my City interests. However, I was surprised to find that, although I had not been very active in the 1950 Parliament, my local Conservative Party did not want me to retire, and so I was unanimously adopted Conservative candidate again. In 1955 the election result was Harvie-Watt, Conservative, 27,628; Barr, Socialist, 14,673; Haynes, Liberal, 5,266. My Conservative majority was 12,955. This was my seventh and last Parliamentary election. I had been in Parliament since

1931 with an interruption of less than two years from 1935 to 1937.

Now, of course, I was heavily involved in the City and I became more so when I was elected to the Board of the Midland Bank in 1956, the Eagle Star in 1957, and later to the Standard Bank. It was clear that my Parliamentary days were coming to an end.

In March 1958 I announced I would not be standing for re-election to Parliament. That was what I should have done in 1950. My heavy engagements overseas in my capacity as Chief Executive of Consolidated Gold Fields made Parliament an impossible commitment for me.

During the remaining days in Westminster I was often abroad on business. I was also frequently in the constituency, where everywhere I went many constituents said how sorry they were that I was retiring. At the meeting when I officially made this announcement I advised them to look for a man of forty or fifty years of age who had been lucky enough to have made a fortune, or a young man who was wealthy and didn't need to bother about earning a living. And so I bowed out of the political scene.

In June 1958 I was one of the twenty-five Territorial Army Officers presented to the Queen at the Hyde Park Golden Jubilee Parade and Review of the Territorial Army by Her Majesty. I had been thirty-six years in the T.A., having joined as a sapper in 1922. I had held every rank, from corporal and sergeant up to brigadier, in that time. I was still one of Her Majesty's Territorial A.D.C.s. I think the Army is one of the most enjoyable hobbies that any man could wish for. This was my last parade in the T.A.

Gold Fields was now my major interest, and a fascinating one at that. I had studied the history of the company thoroughly and closely. The more I pondered its problems the more I considered changes in its interests and in the countries of its operations. Gold was the major basis of our investment and 30% of our income came from gold mines. The largest interests of the company were in Africa. In fact, at one time, we had over 90% of our interests in Africa while the rest—in America,

Australia and the U.K.—were to a certain extent minor interests.

In my view we had come to a cross-roads. We had too many eggs in one basket. The first thing to be done was to unload our investments in the less safe areas of Africa (this was years before Harold Macmillan's 'wind of change' speech). When I first suggested my ideas to my colleagues they were really horrified, especially the older ones. I wanted to get out of all our interests north of the Republic of South Africa. I felt that the Republic had a longer life than the northern states. That was my thinking in 1954.

We, therefore, gradually got rid of our interests in Kenya, Tanganyika and even Rhodesia. In their place I wanted to open up in Australia when we already had two outposts at Lake View and Star and Lake George. There were also New Zealand and Canada, and we had an American office in New York but our interests were small. I wanted to develop old interests and set up new worthwhile ventures. Above all I also wanted to develop in the United Kingdom. I was trying to build up in what I considered to be the safest areas of the world. That was, of course, nearly twenty-five years ago. And I did not want to have our only real interest based on gold, vital though that was and must remain.

I wanted a carousel where all the horses were not down at the same time and I did not want Gold Fields to have all its interests in the one commodity. It seemed a simple policy, but to bring it about was not easy. First of all there was a lot of built-in prejudice in favour of Africa, not only South Africa. Secondly, many of the Gold Fields' directors were suspicious of involving the company in minerals other than gold which had been the basis of our success for so many years. There was never any question of dropping our gold interest, but I was determined to proceed with the policy, for I had been examining the position and prospects of the company for some time. There were a lot of mutterings, and some of my colleagues were apprehensive lest we were taking a step into the dark.

Our first development was in Canada, where we started in 1956 the New Consolidated Canadian Exploration Company in Toronto which was, and is, the great business centre in

Canada. This was a slow starter and has not yet reached our expectations, although we have made money there by buying a company in British Columbia, building it up and selling it at a good profit. We bought another company which is also still going slowly and we have done a lot of exploration, but so far without any spectacular success. I visited Canada regularly to get the lie of the land.

We also started New Consolidated Gold Fields (Australian) with headquarters in Sydney. I went out to see it started and from the beginning this was a more lively animal. Australia soon began to spread its wings, not by exploration but by acquisition.

At the same time Gold Fields and our rival Central Mining, another finance house like ourselves, began discussions to see if we could merge the two companies. In my view it was a natural, but we failed to reach agreement. Not long afterwards Sir Archibald Forbes became Chairman of Central Mining. We were old friends and we often mourned the fact that the merger had not taken place. If he had been in the Chair at the time of the merger talks I'm certain it would have been a fait accompli, with great advantage to both companies. However, I was on the look-out and I studied the position of many companies. Ths was at a time when take-over bids were becoming common in the City. It was prudent to forestall these predators in every way one could.

In 1957 Gold Fields and the British South African Company made an offer for a two-thirds holding in the South West Africa Company. The partners acquired 33% of the shares and Gold Fields took over the administration of the company—a timid step forward. Another step was made a year later in 1958. The Board of Gold Fields, as a protective measure, took the precaution of removing the voting rights of three million preference shares.

In order to secure Gold Fields from the predator it was necessary that we should enlarge our interests by friendly take-overs where possible, and in 1959 we made an offer for the Anglo French Company. It was an old-established mining finance company which held gold, oil, copper and tin interests and they were close friends of Gold Fields. Their interests fitted in with ours and their directors raised no opposition to our offer.

Roland Cottell was the Chairman, with a good financial background. These steps, however, were only mere gropings towards larger things. I therefore kept on examining companies which might be helpful in the expansion of Gold Fields.

One of the companies which was put up to me for consideration was New Union Goldfields. It was controlled by Mr. Harley Drayton, who was a well-known financial figure in the City. Under his control New Union Goldfields was creeping out of the doldrums and was under new management in South Africa. One of the leading figures was Martin Rich, an associate of Drayton who had been sent out to South Africa to pull the company round. He was ably supported by Harry McKay and Sid Segal.

Another company associated with Drayton's interests in South Africa was H.E. Proprietary which appealed to me. They had mining investments not only in South Africa but in Australia and Canada, and three companies in Britain. All these seemed to fit into my expansion plans for Gold Fields.

These Drayton interests were well studied and, in due course, I got in touch with Harley Drayton. He had had a remarkable success, starting as the proverbial office boy. Everything he touched seemed to turn to gold 'in every way'. I met him often, for he was on the Board of the Midland Bank when I joined that Board. One day I told him I would like to talk to him about New Union Goldfields. I told him briefly what was in my mind. He at once asked me to dine with him in his house in Millionaires' Row. I gave him brief notes on the subject I wished to talk to him about and terms. His wife joined us for dinner then left us to our discussions. I outlined my proposals. He asked for only one small concession. I agreed and the deal was concluded, subject to the agreement of our respective Boards.

It was one of the simplest take-overs I had had and was to have. I knew what I wanted and he knew what he wanted and it was beneficial to both companies. He suggested that one of his directors should come on the Gold Fields' Board. I agreed but with two provisions. They were that Harley Drayton himself should come on the Board at the beginning of the merger and that his nominee Martin Rich should come on in about two years' time when he had finished his job in South Africa, by which time I felt that the two companies would be fully integrated. We had also gained an extremely able recruit in Harry McKay who became an executive director and an expert in our Investment Department. He was a quiet, simple man with great ability and I had a profound admiration for his sterling worth not only as an executive but as a man. We also had another first-class executive in Sidney Segal, who, however, went to our growing Australian company and finished up as Chairman of that concern.

The take-over of New Union Goldfields was, therefore, a step which led to great developments in the United Kingdom as well as in South Africa. The pattern of my policy was beginning to emerge and develop. The cost of these transactions to Gold Fields in shares and cash for New Union and its subsidiaries was £4.2 million and for H.E. Proprietary, including subsidiaries, was £3.5 million. In 1959 Gold Fields increased its capital from £11 million to £14 million by the issue of £3 million new shares.

We had taken over interests in tin, diamonds and copper, and from H.E. Proprietary a company called Alumasc, a die-casting and pressing firm specialising in low pressure aluminium castings. That company was a step into industry and was a great success, one of its successful products being aluminium beer barrels.

Another company we acquired by our arrangement with H.E. Proprietary was Moussec Ltd. There used to be an illuminated advertisement in Trafalgar Square, 'She shall have Moussec wherever she goes' with lights showing the golden liquid being poured from a bottle into a glass. It was a champagne type of drink. I remember at the time calling at various bars and pubs and asking for it, to find out if there was any demand for Moussec and whether it was a popular drink. I could usually get it, but the various barmen told me it was not a best seller. In the event, we thought it was a company outside our scope so we sold it, and at a profit.

All these changes were reflected by the profit figures and in 1959–60 the results were the best the company had ever achieved. In 1960 Robert Annan celebrated his seventy-fifth birthday and his sixteenth year as Chairman of Gold Fields. He was a very fit man for his age, both mentally and physically. He delivered his last address to the shareholders and I had the privilege of proposing a vote of thanks on behalf of the staff and shareholders. His sixteen years as Chairman were indeed notable and distinguished.

In that year I succeeded him as Chairman. I don't think we ever had any real arguments in the Board Room, although some of my colleagues were sometimes apprehensive as to what we were doing and where we were going. Mr. Annan became the first President of the company. For me the years had flown. Politics were away behind me and I had no regrets. Gold Fields was my basic interest and I enjoyed every minute of that absorbing task.

Chapter 22

Consolidated Gold Fields

As I have previously said, what I had been aiming at for Gold Fields was a kind of carousel with each horse representing a different country and also a different interest—industry, base metals etc., and not just gold.

We had begun to achieve this policy and ambition, and the reconstruction of the company, which had been my dream, was now starting to unfold itself. During all that time I had been visiting South Africa, Canada, Australia, New Zealand and the United States. I had already visited all these countries as Hon. Treasurer of the British Branch of the Commonwealth Parliamentary Association and also as a British delegate to Commonwealth Conferences, so I was no stranger to them and I had got to know most of the leading political figures which proved to be a great asset in my present task. I had also made many business contacts.

At the Annual General Meeting in 1961 I said, 'While expansion and diversification is our immediate objective I would like to take this opportunity of stressing that the expansion of our business into new fields does not entail any diminution of our interests in the Republic of South Africa. We are proud of our long association with that country and have confidence in their ability to work out a just, realistic and lasting solution of their problems and to develop for the benefit of all sections of the country the vast natural resources which they enjoy.'

Fortunately in 1958 I had brought Mr. Potier into the company. He was a chartered accountant, with a distinguished career in the R.A.F. in the war. He made a first-class Deputy Chairman, for he was full of energy and shared my views about the expansion of Gold Fields. In 1959 Donald McCall also became a director. From then on he played a big part in the new developments. Both men were young, competent and hard-working. I could not have had a better team. Gold Fields in South Africa produced some brilliant engineers and administrators; in 1960 W. J. Busschau was appointed Resident Director. He was a Rhodes Scholar and had a first-class brain.

As Australia was beginning to expand and develop, it was essential I should find someone there of top calibre. I was lucky to discover J. B. Massy-Greene. He was the son of a Federal Treasurer and distinguished political figure in Australian politics. Massy-Greene had a wide knowledge of Australian industry and mining and was a well-known personality. He did a lot for Gold Fields as Managing Director, and subsequently Chairman, in Australia.

I was more than ever convinced that we had to expand and to adapt ourselves to the changes in the New World. I felt rather like a commercial traveller. Like any salesman I had to visit the areas where developments were taking place. In America we already had offices in New York, with two stalwarts in Carl Lindberg and John Nicholls. We had started the Canadian company, as well as the Australian company, in 1956. Our headquarters were in Toronto and Sydney. At that stage they were merely outposts with scouting parties looking for the kind of investments we wanted in those countries.

For many years Gold Fields had interests in America but they were small and as a springboard were disappointing. However, in 1958 contact was made with Howard Young, President of American Zinc Lead and Smelting Company at St. Louis. He was a power in the land of zinc. At that time the zinc industry was suffering one of its frequent periods of depression. Vic Allen of our New York office was always looking for new areas for our own Tri-State Zinc Company before the reserves at Galena were worked out. The plan was for a joint venture at a cost estimated at £1.5 million. It was put up to Gold Fields and a joint venture emerged—The New Market Zinc Venture— and I was invited to become a director of American Zinc. Howard Young and I became great friends. He was an outstanding figure in American mining affairs and was trying to find capital for its reconstruction and expansion of its mining activities. We were naturally interested and Vic Allen, now President of Gold Fields American Corporation, flew to San

Francisco to meet me on my way back from Australia to bring me the up-to-date position.

When I arrived at the American Zinc directors' meeting in New York I was determined to outbid another company which was showing interest, although at that stage I had no idea how it could be done. When I had listened to Howard Young's statement I asked him to defer any decision until I had consulted my colleagues in London. This was agreed to. The rapidity with which we in Gold Fields acted created a profound impression on the directors of American Zinc and, in due course, a deal was concluded.

On 23rd May 1963 I issued a statement to the effect that I was delighted with the relationship of our companies and welcomed American Zinc as part of the Gold Fields Group and as representing our most important interest in the Western Hemisphere. Our aim would be to increase the profitability of American Zinc in every way possible and to strengthen and broaden the foundation on which our joint venture would be built, whether by developing the inherent potential of existing assets or by moving into new enterprises in the United States and elsewhere. Gold Fields financed the purchase of the American Zinc shares by raising in New York an $18 million loan from American banks, led by the Bankers Trust Co. That investment was the biggest single deal we had made up to that time. As a result, Gold Fields now held a major position in the base metal mining and smelting industry in the United States. American Zinc was then one of the giants in that particular field.

Our company's interests were changing fast and I decided to change the parent company's title from Consolidated Goldfields of South Africa to Consolidated Gold Fields. I stated in my speech at the Annual General Meeting in 1963 that for some time we had felt that it was no longer appropriate for the parent company to have a geographic limitation to its title. Gold Fields was undoubtedly international in scope and that is the title by which the company is now known throughout the world.

In Australia also we found a land of venture. There everything was expanding—population, industry and opportunity. Gold Fields had invested many millions in that country and its advance had been spectacular, although in recent times we have had our disappointments we well as our successes. I think one of our most impressive steps was the building of Gold Fields House in Sydney. My wife laid the foundation stone. It is a twenty-seven-storey building on Sydney Cove and when it was completed it was the second highest in Sydney. Remembering the long arguments we had over our decision to go ahead, I think it was a correct decision, for it helped to put Gold Fields on the map and gave us the prestige building so essential at that time.

I first became interested in Australia when I visited all the State capitals on my way to the Commonwealth Parliamentary Conference in New Zealand. On that occasion I had visited Lake View and Star and had met Dolph Agnew for the first time at Kalgoorlie. Dolph's father, John Agnew, had been Chairman of Gold Fields and now Dolph's son Rudolph is one of the leading personalities and Chief Executive of the parent company, with the future Chair of the company within his grasp. It was that visit to Australia in 1950 which stirred my imagination as to what Gold Fields might do in this land of opportunity. Although my first visits to Canada, USA, Australia and New Zealand were all political, there was no doubt that I looked at them to see where mining and other interests might be developed. I knew I would be back.

Early in 1962 my wife opened the extended headquarters of Gold Fields of South Africa in Johannesburg. The extension, costing approximately £400,000, had become necessary as a result of absorption of other companies in the Gold Fields Group. It is a ten-storey building. The Board Room furnishings include some of the original furniture installed by Cecil Rhodes, the founder of the company.

By that time I thought that, as the Group was expanding so quickly in many parts of the world, it was necessary that the heads of the new companies of Gold Fields should meet and get to know one another. I discussed it with my colleagues in London. In principle, we quickly agreed it was a good idea. Most of them thought the conferences should be held in London, or near London, so that in their spare time the visitors could see the sights and go to theatres and enjoy themselves.

I had quite a different idea altogether. I wanted a captive audience that would be forced to stay under one roof and in that way build up a closer friendship. I also thought wives should be invited so that they too would get to know the Gold Fields family. It was quite a bombshell I dropped when I told my colleagues that I thought the best place for the conference to be held was Gleneagles in the heart of the Highlands. There I knew there were golf courses, tennis courts, swimming and bowls, and dancing at night. All the delegates would be together and I would lay on the odd coach tour for wives to see the Highland scenery. This was finally agreed.

The conference was held from 2nd to 9th July 1964 and was subsequently acclaimed by all who attended as a most worthwhile and memorable experience. At the beginning of the conference my wife and I entertained in our own home the Chairman of each of the companies represented—Mr. and Mrs. Massy-Greene from Australia; Mr. and Mrs. Mason Smith from the United States, and also from that country Mr. and Mrs. Howard Young of American Zinc; and Dr. and Mrs. Busschau from South Africa. I laid on my pipers to play at dinner to give them the Scottish touch, and I wore the kilt.

I opened the conference by giving a talk on the British scene, political and economic. Then the heads of each of the delegations did the same for their countries—Dr. Busschau for South Africa, Mr. Mason Smith for America, Ian Crookston for Canada and Mr. Massy-Greene for Australia. There were also lectures on different aspects of our world-wide activities. They included a lecture on technical progress in the gold mining industry by Ian Louw, now the Chairman of Gold Fields of South Africa. There were also lectures on different industries, including American Zinc and Alumasc. A lecture on Tennants was given by the Chairman, Lord Glenconner. The lectures were of a high standard and the subsequent discussions on each were indeed stimulating.

After the conference my wife and I entertained the top technical directors from each of our territories, accompanied by their wives. During it we entertained at our home all the other delegates and their wives, about eighty altogether. Fortunately it was a good day and we were able to have our buffet lunch outside. A few people had a bathe off the rocks in front of our house but those from the warm waters of South Africa were in and out in a matter of seconds. They were staggered to hear that my wife bathed regularly each day in the summer months. On the last night at Gleneagles the conference delegates sang *Auld Lang Syne* amid much good feeling. It had a great impact on the Group, we felt like one family.

In the autumn of that year, the *Guardian* gave me quite a write-up. 'In the ten years since Sir George Harvie-Watt Q.C. became responsible for the expansion and diversification of the Consolidated Gold Fields Group its assets have increased from £34 million to something like £100 million and its profits, after tax, from £1.3 million to £4.2 million. In the five years since he was promoted to the Chair, first occupied by Cecil Rhodes the Group Founder, Sir George has risen to the challenge in a way that has caught the City's attention. While the Group's South African business in gold, platinum, uranium and other interests have been further developed, it is spreading fast into other countries and different fields.'

In the autumn of 1964, not many months after the conference, my wife cut the first turf at Kloof, the latest gold mine of Consolidated Gold Fields. Kloof, which means cleft in the rocks, has now had a town built called Glen Harvie. She had previously cut the first sod at the Harvie-Watt shaft of the Libanon mine. She also launched a trawler built at Hall Russell's yard, Aberdeen, for a South African firm. These are only samples of the tasks that fell upon her as the Chairman's wife. Fortunately her political experience stood her in good stead. As a politician's wife she had to make many speeches of all kinds, even political speeches. As the wife of the Chairman of a large group of companies there were many engagements which fell to her lot. In that way she was a tremendous help, for many M.Ps' or Chairmen's wives I have met have been tongue-tied and could only say a few words, and even those had been carefully rehearsed.

In March 1965 I paid a return visit to New Zealand. I had always meant to go back, for it is one of the most beautiful countries in the world. I also had New Zealand very much in my mind when I was building up Gold Fields, especially in Aus-

Consolidated Gold Fields

tralia. When I arrived in Auckland, in an interview with the Press I stated that I hoped the Gold Fields Group could expand in New Zealand. We had made our first venture in 1964 with the purchase of 51% of the shares in Zip Industries. I was now out to examine this recent acquisition and see if there were any other prospects which should be investigated. Zip Industries was quite a prosperous company which made water heaters, space heaters, frying pans and electric blankets. I got two of their electric fires in 1965 and they are still going strong in Scotland. Zip Industries, which had more than a dozen factories, employed over 500 people with its main production plant at Lower Hutt.

I then visited Australia, where our interests were rapidly growing. Our investments in Australia at that time included a 60% interest in Commonwealth Mining Investments Australia Ltd. This was then our most recent acquisition and I well remember the occasion. It was during one of my earlier visits to Australia. Frank Beggs was then our representative in that country. I had told him to produce, for my inspection, lists of possible acquisitions for us to peruse together. When I got to Sydney he had ready for me detailed information about many companies. We sat the whole day in our shirt sleeves in my suite in the hotel.

It was grillingly hot with no air conditioning. He kept on showing me details of very large companies and I said we must aim our sights a lot lower. We went over those reports many times until I felt it was a useless task. It was at that moment that I picked up papers relating to a much smaller company in which Frank thought I wouldn't be interested. It was the dossier of Commonwealth Mining. It was just the right size and what I had been thinking of all along. I asked him if he knew the people involved. He did, and we started right away to make overtures which, in the end, were successful. That was the start.

We then made further investments in rapid succession in Associated Minerals Consolidated (67%), Wyong Minerals—Rutile Interests (65%), Bellambi Coal and Lawrenson Alumasc (53%). The most recent acquisitions were 57% in Mount Lyell Mining Company Copper and a large interest in Rennison Zinc through Mount Lyell. Apart from A£6.5 million outlay on the iron-ore developments in Western Australia, Consolidated Gold Fields was planning to spend at least A£10 million in other mining ventures in Australia.

It was on that visit that my wife laid the foundation stone of Gold Fields House, Sydney Cove. She said, 'I've cut the first sod twice and I've launched a ship. This is my first foundation stone.'

Another great development was the iron-ore mines in N.W. Australia. The Gold Fields' partners were Utah Construction and the Cyprus Mines, both American companies. That operation was called Mount Goldsworthy. Dredging and construction of a jetty at Port Headland began in July 1965 and mining started in the early part of 1966. The principal market was Japan. Mr. G. J. Mortimer was made General Manager of Mount Goldsworthy Mining Associates. He was seconded from London for the time being, as one of the most promising members of the Gold Fields staff in London. He was a mining engineer from the Royal School of Mines and had held appointments in South Africa. I met him there and was so impressed by him that I brought him home to the United Kingdom. He was a tower of strength to Gold Fields in many of its ventures and held the position of Chief Executive and Deputy Chairman.

My last duty on this visit was to open the Administration Block at Bellambi Coal Company. I was presented with a painting of the Australian countryside by a famous artist, Leonard Long. This is a picture which has given me much pleasure throughout the years and it is a reminder of a notable visit.

Not long after my return I was busy preparing my speech for the Annual General Meeting. It was all gloom outside the Chartered Insurance Institute where the meeting was held—cold, damp and dreary—but inside there was a feeling of warm optimism. Consolidated Gold Fields, the U.K. registered mining finance house, whose assets now amounted to around £100 million, was in the news following my optimistic annual review of its affairs. The meat of my speech was a Cook's Tour of the Group's £100 million assets. We had a very full meeting. I concluded my speech on a Shakespearian note by quoting Brutus from *Julius Caesar*, 'On such a full sea are we now afloat and we must take the current when it serves.'

1966 was another good year for Gold Fields. It was frequently stated at that time that 'much of the credit for this dynamic policy of expansion which broadened the Group's base and brought rewards to its shareholders must go to Sir George Harvie-Watt who has been responsible for the growth programme for the past twelve years'. It is not often one gets a pat on the back. When things go well nobody bothers, but when things go wrong there are plenty of know-all critics who are only too ready to criticise and tell everybody what should have been done. It is always easy to criticise while looking back. It isn't so easy to try to do well in prospecting the future.

In August 1966, when equity issues were scarce enough because of political and other uncertainties, Consolidated Gold Fields had a rights issue involving £5.5 million. That seemed to surprise a lot of financial journalists who said that the Chairman who was doing this was Sir George Harvie-Watt, responsible for Gold Fields' policies for the last twelve years—'a man with a varied career and distinguished in many fields'. I don't know about the latter comment but I certainly had a varied career which probably allowed me to take a wider look at events and see more clearly into the future. At any rate, in spite of many vicissitudes, Gold Fields Group total revenue advanced to the new peak level of £17,160,000.

In 1967 Gold Fields again broke into new ground when it expanded into the sand and gravel industries in the United Kingdom. This was a follow-up to our policy of increasing our interests at home. We had been looking for some time for suitable expansion, particularly in the extractive industries. Quarrying, sand and gravel come within this view. I thought that a company of this character could form the base of our further expansion in the United Kingdom. Gerry Mortimer was our right-hand man in this large new development. We first took over the Greenwood St. Ives Sand and Gravel Company. The following year, 1968, I went to St. Ives, Huntingdon, to meet about 150 of the firm's employees of all grades. The visit had been arranged for me to meet especially the long-standing employees of the company. More than fifty of them were presented with special Gold Fields ties to mark twenty years' service or more with Greenwoods. A company spokesman said, 'Sir George has not come down on business. Our Parent Company is very strong on the human side and we regard him as a very distinguished visitor. He doesn't want to meet the top boys but to meet the workers and the long-term workers at that.' How right he was.

In 1968, after a six weeks' struggle, Amalgamated Roadstone succumbed to a bid from Gold Fields, bringing our mining group into the forefront of the British sand and gravel and rock-extractive industry. Since its offer for Greenwoods St. Ives in 1967 Gold Fields has bought another four private companies for around £3 million. Amalgamated Roadstone at £34 million now brought the direct investment in aggregate in Britain to about £45 million.

Our ambitions lay still higher in that field. I had talks with Ron Amey about his company, Amey Roadstone, which was probably the best-run of its kind in the country. We would have made a deal at that time but our respective staffs could not come to an amicable agreement and so this amalgamation did not take place until I had stepped down from the Gold Fields Chair. The credit for the amalgamation must go to my successors, Donald McCall and Gerry Mortimer. Ron Amey is, of course, on the Gold Fields Board and brings great knowledge of the aggregate industry to that position. The year ended June 1968 was a wonderful year for Gold Fields, and for me. One City financial writer emphasised the wonder of it for Harvie-Watt who reported profits for the year of £16,348,000 before tax, against £11,231,000 in the previous year. In October 1969 the *Investors Guardian* ran a headline 'Sir George departs in a Blaze of Glory'.

My years with Gold Fields were most rewarding, much more so than my years in any one of my other activities, even politics. If I had never been tempted by the City I might have been more interested in politics, but I found Gold Fields a greater challenge. Well known though this company was when I first joined the Board after the war, it was really well down the league table of Britain's largest companies. In December 1951 the issued capital (ordinary) was £4,200,000, share price 49/4½, market capitalisation £10.4 million. That was the year I became Managing Director. In 1969 when I retired from the Chair of Gold Fields it was the twenty-fifth largest company in Britain at £280 million. The Board was not at all keen for me to retire. I was determined I should do so for various reasons.

First, I had done a long stint of some fifteen years as Chief Executive and eighteen years as Managing Director. Second, I did not believe in top executives staying on after the age of sixty-five. This prevented the keen and energetic members of the staff from getting a chance to climb to the top of the ladder at a reasonably young age. My predecessor had stayed on as an executive until he was seventy-five. Actually I had to stay on for a further period of six months because the man I had chosen to succeed me fell ill and died. It was a tragedy, for Mr. Potier would have made an admirable Chairman. However, Donald McCall, who had been number three in the hierarchy, was ready for the Chair and indeed followed me with great success. When Donald McCall retired from the Chair he was followed by Lord Erroll of Hale—an old friend of mine in Parliament. He had joined the Board after he left the Commons where he had filled several important Government posts—in particular that of President of the Board of Trade; he also had a leading position in the business and City world.

I remained a director and became Consultant to the Company until I was seventy. I then became President which I considered a high honour indeed. I continued to be a director of the Midland Bank, the Clydesdale Bank, the Standard Bank, the Eagle Star Insurance Company, and the North British Steel Group at Bathgate in Scotland. This company included the Atlas Steel Works founded by my father. In my teens I had spent several years there as an apprentice mechanical engineer. Thus I can say I started in steel and finished my working life in steel. The North British Streel Group was managed for many years and greatly expanded by an outstanding trio of brothers named Menzies. Sadly, two of them—Douglas and Ian—died prematurely within the last few years, leaving the eldest brother Macbeth Menzies to continue as Chairman, a man well known and respected for his enterprise and leadership.

In 1970 I was awarded the Gold Medal of the Institution of Mining and Metallurgy in recognition of my 'distinguished services to the world-wide mining industry'. My cup was full.

In a life packed as mine has been with so many interests it has been impossible to recount everything in greater detail. From humble beginnings I have seen the world from many angles—the law, the City, politics, industry and the army. But the outstanding experience of my life was my four years with Winston Churchill, architect of destiny and the greatest man of my time.

Index

A.D.C. to George VI, 209
— to Elizabeth II, 209
Agar, Herbert, 131
Agnew, Sir Andrew, 170
Agnew, Dolph, 248
Agnew, John, 248
Agnew, Rudolph, 248
Airlie, Lord, 122
Alexander, A. V., 58, 69, 111, 123, 227, 230
Alexander, General (later Field Marshal Earl Alexander of Tunis), 100, 217
Allen, Vic, 246
Alness, Lord, 130
Amery, Leo, 50, 111, 130, 139, 153
Amey, Ron, 254
Anders, General, 83
Anderson, Sir John (later Viscount Waverley), 98, 117, 129, 130, 150, 199
Annan, Robert, 162, 208, 237, 244
Assheton, Ralph (later Lord Clitheroe), 154, 157, 181
Astor, Gavin, 232
Astor, Lady, 182
Atlantic Charter, 45
Atlas Steel Works, 7
Attlee, C. R. (later Earl), 54, 58, 69, 86, 90, 99, 129
Auchinleck, General Sir Claude (Later Field Marshal), 59, 92

Baldwin, Oliver (later 2nd Earl Baldwin of Bewdley), 88
Baldwin, Stanley (later Earl Baldwin of Bewdley), 24, 41, 164
Baronetcy, 204–5
Bathgate Academy, 5
Baxter, Herbert J., 16
Beaverbrook, Lord, 44, 48, 58, 61, 71, 73, 78–9, 85, 131, 142, 192

Beecham, Alec, 172
Beggs, Frank, 251
Beit, Sir Alfred, 139
Bellenger, Fred, 68
Benn, A. Wedgwood, 62
Bernhard, Prince, 69
Berry, Lionel, 128
Bevan, Aneurin, 93, 100, 167, 173, 180, 196
Beveridge, Sir William, 71
Bevin, Ernest, 58, 90, 97, 129, 134, 148, 160, 180, 182
Bevir, Anthony, 45
Birkenhead, Lord, 8
Birkett, Mr. Justice (later Lord), 102
Blair, Sir Reginald, 174
Bonham Carter, Sir Maurice, 47
Boothby, Bob (later Lord), 152
Boscawen, Lady Mary, 123
Bowyer, Sir George (later Lord Denham), 12
Boyd Merriman, 111
Boyle, Lady, 123
Brabazon, Moore (later Lord Brabazon of Tara), 50
Bracken, Brendan, 2, 42–3, 56, 63, 66, 71, 78, 89, 109, 110, 142, 144, 162
Braine, Bernard (later Sir Bernard), 27
Brass, Sir William, 112, 174
Bridgeman, Viscount, 60
Bridges, Sir Edward, 134
British Economic Federation, 9
Bromhead, Colonel, 120, 125, 156, 169, 197, 202
Brook, Senator, 212
Brooke, Sir Alan (later Viscount Alanbrooke), 61, 94
Brooke, Henry, 65, 154
Brown, Ernest, 50, 56, 84, 88, 121
Browning, General, 208
Bruce, Stanley, 144

Bucknill, Mr. Justice, 111
Busschau, W. J., 245, 249
Butcher, Captain, 96
Butler, R. A. (later Lord Butler of Saffron Walden), 65, 90, 147, 154
By-elections,
 Brigg 210, Brighton 142, Croydon 210, Daventry 120, Derby 142, Lancaster 51, Leeds 221, Putney 84, Rotherham 210, Scarborough 51, Shipley 18, Wrexham 51

Cadogan, Sir Alexander, 44
Camrose, Lord, 160
Canterbury, Archbishop of, 80
Carlton Club, 46, 177
Carvel, John, 88
Castle, Barbara, 221
Catlin, Professor George, 157
Cazalet, Thelma, 127
Cazalet, Victor, 127
Chamberlain, Neville, 42, 77
Chapman, Alan, 65
Chequers, 46
Cherwell, Lord, 44, 47, 61, 63, 77, 116
Christopherson, Stanley, 118, 162, 208
Churchill, Clementine (later Lady Churchill), 47, 48, 51, 73, 85, 91, 93, 99, 109, 136
Churchill, Diana, 85
Churchill, Jack, 45, 47, 66, 104, 110, 130
Churchill, Mary (later Lady Soames), 47, 48, 73
Churchill, Pamela, 88, 130
Churchill, Randolph, 80, 99, 104, 107–8, 134–5, 199
Churchill, Sarah, 126, 217–18
Churchill, Winston S.
 Alexander, A. V., Incredible story, 227
 Beaverbrook, attitude to, 131
 Boer War incident, 139
 Bombproof shelters, views on, 62
 Books published, 112
 Broadcasts of speeches, 36
 Cat, incident with, 146
 Cigars, 53
 City of London, Freedom, 126
 Clydesiders, attitude to, 76
 Coventry air raid, 66
 Division Lobby, 33, 120
 Dress, 46–7, 52, 86
 Edinburgh Freedom, 104
 Election letter to author, 200
 Favourite restaurant (Savoy), 65, 133
 Gift of lion, 114–15
 Humour, sense of, 134, 172, 176–7
 Illnesses, 117, 134, 140, 150
 Likes and dislikes, 56
 'Men of Munich', attitude to, 128–9, 130
 P.P.S., appointment, 2
 Parliamentary reports to, 66
 Personality and wit, 47, 56
 Portrait by Salisbury, 95–6
 Return to Parliament after convalescence, 140
 Richmond Green, speaking for author, 200–1
 Roosevelt, death of, 179
 Sawyer (valet), attitude to, 127
 Speeches, formation of, 48
 Temperament, 43, 50, 59, 63–5, 68, 74–6, 80–1, 98, 100, 128–9, 140–1, 167, 172
 'The Boss', 141
 Ulster, 84
Citrine, Walter, 53
Clark, General Mark, 94
Clavering, Sir Albert, 25–6
Clifton-Brown, Douglas, 118–19
Clydesdale Bank, 255
Coalition break-up, 186–92
Codner, Maurice, 133, 160, 163, 202
Collins (Smoke Room waiter), 167
Colville, John (later Sir John), 2, 45, 174
Consolidated Gold Fields, 208
 Alumasc 243, Amalgamated (later Amey) Roadstone 254, Anglo French Co. 241, Associated Minerals 251, Australia 241, Bellambi Coal 251, Canada 240, Conference at Gleneagles 249, Commonwealth Mining Investments 251, Cyprus Mines 252, Greenwood St. Ives 253, H.E. Proprietary 242, Lawrenson Alumasc 251, Mount Lyell 251, Moussec 243, New Union Gold Fields 242, Rennison Zinc 251, Rutile Interests 251, St. Louis 246–7, S.W. Africa Co. 241, Utah Construction 252, Wyong Minerals 251
Cooper, Duff (later Viscount Norwich), 25, 121
Cooper, Tommy, 150

Index

Crerar, General, 153
Cripps, Sir Stafford, 78, 80, 90, 98, 100, 104, 206, 210
Croft, Lord and Lady Page, 156
Crowe, Sir Edward, 158
Cunliffe-Lister, Sir Philip (later Viscount Swinton), 14, 24, 174
Cunningham, Admiral Sir John, 96
Cunningham-Reid, Capt. A., 158
Curtin, John, Prime Minister of Australia, 151

Dalton, Hugh, 50, 58, 77–8, 121, 134, 166, 210
Darlan, Admiral, 109
Davies, Clement, 109
Davis, Arthian, 16
Davis, Joe, 212
Dawson of Penn, Lord, 116
Dean, Frederick William, 25–6
De Gaulle, General, 115, 157–8, 180
D'Egville, Howard, 159, 210, 216
Devas, Anthony, 160
Devonshire, Duke of, 114
Dick, Sir William Reid, 160, 163
Diefenbaker, John, 229
Doolittle, General, 216
Douglas, Sir William, 170
Dowding, Lord, 37
Drayton, Harley, 242
Drew, George, 217
Dudley, Lady, 135, 153
Dugdale, T. L. (later Baron Crathorne), 46, 58, 62, 65, 91, 107, 128, 135, 141, 156, 166
Duncan, Sir Andrew, 49, 50, 110, 121, 122, 146, 158, 170
Dunglass, Lord (see under Home, Alec Douglas)

Eager, Sir Clifden, 226
Eagle Star Insurance Co., 239
Eden, Anthony, 50, 90, 99, 123, 176
Eden, Guy, 148
Edmondson, James (later Lord Sandford), 194
Eisenhower, General, 94
Elliot, Walter, 91
Ellis, Sir Geoffrey, 14, 232
Empire Parliamentary Association, 210
Ennals, David, 222
Erroll of Hale, Lord, 255

Erskine-Hill, Sir A. G., 55, 65, 74, 131, 155
Evatt, Dr., 86–8

Fifty-Second Lowland Division, 8
Fildes, Sir Harry, 88
First London Division, 11, 17
Fish, Dr. Wilfrid, 194–5
Fisher, G., Archbishop of Canterbury, 231
Fitzroy, Mr. Speaker, 64, 118
Fleischer, Colonel, 212
Fleming, Sir Alexander, 170–1, 194
Fleming, Rev. Archibald, 21
Fletcher, Commander, 62
Flying bombs, 159
Forbes, Sir Archibald, 241
Forbes-Watson, Sir John, 6
Franks, Sir Oliver and Lady, 220
Frazer, Rt. Hon. Peter, 152

Gallacher, W., 175
Garvin, J. L., 134
Geddes, Sir Auckland, 5
Geddes, Sir Eric, 5
General Elections
  1929 10
  1931 18
  1935 24–5
  1945 197
  1950 222–3
  1951 232
  1955 238
George Watson's College, 5, 150
Gerbrandy, 81, 180
Glenconner, Lord, 249
Globe & Phoenix, 34, 208, 213
Gomme, Duncan, 229
Gordon, Dr., 194
Graduation, 8
Graydon, Gordon, 217
Great Boulder, 226
Great Western Railway, 207
Greenwood, Arthur, 58, 67
Greig, Arthur, 163, 170
Greig, Louis, 73
Grendon Trust, 237
Grenfell, David, 50, 58
Gridley, Sir Arnold, 67
Griffiths, Jim, 173
Grigg, Sir Edward, 162

Index

Grigg, P. J., 49, 101, 104, 128, 129, 157, 179
Grimston, R. V. (later Baron), 197

Hacking, Sir Douglas, 51
Halifax, Lord, 50, 115
Hamilton of Dalziel, Lord, 155
Hamilton, Sir Frederick, 172
Harlech, Lord, 118
Harriman, Averell, 47, 96
Harriman, Kathleen, 85
Harris, Air Chief Marshal Sir Arthur, 96
Harris, Sir Percy, 64, 74, 97, 164
Harvey, Ian, 27
Harvie-Watt, Euan, 113
Harvie-Watt, James, 36
Harvie-Watt, Rachel, 155
Henderson, Arthur, 156
Herbert, A. P., 93, 144
Hewitt, Sir E. Ludlow, 123
Hinchinbrooke, Lady, 139
Hoare, Sir Samuel, 149
Hogg, Quintin (Lord Hailsham), 145, 173
Holland, S., Prime Minister of New Zealand, 229, 230
Holmes, Valentine, 102
Home, Alec Douglas (Lord Dunglass), 21, 42, 176
Hope, Lord Charles, 155
Hope, Lord John, 206
Hopkins, Harry, 44, 47
Hore-Belisha, Leslie, 34, 78, 85, 123, 136
Horne, Sir Robert, 5, 77
Hornsby-Smith, Pat (later Baroness), 27, 154
Huggins, Sir Godfrey, 214
Hughes, Moelym, 88
Hughman, Sir Montague, 158
Hutchison of Montrose, Lord, 172
Hyndley, Lord, 58

Inner Temple, 9, 10
Inverclyde, Lord, 122
Ismay, General, 60, 86, 88, 90, 110

Jessel, Hon. Edward, 25–6
Johnston, Tom, 46, 58, 106, 141
Jones, David, 229
Jones, Emlyn, 16
Jowitt, Sir William, 116

Kaufman, Admiral, 122
Kefauver, Senator, 218
Keighley, 12, 13
Kelly, Gerald, 160
Kemsley, Lord, 128
Kennedy, Sir John, 214
Kennedy, Joseph, 47
Kensington Council, 23
Keyes, Admiral Sir Roger, 67, 70
Kidd, James, 9
King, Admiral, 96
King George VI, 120
King, McKenzie, 152–3
King Peter of Yugoslavia, 57, 123
Kirkwood, David, 120
Kloof gold mine, 250
Kopanski, General, 83
Kukiel, General, 55

Lake View & Star, 226
Lamb, Sir Walter, 160
Lambert, George, 119
Lascelles, Sir Alan, 148
Lauder, Harry, 106
Law, Bonar, 14
Law, Richard, 14, 131
Leathers, Lord, 49, 50, 111, 121
Lee, Captain, 96
Lees-Smith, Rt. Hon. H. B., 12–13, 25
Levy, Tom, 152
Libanon gold mine, 213, 250
Libel action, 101
Lindberg, Carl, 246
Linlithgow, Lord, 133–4, 155
Lipski, Count, 55, 107
Lipson, Marcus, 173
Llewellin, J. J. (later Lord), 22, 65, 79, 111, 144, 227, 229
Lloyd, Geoffrey (later Baron), 14, 46, 50, 90, 99, 153, 163
Lloyd George, David, 64, 107, 155, 187
Lloyd George, Gwilym (later Viscount Tenby), 71, 88, 89, 99, 118, 121, 155, 197
Lloyd George, Megan
Long, Leonard, 252
Luipards Vlei gold mine, 238
Lund, General, 209
Lyttelton, Oliver (later Lord Chandos), 90, 96, 111, 130

Index

McAlister, Gilbert, 229
McCall, Donald, 245, 254–5
McClaren, Andrew, 176
McColl, Alex, Sir, 158
McColl, Bob, 216
McCorquodale, Malcolm, 58, 65, 128
McCulloch, Donald, 154
McCulloch, General, 122
McDiarmid, Alan, 170
MacDonald, Malcolm, 3, 157
MacDonald, Ramsay, 18, 24, 99
McDonald, Tom, K. C., 221
McGovern, John, 76, 93
McGowan, Lord, 122, 158, 163, 170
McIntyre, J. S., 155
McKay, Harry, 242–3
McKenna, Reginald, 118
Maclachlan, Malcolm, 237
McLean, Alistair, 55
McLean, Neil, 20
Macmillan, Rt. Hon. Harold, 232, 240
Macmillan, Rt. Hon. Maurice, 232
McNeil, Hector, 134
McNeil, Professor, 170
Macpherson, Sir Ian (later Lord Strathcarron), 5
Mabane, Bill, 172, 234
Madeira shipping case, 30
Maiden speech, 20
Maisky, 123
Mandel, Georges, 116
Margesson, David (later Viscount), 31, 62, 132, 141, 177
Marriage, 21
Marshal, General, 96
Martin, John, 2, 45, 47, 73, 86, 88, 104, 108, 110
Masaryk, Jan, 56, 122
Massy-Greene, J. B. (later Sir Brian), 246, 249
Mathers, George, 141, 156
Matson, Jack, 233
Maxton, James, 64, 76, 110, 119, 161
Maxwell-Fyfe, David (later Earl of Kilmuir), 6, 30, 103, 150, 170
Menzies, Macbeth, 255
Merrit, Cecil, V. C., 221
Methven, Sir Harry, 148
Midland Bank, 239
Mid-Surrey Golf Club, 161
Milne, Lord, 148
Mitchell, Harold (later Sir Harold Mitchell, Bt.), 55, 65, 90, 107, 135, 156, 181, 194, 203
Molamure, Sir Francis, 229
Monotype Corporation, 208, 232–7
Montrose, Duke of, 123
Morgan, Sir Herbert, 160
Morris, John, W., K.C. (later Lord Morris of Borth-y-Gest), 16
Morrison, Herbert, 32, 117, 136, 196
Morrison, T. B., 5
Morrison, W. S. (later Viscount Dunrossil), 50, 72, 99, 121, 128, 150, 227, 229
Mortimer, G. J., 252–3
Morton, Desmond, 72
Mosley, Sir Oswald, 136
Mountbatten, Lord Louis, 129
Munnings, Sir Alfred, 160, 163
Murphy, Colonel, 155
Murray, Dr. Stark, 180, 194

Nash, Walter, 229
Nathan, Lord, 62, 71
Nation, General and Mrs., 167
Nicholls, John, 246
Niemeyer, Sir Otto, 160
North British Steel Group, 255

Oram, Sir Matthew (Speaker of N.Z. Parliament), 230–1
Owen, Frank, 129

Palmer, Gerald, 90
Pearl Harbor, 68
Peat, Charles, 90
Peck, John, 2, 45
Petherick, M., 176
Philip, André, 116
Phillips, Admiral, 70
Phoenix Mining & Finance Co., 34
Phoenix Prince gold mine, 34–5, 213
Piggott, Sir John, 218
Pile, General Sir Frederick, 37, 39, 40, 99
Pound, Admiral Sir Dudley, 122
Portal, Sir Charles, 103, 111, 121
Potier, G., 245, 255
P.P.S.,
  Duties of, 29
  to Euan Wallace, 29, 31
  to Premier, 41
Pretoria, 213
Princess Elizabeth, 120

262 Index

Princess Margaret, 120
Princess Royal, 156
Purbrick, Reggie, 123
Pym, Leslie, 65

Raikes, Victor, 176
Ramsden, Eugene, 52, 232
Ray, Sir William, 25
Reading, Lord, 16
Rendell, George, 123
Rettinger, Dr., 83, 96, 115
Rich, Martin, 242
Richmond By-election 1937, 25–8
Ritchie, General, 92
Robert, Archduke of Austria, 107
Roberts, Margaret (later Margaret Thatcher), 154
Roberts, Wilfrid, 64
Robins, Ellis, 35
Robinson Deep gold mine, 213
Rogers, George, 27
Roosevelt, President, 44, 75, 179, 181
Rosebery, Lord, 104, 106, 122, 170, 172
Rowan, Leslie, 2, 45, 80, 110
Royal Borough of Kensington, 23
Royal Engineers, 7
Royal Technical College, Glasgow, 7
Rushcliffe, Lord, 148

Sadd, Clarence, 162
Salisbury, Frank, 95
Sandys, Duncan, 85, 89, 101, 129, 139, 169
Sankey, Lord, 50
Sawyer (W.S.C.'s Valet), 127
Segal, Sidney, 243
Selborne, Lord, 123
Shakespeare, Sir Geoffrey, 71
Shinwell, Emanuel (later Baron), 9, 74, 97, 149
Shipley, 18
Shipping Federation, 16
Sikorski, General, 49, 55, 83, 96, 115, 127
Simmer & Jack gold mine, 213
Simon, Sir John, 14, 50, 76–7, 121, 202
Simovitch, General, 56, 84
Sinclair, Archibald (later Viscount Thurso), 56, 64, 73, 84, 111
Slade, G. O., 102
Smiles, Sir Walter, 174
Smith, Ben, 111

Smith, Mason, Mr. and Mrs., 249
Smithers, Waldron, 63, 76
Smuts, Field Marshal Jan, 107, 137, 153
Snedden, Sir Richard, 6, 16
Snowden, Philip, 14–15, 18
Somervell, Donald, 90
Soulbury, Lord, 226
Southby, Lady Anne, 155
Southby, Sir Archibald, 183
Spens, Willie, 111
Stalin, 100, 176–7
Standard Bank, 239
Stanley, Oliver, 130
Stephens, Frances, 155
Stephenson, Colonel, 155
Stirling, Miss of Glorat, 123
Stokes, Richard, 111, 173, 180
Stone, General, 84
Strathcarron, Lord, 5
Strauss, Harry, 176
Stuart, James (later Viscount Stuart of Findhorn), 2, 51, 58, 65, 73–4, 79, 91, 104, 107, 109, 110, 135, 163, 175, 179, 194–5
Sub Nigel gold mine, 213
Swaffer, Hannen, 75, 101, 103
Sylvester, A. J., 88

Tate, Mavis, 183
Tauber, Richard, 35
Tedder, Air Marshal, 69
Tennant, C., Sons & Co., 249
Territorial Army, 7, 8, 11, 17, 22–3, 33, 209, 223, 239
Teviot, Lord, 158, 172
Thesiger, Gerald, 16
Thomas, Jim, 62, 131
Thomas, J. H., 184
Thompson, Commander, 47, 86, 88
Thompson, Dorothy, 46–7
Thorne, General, 122
Tinker, Joe, 119
Titchfield, Marquess of, 49
Topping, Sir Robert, 51, 154
Tree, Ronnie, 66
Truman, President, 219
Truscott, Sir Denis, 235

V.E. Day, 193
Vlakfontein gold mine, 213

Index

Wake-Walker, Admiral, 123
Wallace, Euan, 2, 130
Wallace, F. W., 10, 29
Wardlaw Milne, Sir John, 92
Waterhouse, Charles, 65, 151, 194
Webb, Sir Alfred, 160
Wemyss, Lady Victoria, 155
West Driefontein gold mine, 213
Whips' Office, 31-2
Whitely, Brigadier, 127
Wilkinson, Ellen, 122
Williams, H. G., 63
Williams, Shirley, 157
Willingdon, Lady, 85
Willink, Harry, 65
Wills, John Spencer, 232-3

Wilmot, Rt. Hon. John, 216, 229
Wilson, Charles (later Baron Moran), 90, 98, 126
Wilson, Rt. Hon. Sir Harold, 220
Winant, John, 60, 126
Winterton, Lord, 70, 74, 149
Wood, Kingsley, 58, 117, 129, 130
Woodburn, Arthur, 156
Woolmer, Lord, 121, 154
Woolton, Lord, 49, 71, 111, 121
Wright, Provost, 155

Yalta, 175-6
Young, Howard, 246, 249

Zip Industries, 251